1995

*Phyllis M. Brooks*

# Overcoming Learning Disabilities:

## A Team Approach (Parent—Teacher—Physician—Child)

**Martin Baren, M.D.**
**Robert Liebl**
**Lendon Smith, M.D.**

Reston Publishing Company, Inc.
*A Prentice-Hall Company*
Reston, Virginia

**Library of Congress Cataloging in Publication Data**

Baren, Martin.
  Overcoming learning disabilities.

  Bibliography: p. 293
  Includes index.
  1. Learning disabilities.    2. Teaching teams.
I.  Liebl, Robert, joint author.  II. Smith, Lendon H., joint author.
III.  Title.
LC4704.B4        371.9        77-27093
ISBN 0-8359-5365-3

*To Sandy, Danny, Ellie, Amy, and Steve,
who showed so much patience and understanding
during the "dog days;"*

*and to Jo for her encouragement and understanding
and Cindy for her secretarial skills
that made this work possible*

10   9   8   7   6   5   4   3   2   1

Printed in the United States of America

# Contents

# *Preface*

The main activity in which most children are engaged is some type of schooling. The vast majority of these children are able to attend school and participate in the educational process with a fair degree of success. While many people display some degree of educational disability at some time (evident when we consider that some people have difficulty with foreign languages, others with math, and still others with subjects such as music), the degree of disability and its relative importance or non-importance is dependent upon the person and the situation or setting. Our concern is with those children who, for various reasons, display more than just a superficial or cursory learning problem and cannot benefit fully from the usual school experience. It has become necessary, in such cases, for those of us who are interested in these children to try to form some strategies to help them.

In this book we will discuss the types of things that can go wrong and will explain how various disciplines can work together to help the school solve these problems.

There are many reasons why a child may fail to become educated to his full potential. These may include physical, emotional, psychological, neurological, cultural, and environmental causes—or often combinations of these. Some children are identified quite early in life as potential problems, others only when they actually enter school. No matter what the basic problem may be, it is necessary to try to provide the best possible education for all children. The people who are faced with this task, sometimes an enormously difficult one, are those who are responsible for all educational matters—that is, the schools and the teachers!

The child's problem may be quite complex, or in some cases may have existed for a long time before the teacher ever had a chance to work with that particular child. Because of the diversity of the problem areas, it has become necessary to train many different types of teachers in various skills so that each child will be educated in the best manner for his or her particular situation. It has also become evident that in many cases the teacher not only has to learn specific new skills within the educational process itself, but also at times will need to draw upon the expertise of other disciplines, including those within the school (psychologists, nurses, counselors) and those outside (such as physicians and, most importantly, the parents).

Over the past several years it has become quite common for the various parties interested in a particular child to work together to provide as much input for school personnel as possible. This ensures the best possible educational situation for each child. However, it should be clearly recognized by all parties involved that the *final decisions* regarding a child's classroom activities *are to be made by the school*—with parental approval. Because of the complexities of the medical, physical, social, and emotional background of each child, many educational institutions have begun to work quite closely with other disciplines, freely sharing information and ideas.

The most important result of this type of cooperation is the closeness and communication that can develop between the interested parties and the child and his parents. Through such cooperation, the authors have personally experienced a very satisfying professional relationship which has grown to encompass a large urban school district. Initial contacts at special meetings between educators, school psychologists, nurses, physicians, counselors, and parents have now grown into a network of communications involving an entire school district. At the present time the actual practice of assessment and remediation of individual children with learning problems includes staff meetings; telephone calls between physicians, teachers, psychologists, and other school personnel; meetings in the classrooms; parent discussion groups; question and answer sessions with all parties involved; and free and open communication among all persons interested in the child at all times. Obviously the parents are totally informed all along the way by all parties involved.

This type of open educational network of communication has worked beautifully in our experience and is spreading into other nearby areas. We are also aware that other parts of the country are experiencing similar results. To represent more clearly exactly what we are attempting to accomplish, we have coined the term *educational triangle,* which is illustrated in the following diagram:

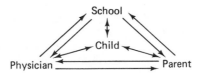

We can see that the flow of information between the three corners of the triangle is free, and that each discipline must hold its own or the triangle may collapse on the child. This type of approach shows how important it is for all those who are involved with the child to work together to assist the school and permit use of its resources to full capacity in the educational process.

As the authors have become more deeply involved in the total commitment necessary to make things work well, we have learned that a prime necessity is the ability of each discipline to be able to understand the other and to communicate in language that everyone understands. Since this is often rather difficult because of the nature of professional terminology itself, we knew that one of the most important things we had to accomplish in our own intercommunications was complete comprehension of everything we were talking about concerning each child—by all personnel—and especially by all parents. Our group meetings, seminars, phone calls, and memos have accomplished this to a great degree. The educators, medical people, and psychologists also have made every attempt to state the problems and possible solutions in simple, easy-to-understand and goal-oriented terms. This has been a great help to us all.

However, because of the nature of the problem, there are still many terms, labels, diagnoses, and therapies that are confusing, poorly understood, and often controversial. Therefore, we felt that it would be helpful to have all of the information usually passed about concerning children with school problems compiled in a way that would make it utilizable and easy to assimilate for the teacher (and certainly other people interested in the child).

Along these lines, the goals of this book are as follows:

1.  To help the teacher understand what various labels such as "Minimal Brain Dysfunction," "hyperactivity," "dyslexia," and "aphasia" mean—or don't mean.

2.  To establish a comprehensive guide to the causes of educational difficulties.

3.  To explain and describe some of the common medical problems seen in the classroom. Also to help the teacher learn something about "familiar" disorders such as hypoglycemia, seizures, brain damage, and perceptual problems, and the effect of all of these on the learning process.

4.   To show how a child might be identified as early as possible as having a learning problem.

5.   To explain how to utilize this information in forming specific strategy for that child.

6.   To help the teacher understand how biochemical, nutritional, and physical disorders can cause learning problems and to explain some of the current theories about these disorders.

7.   To describe how the various disciplines can work together to help the child in all areas.

8.   To explain the educational approach and the different types of programs for various problems; also to acquaint the teacher with on-going developments and future planning in the field of learning disabilities.

9.   To describe the different approaches to the emotional therapy of a child and his family.

10.   To provide a brief description of the various medical interventions used to help a child in the classroom, including the use of medications, special diets, and vitamin therapy.

11.   To establish a practical approach to the classroom management of the child with a problem, and to describe the actual setting up of a classroom.

12.   To review the pertinent points of "The Education of All Handicapped Children Act of 1975" (PL 94-142) in order to make the teacher and other school personnel familiar with such concepts as service to *all* handicapped children, due process rights of parents and children, appeal of placement opportunities, and individual education plans.

13.   To make it easier for all concerned with the child to understand what other professionals mean when they discuss the child.

As a start in this direction, we have even coined a term of our own that is indigenous to no one special discipline. We will refer to a child who is not able to succeed in the normal school situation as having "educational dysfunction." We hope we are not adding to the terminology pollution with this coinage, but since the term can be used to describe any child with a particular set of problems, we feel it may be useful for *all* disciplines.

Finally, we would like to repeat the primary goal of our book. This is the very important credo that *the ultimate responsibility for a child's education lies with his teacher.* We might add that the child's parents will also be responsible, since they are such an integral part of the child's educational experience. We feel that every child can be expected to learn within the confines of his own limitations and disabilities. To assist the child in this process, the teacher may often need the help of other professionals such as psychologists, language specialists, physicians, physical and occupational therapists—and certainly parents—and also a clear and free situation within which to work. We hope to be able to add our own contribution with this book.

We think this book will be helpful not only to the teacher, but also to other professionals involved in the education of children. This includes nursery and preschool personnel, school nurses, psychologists, counselors, students of child development, and most certainly parents.

We have totally enjoyed our own experience working together over the past years and have greatly enhanced our own learning process and knowledge through the open communication we have experienced. We sincerely hope that the culmination of our experience with this book will do the same for others who are similarly involved.

POSTSCRIPT:   In order to save space and not to offend the reader's sensibilities, we have used the masculine pronoun for all children and students (since the majority of students with problems are boys). For the same reason, we have used the feminine pronoun for teacher. We hope we have not caused offense to either group by these arbitrary, space-saving choices.

# *Foreword*

Why is this book different? What does it say? How can it help? Who should read it?

The authors have attempted to provide a comprehensive, practical, and yet simplified and understandable approach to the complicated field of learning problems. We have included material from the educational, psychological, and medical fields, stressing cooperation and communication between all of these disciplines. This idea of teamwork is extremely important, and we show how it really can work. We feel that each child with a learning disability should be considered unique and should be treated as a specific child with a specific problem of set of problems—not as a syndrome or label. This book is practical, utilizable, and workable, as well as comprehensive, which is a unique concept in itself.

The material covered includes a discussion of the labeling problem and how this has complicated the subject; a list of the various causes of learning disabilities; medical, neurological, and nutritional theories of learning problems; a glossary of common medical illnesses and terminology; a discussion of how educators, parents, and physicians can work together; charts, indexes, and forms to expedite this communication; and a summary of the educational, psychological, and medical approaches, including special-education programs, prescribed medication, nutritional aspects, and psychological theories. This type of comprehensive interdisciplinary approach is quite unique in this field.

The book is meant to be a concise and easily used guide, handbook, or reference. Many of the concepts are repeated in different parts of the book in various forms in order to stress the importance of such information.

The entire final chapter consists of a summary in a concise format. That chapter also includes some brief case histories of children with learning disabilities in order to show how the various disciplines were actually brought into play in dealing with these children. We hope this will further demonstrate how cooperation between all interested parties can help these children achieve their full potential.

The message of this book was reinforced by the passage of Public Law 94-142 (PL 94-142), the "Education for All Handicapped Children Act." This is the most significant legislation in the history of special education in the United States. The House of Representatives passed the law by a vote of 404 to 7, the Senate gave its approval by a margin of 87 to 7, and Presidential approval followed on November 28, 1975. Because the law will affect most teachers in this country in the years to come and because all education agencies must comply with it, some of the important concepts of PL 94-142 are discussed. The role of teamwork will become even more important as PL 94-142 is brought into the classroom.

Because of the rapid changes inherent in such concepts as new legislation, nutritional and medical advances, and educational innovations, there must be methods of communication of such information. This book will attempt to bring together the important concepts in such a way as to help the teacher utilize more effectively that which is necessary to educate each child optimally. We feel that the classroom teacher who is in the unique position of having the ultimate responsibility for the child's education should benefit most from a book of this type. In addition, the book should be helpful to parents, other educators, students involved in education courses, school nurses and psychologists, pre-medical and medical students, nursing students, physical education students, speech and language therapists, occupational and physical therapy students, psychology students on both the undergraduate and graduate levels—and for anyone interested in learning disabilities.

The authors' experiences while working together on a day-to-day basis with children with learning disabilities have made this book possible. We hope that it will make the task easier for others who are similarly engaged.

# Acknowledgments

The authors are indebted to Robert and Patricia Howell, who added so much to this book through their critical, comprehensive, and gracious help and ideas during the preparation of the manuscript.

We also gratefully acknowledge the help of Robert Joy in the preparation of Chapter 10, "The Psychological Approach."

We offer our sincere thanks to Nancy Inglehart, who drafted the illustrations found in Chapter 5; and to James Burns, who was so helpful in the preparation of many of the photographs that appear throughout the book.

Finally we wish to acknowledge the help of all of the teachers, parents, school personnel, and others with whom we have worked so closely through the years while gathering material for this book.

### PART I

# Identification

# CHAPTER 1

# Definition of the Problem

The average child in the United States enters school at approximately five years of age with the expectation that he or she will be educated to his full potential. This is usually accomplished through the normal educational channels in the community, including the public and, in some cases, private schools. Within a certain period of time, however, it often becomes evident that an estimated 5 to 20% of children are having problems in this endeavor.

Because our society has become quite complex, we now recognize the fact that success in school has become more and more important. For the school-age child, success or failure in mastering an education frequently will determine his future career as well as his role in society. Therefore, school failure can represent a major catastrophe affecting both the child and his family.

Over the past few years a growing number of people in all walks of life have become involved with children who have learning disorders. And a mammoth amount of written material has accumulated concerning this type of child. As with any popular cause or crusade, however, differences of opinion on the part of many workers in the field have led to a great amount of confusion in the recognition of, as well as the management of, this problem.

There are several reasons why such confusion has occurred. The most important factor is probably the diverse backgrounds and different approaches of the various interested parties. At the present time the child with learning problems may be seen and evaluated by any one or all of the following: classroom teacher; psychologist; special-resource teacher; counselor; social worker; physician; speech, hearing, or language specialist; nurse; nutritionist; occupational therapist; physical therapist; and many others in related fields. Even the type of physician involved may vary from generalist to pediatrician to neurologist to psychiatrist. Since each field uses its own background, approach, and terminology, it is no wonder that confusion reigns supreme.

Another very definite problem is the failure of the various workers to communicate with each other, as well as with the parents and with the child himself. Certainly one of the reasons for this one-sided type of approach is the lack of a common ground on which to establish lines of communication. Another reason is the fear that one discipline or the other will "take over" the child and will exclude all of the other interested parties. And, of course, the result is often a lack of important information by one party or another.

A third and obviously vital difficulty lies in the failure of the child and his parents to be included in the deliberations on his fate. A poor learner knows he is having problems, just as he would know if he couldn't throw a ball or skip rope as well as some other children. The parents of this particular child also know there is a problem. However, it is not necessarily an easy matter to move on to the next logical step—that is, having the child and his parents accept the problem and getting them to work with the proper specialists to help solve it.

For the above reasons we have tried to set up an approach to children with educational difficulties that will encompass the following precepts:

1.  There are a large number of causes for learning disorders. No one discipline or investigator can hope to know everything about the nonlearner. We must all learn to work together and share our knowledge as well as our resources, so as to direct this pool of information at the child with a problem.

2.  It is of the greatest urgency to identify the child with a problem as quickly and as early as possible. Once this is accomplished, a program of remediation should be undertaken, one that will include all the various disciplines working together with a common goal—the education of the child.

3.  The child and his parents must be included in every step of planning. The entire program for any particular child will be doomed to failure unless there is understanding and mutual cooperation between all involved parties.

4.  No one form of diagnosis or management should be held above any other. There is an overabundance of theories concerning children with learning problems, many of which are yet unproven. When we

become evangelistic in our approach, we are more interested in our own approach than in the child.

5.   In the final analysis, it must be firmly established that there is but one person who is responsible for the ultimate learning progress of the child—and that is the teacher! The physician may make the child feel better by treating his illness; medication may help the child concentrate more appropriately; the psychologist may help him understand and deal with his problems better; the counselor may help the family pull together better; and so on. Yet all of these are only corrections and embellishments; we can bring as healthy a child to the educational waters as we are able to, but it is the teacher who must establish the best way for this particular child to satisfy his learning thirst.

This last point is quite important and is often misunderstood. Children with educational problems can often be helped by various parties such as physicians, psychologists, physiotherapists, and others working in related fields. It is certainly necessary to enlist the aid of these professionals. However, the person who works most closely with the student is the classroom teacher. Therefore, the actual final strategy for each child can best be planned and carried out *within the classroom.* Of course it is very important for the teacher to be able to communicate with all of the other disciplines, as well as with the parents and the child about the identification and management of the child's problems. The school welcomes communication at all levels. However, the fact remains that the teacher often spends more time each day with a particular child than the parent does, and certainly more time than the doctor does. Therefore, it is important that the teacher should recognize when something is going wrong and should begin treatment of the child's problems within the school setting, with the aid of all other concerned parties.

What we are talking about is a free-flowing, accurate, sharing, helpful type of communication between all parties involved: *child, parent, school,* and *physician.* In the preface we set up a diagram that we feel is a useful way to approach this problem. This is our *educational triangle,* shown again below (see Figure 1-1). As we have indicated, each part of the triangle is totally dependent on the others, and the child is surrounded by, and interacts with, each corner of the triangle. If we now take each part of the triangle separately, we can see how some of the problems have arisen, and how they might be dealt with.

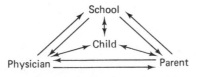

*Figure 1-1.   Educational triangle.*

## CAUSES OF A CHILD'S
## LEARNING DISABILITIES

There are innumerable reasons for learning difficulties, and the literature in this area is filled with a diversity of etiological classifications. As stated previously, one of the big reasons for so much confusion in this entire field is the large number of surveys of children with learning problems offered by such a diverse number of disciplines. Even the method of classifying these problems may be confusing.

Categorization of the causes may be derived from any of the following areas:

Physical

Social

Emotional

Cultural

Medical

Intellectual

Hereditary

(Each of the above could also be further split into many parts.)

Some experts in the field will divide the causes of learning disabilities into only three areas—environmental, emotional, and developmental. Others will not include the retarded child in the classification of children with learning problems and will speak only of "pure learning disorders."

The worst problem in the etiological classification during the past decade has been the widespread usage of the term *minimal brain dysfunction*. We will try to deal with (or more properly—eliminate) this term and its unfortunate cousins in later chapters (see Chapters 2, 3, and 4). However, because of the notoriety and general usage of this term, it might be worthwhile mentioning some pertinent facts at this time. During the past 60 to 75 years, an explosion of terms in the medical, psychological, neurological, educational, and lay literature has occurred—terms that can be applied to children who don't learn to their full potential. Most teachers will recognize some or many of those listed below. (See Chapter 2 for a more complete list.)

| | |
|---|---|
| Dyslexia | Chronic Impulse Disorder |
| Developmental Dyslexia | Perceptual Problems |
| Hyperactivity | Minimal Cerebral Palsy |
| Hyperkinesis | Learning Disabilities |

Hyperkinetic Impulse Disorder    Maturational Delay

Chronic Brain Syndrome    Minimal Brain Damage

Minimal Cerebral Dysfunction    Minimal Neurological Dysfunction

There are actually over 30 terms that have been used to describe certain children who are loosely lumped together into this type of category according to their symptoms, behavior, psychological test results, physical examinations, or other observations. The attempt to classify children in this manner is probably one of the main reasons why there has been so much confusion and poor communication regarding children who have educational problems.

Many people in this field develop a "labelology" game hoping that other workers will know what they are speaking about. However, this has often had just the opposite effect. A label of "hyperactivity" can mean almost anything to anyone. "Dyslexia" is in the same category. In an attempt to bring some order to this field, in 1966 a national commission[1] dealing with this problem selected the term *minimal brain dysfunction* to represent many of the other above labels and then carefully defined it (see definition below). However, even this definition is questioned by many experts and workers in the field and really does nothing but further distort the entire picture since the terminology used is so general. The commission's definition of minimal brain dysfunction refers to "children of average intelligence with certain learning or behavioral disabilities which are associated with deviations of function of the central nervous system. These may arise from genetic causes, biochemical dysfunctions, birth injuries or from other causes." It is easy to see how a definition so broadly based is really of no particular aid to someone dealing with one particular child.

Because of the mass confusion in terminology and definition in this field, we should disregard this type of approach where possible. It is much more reasonable to regard each individual child as having his or her own set of problems that must be dealt with individually and not in the context of some all-inclusive diagnosis. This theme of an individual treatment for each child is important and will be stressed throughout the book. We may see children with all types or combinations of difficulties that do not fit into one or another diagnostic label. For example, there are many "overactive" children with no learning problems at all. And some children with severe perceptual difficulties learn beautifully. Many emotionally disturbed children are fine learners, too. And many

[1]*Minimal Brain Dysfunction in Children, Terminology and Identification, Phase One of a Three-Part Project,* Sam D. Clements, ed. National Institute of Neurological Diseases and Blindness, Monograph No. 3. Washington, D.C.: U.S. Department of Health, Education, and Welfare, Public Health Service Bulletin No. 1415, 1966.

students who are not learning well have no perceptual, overactivity, or major emotional problems. Therefore, we again stress—it is urgent to look at the child who is having a problem and see what *his particular* difficulties are and how we can *help him.*

As part of the evaluation of the child we previously mentioned some of the causes, such as cultural, medical, etc. These will be more carefully explored in another chapter (see Chapter 3), but by way of introduction, a few words might be said here concerning etiology.

There is major confusion concerning terms such as *hyperactivity, dyslexia, minimal brain dysfunction,* etc. If we even look at some other seemingly better "defined" areas of causation for learning problems (e.g., retardation), we can see similar problems. Most workers in the field will agree that the retarded child is one who might have a learning problem because of a subnormal intellectual function. However, even here there is controversy since the types of tests used in the testing situation and cultural differences must be taken into consideration. The definition of mental retardation in some cases can be and is disputed. Therefore, a child who on the surface seems to have subnormal intelligence may have other problems interfering with the very testing that marks him as a retardate. Thus again—individual evaluation and attention are necessary!

And what of the medical evaluation of the child who is having difficulty learning? It is obvious that a child with a chronic illness such as heart disease or leukemia may have school problems. However, there are many so-called medical problems that are quite controversial, both in medical and related fields. For example, there has been quite a bit of recent interest and controversy in the field of nutrition as it relates to learning problems. Terms such as *hypoglycemia* (low blood sugar), *food additives,* and *megavitamins* have become part of the "folklore" concerning these children. *Orthomolecular brain structure, biochemical building blocks,* and *food allergies* all now have a place in this field— rightfully so or not. Doctors, nutritionists, and educators have sometimes locked horns or at times joined forces on the subject of what a child ingests and its relationship to his learning abilities. So even in the well-defined "medical" approach to learning problems there is enough controversy to make a simple approach to the poor learner extremely complicated. Of course if we add the entire controversy of medication to this discussion, the pot really boils over.

We will explore the medical background of learning problems more fully in future chapters (see Chapters 4 and 5), but we would like to caution the teacher who first identifies these children. It is usually most productive to keep an open mind in this area. It would be helpful for the teacher to *describe* what problems are seen in the classroom and to *discuss* the significance with the doctor and other interested individuals. In this way the child will benefit from an individual multidisciplinary approach to his own problem, and he is less likely to become part of any fad or debatable treatment.

Before leaving the center of our triangle—the child—it would be well to say a word about another very controversial aspect of the problem. Just how important is the endowment of the child himself in regard to his learning situation? It is very difficult to really say for sure, but it is widely accepted now that certain children are more vulnerable to all kinds of stresses than are others. Just as the child with an allergic pre-disposition may not be in trouble unless he is exposed to a particular allergen, so may a child in the classroom not be in trouble until he is subject to certain stresses that may then cause a problem in the vulnerable or "at risk" child. Of course the home environment is of very definite importance in the molding of a child, and vulnerability will certainly be exposed in a poor situation there.

Each child will respond to the stress, structure, or distraction of the classroom in his own unique style. Some become quite active, some withdraw, and a few may appear sick or complain of various physical ills. Then there is always the "class clown" who covers up deficiencies or anxieties by making jokes or faces. Again, the end result will depend on the vulnerability of the child and the situation he faces.

We must also consider the hereditary aspects of the learning problem itself. There are many children who have an inborn problem in their nervous systems that makes it impossible for them to acquire certain skills. Some of these children will never learn how to read (at least not in the ways we are currently trying to teach them—or perhaps there *is* no way for a limited number of children). This type of child must be handled in a very different way than the majority of children who *can* be taught in the established way.

So we see that the center of our educational triangle is a complicated creature. All three corners of the triangle must carefully focus on the individual child in a nonjudgmental, discriminating, and cooperative manner to make sure he really gets the benefit of our combined efforts.

## THE SCHOOL'S RESPONSIBILITIES

As we have mentioned, it is urgent that the school and its component parts take an active part in the identification of the problem child. The teacher and other school personnel can provide very useful information to both of the other corners of the triangle—the parents and the physician. The teacher must point out specific problem areas that have been observed in terms of academic performance, classroom behavior, and peer relationships. Certainly any physical problems the child may exhibit that the teacher feels is in some way different from the norm must be identified. The teacher can also provide important information concerning the child's day-to-day activities and performance and can decide whether this meets the school's expectations for this particular child.

The most important thing to consider in this communication is the type of specific information needed. It is urgent that both the physician and the parent know exactly *why* the teacher feels that there is a problem, what she thinks precipitated it, and how long it has been going on. The teacher can also be quite helpful to the doctor by providing a descriptive account of the child's behavior with comments on why it is considered abnormal behavior for that particular child. Finally, the school personnel should fully explain to the parent and the physician just what the school expects from them. A concerted effort must be made to let the doctor and parents know exactly how the school views the child and what types of strategies might be employed to help that child get back on the right path to his normal potential. (A complete description of these avenues of communication is provided in Chapters 6 and 7.)

## THE PARENTS' ROLE

A most important part of our triangle is the role of the persons ultimately responsible for the child—the parents (or other caretakers). Without the help, cooperation, advice, and understanding of the parents, there will be very little long-lasting remediation. In many instances the parents are well aware that there is a problem long before schooling begins. The child may have shown some deviation in development through the first years of life, such as a delay in motor, language, or social areas. Certainly a child who has any type of chronic medical illness is a likely candidate for some type of learning problem.

If a question is raised concerning the child at any point in his progression through the learning experience, whether in preschool, kindergarten, or beyond, the parents must immediately be made aware of what kinds of problems are perceived by the observer. The physician and the teacher are in a very good position to serve as identifiers and clarifiers anywhere along the way. Developmental and medical problems should be shared with the parents as soon as they are discovered.

As the child advances through the school years, problems perceived by the teacher can be shared with the parents. The parents must fully understand the entire scope of what is being said about their child at all times. Occasionally they will disagree, sometimes violently, with the school's perception of their child. The teacher should try not to take issue with this type of response but perhaps could attempt to understand what prompted it in the first place. Remember—*It does no one any good to have the parent working against the school!*

When possible, it may be wise to use the physician as a mediator in these disputes. Perhaps the matter is only one of a minor misunderstanding, although in some cases there may be a major disagreement. Some parents will attempt to blame all of the child's educational difficulties on the teacher and the school. When this happens, it is even more important to attempt to come to some kind of meeting of the minds so that the child will not suffer.

The parent not only must understand what the child's problem is in the classroom, but he must also be made a working part of the solution. There are many approaches to remediation, all of which will be discussed later, but suffice it to say none of these will be successful without the full cooperation of the parent. The important point to remember here is that the parent should not be expected to introduce new concepts or to develop strategies, but should only assist and support the teacher when possible, feasible, and productive. It can be useless and perhaps dangerous to expect a parent to teach a child a subject at night that the teacher had problems with during the day. Not only can the learning experience fail, but the child-parent relationship may then start to deteriorate, which is the last thing we want to see.

## THE PHYSICIAN'S ROLE
## AND RESPONSIBILITIES

The first point we wish to establish and hope to make fully understood is that the *doctor cannot solve the educational problem(s) of the child.* He may deal with the physical and emotional disabilities that may be present, but the child's education occurs *in the classroom.* The medical component of the approach to the child with learning problems may be likened to a musician in an orchestra. The physician can see and hopefully appreciate all of the other many "instruments" of a child's learning capabilities and can help to merge them into a harmonious result. The doctor takes a medical and physical history from the parents, conducts a physical and neurological examination of the child, receives important information from the school, and then blends his idea of what type of difficulty a child may be having into harmony with the other educational musicians and instruments.

The next step is one that is frequently poorly executed. The physician must *communicate* his findings to the school and parents just as specifically and clearly as he expects to *receive* information from the others. The medical reports must be quickly and completely available to school personnel (with parental permission), and then together the parents, the doctor, and the school should consider what best can be done for the child. It is often impossible for a physician to care for a child with school problems without personally speaking with the child's teacher, counselors, principal, school psychologist, and often the school nurse. This type of personal communication is often difficult to attain, however. Some discussion of this aspect is included in the preface and also in Chapters 6 and 7.

There are many appropriate suggestions for physicians to make to the school concerning the influence of the medical aspects of the child on his educational environment. However, medical decisions on educational remedies are often not only inappropriate but may be actually detrimental. The doctor is an extremely important part of the educational triangle, but only *one* part. He can help the child, his parents, and his teacher. In turn he can *be* helped by the parent and teacher. If after all of this, the *child* is helped, the component parts are in proper working order.

## SUMMARY

We have briefly discussed the educational triangle and its parts. In future chapters we will show how each component is more thoroughly involved in the identification and remediation of the child with learning difficulties. Before moving ahead, however, it would be in order to summarize and briefly describe our philosophy and approach to this entire problem.

1. There are many reasons for a child to develop learning problems. Therefore it is more important to accurately describe what the child is actually doing or experiencing rather than to try to categorize him.

2. There are many names given to a child who doesn't learn. It is best to disregard terms such as *dyslexia, minimal cerebral dysfunction, brain damage, perceptual defects,* and *hyperactivity,* and just describe how the child actually functions.

3. There are many *different* personalities represented by the children in our classrooms. Some individuals are more vulnerable or "at risk" than others. It is *urgent* that we find out what makes each individual child vulnerable and then deal with his or her *own* educational problem. Remember: *Each child has his own educational problem with its own individual solution!*

4. There are many individuals interested in a child with learning problems. They should all be working *together* for the child, not by themselves and independently.

5.   There are many theories dealing with the treatment of the child who doesn't learn, from the medical to the psychological to the educational. If the people who are trying to help the child are more interested in their own particular brand of treatment than the child himself, there is no way a child can be helped.

Finally, because of the chaos produced in the field of learning disabilities by all of the counterproductive terminology that has been advanced in this area, we would again like to impress upon the reader the need to disregard labels, syndromes, catch phrases, and other non-meaningful designators of the child with a learning problem. We feel that it would be most helpful if any child who has a problem with any type of educational situation—whether he is labeled as retarded, blind, deaf, emotionally disturbed, orthopedically handicapped, cerebral palsied, hyperactive, or dyslexic—should *not be so narrowly labeled* with finality. Perhaps a new all encompassing term, with a description of the various problems the child actually *does* exhibit, would be a much better approach to the problem.

Therefore, at the risk of adding yet another term to the already confusing array of titles that are thrown around, we have proposed the term *educational dysfunction*. By this we mean the child with a learning or educational problem—for whatever reason!

# CHAPTER 2

# "Labelology"— The Labeling Problem

One of the most frustrating and difficult to deal with problems facing the teacher, and parents or anyone else in this field for that matter, is the labeling that has been attached to children who are having school and learning problems. As we mentioned in the first chapter, there have been many approaches to these children from different disciplines—and hence a deluge of confusing terminology. And because of the semiscientific background of many of the labels and categories formulated by different workers, a certain validity has been attached to these classifications. Hence a diagnostic and therapeutic classification may be established, which is often based on purely speculative, descriptive, and mostly nonreproducible information. The end result of this type of approach is to try to lump a child with a problem with a group of other children with similar difficulties on the surface, but who are often educationally and otherwise quite diverse. When you add to this the very different educational background of teachers, psychologists, physicians, and others in this field, it is easy to see how we have gone astray. Squeezing a child into some type of established category is often frustrating for everyone concerned with the child, and without benefit to the child himself.

Most of the problems in the labelology game arise when different disciplines attempt a common description of the child to accommodate the gathering of diagnostic information. For example, the physician will often seek out information relevant to treating or preventing causative factors relating to disease or injury; whereas the educator will approach the problem in terms of identification for the purposes of classroom management. Rather than either of these approaches, it would seem more appropriate to use a more functional and behavioral definition in order to facilitate proper remediation.

This chapter will attempt to show how confusing the situation has actually become. Perhaps some sense can be made out of the chaos if we stop to analyze what these labels really mean (or in most cases—don't mean). However, in order to try to unravel the fabric of educational labeling, we will have to sheepishly make some labeling decisions of our own. Any enemy must be sighted before sinking, so we will expose the culprits before putting them to rest.

For purposes of identification we will divide the discussion into the following classifications. Most children with learning problems occurring in the absence of any other obvious cultural or physical disabilities can be found in one of the following groups.

1. Retardation

2. Hyperactivity—Minimal Brain Dysfunction—Learning Disabilities—Dyslexia

3. Language Disorders and Aphasia

4. Emotional Disorders

5. Neurological Handicap (NH)

Even this breakdown is totally artificial since there can be overlapping of many categories within each child. However, we must start *somewhere* to try to show how misleading this labeling has become. In the following pages we will attempt to show just how artificial these barriers really are as we discuss each category.

## *RETARDATION*

*Retardation,* or *mental retardation,* is a term reserved for children (or adults) who generally are considered to have subnormal intelligence. This means that their reasoning and learning abilities are substantially below a standard accepted in the community as being "normal." The standard of normalcy has been arrived at through the use of innumerable testing procedures well known to all teachers, psychologists, physicians, and parents. Thus a certain point has been established that suggests that a child whose test results fall below the magic number or range is retarded. Above this point, the child is either low normal, normal, or above normal. And the retarded group is divided into mild, moderate, and severe retardation. This has been carried over into the therapeutic area with the classifications of educable mentally retarded, trainable mentally retarded, and custodial mentally retarded groups.

Part of the testing apparatus has been refined to subdivide various functions or groups of functions, so that such classifications as verbal IQ and performance IQ may be quoted. The IQ or intelligence quotient is the specific number given to the child's performance to show how he rates in comparison to all other children. Simply stated, a result of 100 is usually around the norm in most, below 70–75 is considered retarded, and above 125 or 130 is considered superior. Another way of looking at this is to state that if a child is functioning at a five-year level and he is actually ten years old, his IQ would be 50.

Because of the difficulties inherent in the very act of testing children with diverse problems, different types of tests have been developed. In general, the various so-called intelligence tests are usually divided into three groups.

1. Global

2. Verbal (or vocabulary)

3. Performance

In order to familiarize the reader with some of the terminology in the field, we will list below some of the more popular tests used in each area. (For a more complete discussion, see Chapter 10.)

1. *Global Intelligence Tests*

 a. Stanford-Binet—(ages 2 to 18)—primarily a verbal test.

 b. Wechsler Intelligence Scale for Children—Revised (WISC-R) —separate verbal and performance scores—(ages 5 to 15).

 c. Wechsler Preschool and Primary Scale of Intelligence (WPPSI)—(ages 4 to 6).

2. *Verbal Intelligence Tests*

 a. Full Range Picture Vocabulary Test—(ages 2 to 6 to adult).

 b. Peabody Picture Vocabulary Tests—(ages 1%₁₂ to 18).

 c. Lorge—Thorndike Intelligence Test.

3. *Performance (Visual-Motor) Intelligence Tests*

 a. Draw-a-Man Test—(ages 3%₁₂ to 13).

 b. Leiter International Performance Scale—(ages 2 to adult).

There are many other types of tests that measure other functions such as academic achievement, perception, language, reading readiness, and social competence. These will be reviewed as they pertain to specific problems. At the present time we are referring only to global measures of intelligence as they relate to a child suspected of being of subnormal intelligence or retarded.

It is certainly quite true that if a child is functioning at a low intelligence level, he *will* have major problems in learning. However, the attempt to completely categorize the "retarded" child without considering the individual merits of each case will often be grossly unjust to the child and to his teacher. Consider the following examples.

1.   A child with a severe sensory handicap such as in vision or hearing will be unable to function in class *or be tested properly* unless his defect is discovered and treated, or at least allowed for.

2.   A severely emotionally disturbed child, for whatever reason, will often act like—and test like—a retardate. Because of the emotional disturbance, the child relates abnormally to his environment and to the testing situation; thus he is *considered* retarded.

3.   The nonretarded child who is unable to function in class may also score poorly on an intelligence test.. A good example of this is the child with a severely shortened attention span. If he cannot function in the classroom, he surely cannot sit still long enough to properly take a valid examination.

4.   It should be evident that a child who is not fluent in a certain language will have difficulty taking a test in that language. However, this fact is very often disregarded in many testing situations.

5.   Any cultural differences that prevent a child from understanding may also prevent his true abilities from surfacing when tested by language and symbols that are foreign to him. A good example of this is the ghetto child who has been exposed to "street language" and cannot function in the "foreign" tongue used in the school situation.

It is simple to see how this type of list could go on and on. What we are trying to show here is that it is necessary to find out the approximate underlying capabilities of a particular child. This must be considered in the context of who that child really is. We certainly must find out if a child *is capable* of learning before labeling him a failure. However, in doing this we must be sure we consider all of the possible limiting factors present in the actual measurement of that capability!

There are a large number of children for whom no one doubts the categorization of a subnormal mentality. Most of the time these children have other physical defects as well as one or more added problems such as seizure (convulsive) disorders, weakness or paralysis, movement disorders, language disabilities, social ineptitude, or other such problems. In this type of case there is usually no major difference of opinion between parent, educator, and physician as to the scope of the child's problems.

It should be noted here that we often face a situation in which we are dealing with a child who is operating very much below his chronological age level in all areas of development. Quite often many diverse diagnoses, both educational *and* medical, may have been made of this child. It must be clearly stated to the parents of such a child (often in the preschool age group where specific testing is difficult at best) that their child is *acting* like a much younger child in every way. Thus, even if he is not *truly* mentally retarded, he should at least be thought of as *functionally* retarded for the present. This will ensure that he will not be pushed into an educational program that is unsuited for him at this time.

It is that large "gray area" of children who pass in and out of the diagnosis of retardation that we must be most vitally concerned with. The unmotivated, the socially maladjusted, the immature, the emotionally disturbed, and those with language disorders often fit into this category. It is in this group where we see so much emotionality involving the school and parent. It is this borderline or hard-to-diagnose child who must not be labeled early and then be forgotten. If we're not careful, we can lose both the child's and the parents' cooperation.

We should not be afraid to use the term *mentally retarded* in discussing children. It serves no purpose to label a child as "educationally immature" or "limited learner" or "slow" just to placate parents. At the same time, we must not use this label as an indictment forever excluding this child from the mainstream of normal education. We should not be afraid to tell a parent that the child is functioning as a retarded child at the present time. However, we must be sure that we carefully follow and retest the child as he develops so that we may be able to change our thinking about him if his performance warrants such action in the future.

Thus, the label "retardation" is certainly suitable to describe the functioning of certain children. Sometimes the term describes a temporary condition that may be alleviated, and sometimes the condition indicates a permanent learning disability. The educational approach to retardation will be discussed elsewhere (see Chapter 8).

## *HYPERACTIVITY, LEARNING DISABILITY (DYSLEXIA), AND MINIMAL BRAIN DYSFUNCTION*

These three groups of descriptive disorders—hyperactivity, minimal brain damage, and learning disabilities (dyslexia)—should all be discussed together since the confusion surrounding them has led to a blind alley. A huge number of terms have been used in this particular area. However, most of these have been misused, intermingled, defined, redefined, and recently discarded. The confusion has been so rampant that there have been symposia, conferences, and publications solely dedicated to clearing the air about this subject.

The attempt to classify all of the disorders in this area into the "trash-basket" category called "minimal brain dysfunction" or "minimal cerebral dysfunction" has recently been questioned by most authorities in the field. It is well recognized that the more terms coined for a certain condition, the less we are likely to really know regarding that condition!

The large group of disorders we are speaking about includes inherited traits, actual brain disorders, disturbances of brain structures, psychological problems, cultural difficulties, and many other diverse factors. Regarding the term *minimal brain dysfunction,* it is certainly *not minimal* to the child it affects. Also we cannot prove there is anything wrong with the brain when and if it could be examined; and we are certainly not aware of exactly what the actual dysfunction is in many cases! As was pointed out in Chapter 1, there have been many terms affixed to children who exhibit problems in this area. Some of the more popular include:

| | |
|---|---|
| Minimal Brain Dysfunction | Minimal Brain Damage |
| Specific Reading Disorder | Organic Brain Damage |
| Minimal Chronic Brain Syndrome | Dyslexia |
| | Hyperactivity |
| Organic Driveness | Minimal Cerebral Dysfunction |
| Hyperkinetic Syndrome | Clumsy Child Syndrome |
| Choreiform Syndrome | Visual-Motor-Perceptual Disability |
| Learning Disability | |
| Hyperkinetic Behavior Syndrome | Congenital Word Blindness |
| | Primary Reading Retardation |
| Strephosymbolia | Minimal Cerebral Palsy |
| Perceptual Handicap | Attention Disorder |
| Neurophrenia | |
| Character Impulse Disorder | |
| Interjacent Child | |

There are other terms that have at one time or another been included in this category, but we feel the list is already long and confusing enough.

Because of the frustrations of workers in this field over the past several years, there has been an attempt to cut down and refine some of the terminology. Therefore, we have become "lumpers" instead of "splitters." And instead of using all of the various terms mentioned above, we feel it is easier to describe the children we are talking about if we consider just three general headings. These are: (1) learning disability (dyslexia), (2) hyperactivity (hyperkinesis), and (3) minimal brain dysfunction.

Let us look at these three areas as they have evolved to see if the question of clarity is any closer to being approached. The best way to examine this problem is to consider the various definitions of these three terms.

### Learning Disability (Dyslexia)

Children with learning disabilities can be thought of as those who have normal intelligence but achieve below expectations in one or more school subjects. These individuals may fail to learn when using techniques suitable for the average child, yet they often do well when given special instructions that bypass their specific intellectual block or that build upon other skills not ordinarily used for mastery of the particular task. This category of child is thus very often representative of *unexpected* school failure. If the disability is in the area of reading, the term *dyslexia* is often found somewhere around. This word is derived from the Greek and means "hard," "bad," or "difficult," as pertaining to words or vocabulary. The word was originally used to describe reading disturbances due to definite brain damage or injury. However, most children so categorized have *no* history of brain damage, and so the term *developmental dyslexia* was invented. This was meant to refer to a disorder of reading that was due to a developmental lag in reading skills. Over the years other terms have crept into this area, and we now see such labels as "developmental dyslexia," "specific reading disability," "word blindness," and many others.

Since the poor reader is usually a poor speller, often has poor handwriting, many times shows problems of fine motor coordination, frequently exhibits some speech disorders, and usually has emotional difficulties as well, we can see how *specific* reading disability is *not* very specific anymore.

When the reading disability is broken down into causative and therapeutic areas, the real confusion begins. We are fairly certain that there are at least three major etiologic categories of reading disabilities, as noted below. (For a complete list of all of the "causes" of educational problems in general, the reader is referred to Chapter 3.)

1. Environmental or social-emotional problems—including poor home situation, unsuitable classrooms, poverty, poor nutrition, medical illness, and lack of opportunity.

2.  Physical problems—including brain injury such as in child-birth, central nervous system infections such as meningoencephalitis, or actual head trauma.

3.  Hereditary problems.

In suggesting that any of these causes will produce only a reading disability, we often strain credibility. Therefore many other disturbances seem to encroach into the area of pure reading or learning disability, and that is when the labeling problem becomes monstrous. We often see a child diagnosed as having "learning disability"—and then this is followed with a few more terms such as *visual-perceptual problems, developmental lag, hyperkinesis,* and *mixed dominance!* These added terms are usually meant to be used as helpers or explainers for the original diagnosis. Unfortunately, what they really tell us is that we don't know why the child is not learning, and we are trying to explain it with some other terms we don't understand either.

We do know that there are a certain number of children who do not learn properly in one area or another, and we have a general idea of some of the possible causes of these problems. We also are aware of certain strategies we can use to try to help these children to learn better. What we do not want to do is attach a label to the child and teach to the label instead of to the child. This will become clear as we look at the second category of descriptive terminology that has crept into the learning field—*hyperactivity.* For a more complete discussion of specific learning disabilities, see Chapter 4.

## *Hyperactivity (Hyperkinesis)*

The hyperactive child has become one of the most controversial figures in education and pediatrics over the past few years. It has gotten to the point where parents are now asking the physician if their three-month-old infant is "hyperactive." The question of therapy as it relates to things such as drugs and diet has added further fuel to the fire. And recently the label of "hyperactivity" itself has become tainted with terms such as *hyperkinetic, perceptual problems, motor impulse disorders,* and many others. The final touch of chaos was reached when hyper-activity evolved into the *minimal cerebral dysfunction* mess.

Regarding just the term *hyperactive,* without any of its side embel-lishments, we can state a few facts. The most important thing to remember is that this term is *purely descriptive—not diagnostic!* Although there are many theories as to the causation of hyperactivity, it is often impos-sible to get two "experts" to describe a hyperactive child the same way, let alone find a cause for his overactivity. We also know that the descrip-tion of a child's activity varies from observer to observer and from situation to situation. We are certainly looking at a very elusive concept when we try to discuss a hyperactive child.

It is very important to know who is describing the child in the first place. For example, most of the children who are described as hyperactive by their mothers are not so regarded by their fathers. And two teachers seeing a child in the same day can differ greatly when describing his level of activity. We certainly know that the more tired, impatient, or unhappy an adult is, the more hyperactive a child in his presence will be considered to be!

However, let us suppose that everyone is describing a certain child in the same way, and they all say that he is quite a bit more active than other children in the same situation. There may be many reasons why this child shows that particular behavior (see Chapter 4). The following list discusses some of the reasons why certain groups of children are considered to be hyperactive.

1.   Normally overactive or exuberant children with no problems.

2.   Difficult background and poorly developed social skills. Children in this group show quite a few behavioral problems and are usually quite impulsive. They do not know how to act in most group situations; hence they often are inappropriately over- or hyperactive. These children will lose their overactivity with the proper understanding of what is wrong, and with the necessary support.

3.   Emotional stress or anxiety. A child who is upset or bothered by his life stresses will not be able to concentrate and often cannot sit still. If the child is not sure his home is going to survive the next few weeks, he certainly will not be able to sit still in the classroom. This type of hyperactivity is quite common but often very difficult to separate from other types.

4.   Mental retardation—global or specific. If a child does not understand what is going on in a classroom, he will not be able to sit still. For example, if he is expected to read but cannot do this, he may run around the class until math period when he *can* perform. This type of hyperactivity is also quite difficult to separate out since it may be either a cause or an effect; hence a super detective job must be done by the school to help this child.

5.   Medical hyperactivity. There is a long list of medical conditions such as hypoglycemia (low blood sugar), allergies, and sensitivity to various foods and environmental pollutants that have been associated with hyperactivity. This is certainly the most controversial group of hyperactive children and will be discussed later (Chapter 4). Many of the children in this group can also be considered neurologically hyperactive

(see group 6 below). In some cases the medical condition might be either the cause or the precipitating factor bringing out the neurological problem. Many of the conditions in this group of hyperactive children remain somewhat elusive to diagnosis and treatment.

6. *True neurological (organic—physical) hyperactivity.* There certainly exists a small group of children, most often boys, who *do* seem to have some sort of inherited disorder that causes them to exhibit certain behavioral characteristics that are the ones most often alluded to when people speak of hyperactivity. These children probably have a disorder of the central nervous system whereby their ability to concentrate and screen out undesirable environmental stimuli is impaired. This is most likely a combination of chemical and neurological factors (see also Chapters 3 and 4). These children have been described in many different ways by many different people. Out of all of the various descriptive behaviors appended to these children, a certain few seem common to all reports. Thus we see the terms *short attention span, easy distractibility, low frustration tolerance, impulsivity, driven behavior,* and *perseveration* almost universally used in this context. All of these terms are fairly well accepted as being part of the "hyperactive complex" and remain very descriptive. They are all secondary to the neurological attention-span problem. However, the picture immediately becomes muddled when other descriptive terms creep into the picture. When we include in the description of the hyperactive child terms such as *perceptual problems, learning disorders, neurological deficits, emotional lability, sleep disturbances, coordination problems,* and the many other terms that have come to be associated with this "diagnosis," we lose both objectivity and therapeutic distinctiveness.

We must come back to the word itself. What exactly is a hyperactive child? Is there really such a thing? What are the characteristics? Should the label be used at all? The answers to these questions are still in a state of flux and certainly will be continuously debated among workers in the field because of the intense differences of opinion in diagnostic and therapeutic implications of this matter. Recently there has been agreement in some ways as to the way this problem should be handled and we will try to present the most widely accepted opinions on the term *hyperactivity (hyperkinesis).*

The small number of children who *do* fit the criteria of neurological hyperactivity present a combination of two different manifestations of neurological dysfunction. The main ingredient of hyperactivity is a short attention span. The other important component is probably some sort of delay in the development of impulse control. These two components of nervous system dysfunction—especially the attention problem—are the prime causes of all of the other manifestations of this group of disorders.

The true neurologically hyperactive child cannot focus his attention consistently, but *may* do so in special situations that are frightening to him, such as at the doctor's office. (Thus the physician may often not see the same manifestations of behavior as are reported by the parent and/or the school!) Because of the attentional problem, such children are very easily distracted and certainly cannot learn well under many types of conditions. And because of immaturity in handling their impulses, many of these children *do* show an ever increasing loss of behavioral control and often seem like they are in constant motion. These children are called organically or neurologically "hyperactive." Many people say that you can differentiate them from the other non-organic "hyperactives" by various symptoms, signs, or laboratory tests. We shall go into this at a later time (Chapters 4 and 11), but suffice it to say for the present that there are no effective ways to specifically pinpoint the organically hyperactive child—with one possible exception (and that is a very controversial one)—this is a response to stimulant medication. Thus it is almost impossible to label a child as a true neurological or organic hyperactive by any method known today (with exception as noted).

*To restate the problem:* Many children are *called* "hyperactive" who are not truly hyperactive. The best way to approach this problem is to understand that there is a group of children who have true "neurological hyperactivity," but most children who are labeled as "hyperactive" do not fit into this neurological group. This is an extremely important point and we will focus on it somewhat longer. The best way to emphasize the problem is to present some of the characteristics that have been ascribed to hyperactive children and see how helpful these really are in making a diagnosis.

There have been many characteristics of the hyperactive child listed that have been accepted as diagnostic criteria for making the diagnosis of "neurological hyperactivity." It has been taught that the neurological hyperactive often is recognized in early infancy, or even during pregnancy as a very active fetus. Such infants often are reported as having colic, being very restless, never satisfied, and constantly crying. They also are associated with feeding problems, sleep difficulty of various sorts, and in general are very difficult infants. This is true in many of these "hyperactive" infants. However, it is very important to note that many infants do *not* have neurological hyperactivity, and never go on to exhibit any problems like this later in life, although they may have many or all of the above characteristics in infancy.

If we move on to the toddler years, the description of a child with "unfocused motor activity" is often made. This is suggested as being different from the concentrated exploration of a normal two- or three-year-old, or the attention seeking of many young children. The neurologically hyperactive child is described as a "dynamo" or "bundle of energy." Many parents will say that as soon as the child started to walk, he ran—and never stopped. These children are described as always on the go and always into everything, always touching people and objects. They frequently are reported as running away from home, dashing into the street, or getting into all kinds of trouble. They frequently bring on physical injury to themselves and are constantly at the doctor's office having themselves "stitched-up."

All of these descriptions of the neurologically, organically, or physically hyperactive toddler are often valid. Some children who go on to have major problems in school *do* have a history of this type of behavior when they were younger. However, there are many children who do *not* exhibit any of the foregoing behaviors at the toddler stage, yet show classical signs of impulsive behavior and lack of concentration *when they do get to school.* It can be argued that these children had a physical or nervous system problem all along that didn't show up until the stress of school and learning came upon them. This is certainly a possibility. However, rather than labeling these children as "neurologically hyperactive" or "hyperkinetic" (both terms are used interchangeably), it would make more sense to just describe the child's activity at that particular time—i.e., Johnny is having trouble sitting still and concentrating at *this* particular time with *this* specific teacher in *this* type of classroom. Next year, or even next month, things could go quite a bit better for Johnny. He will mature, the teacher may change, the classroom will be different—some of the stress will be lifted—and Johnny will sit still. Is he still to be considered "hyperactive"? Of course not! He was just a child with a passing problem and now he is acting like a "normal" child. Thus the labeling of Johnny was unnecessary. It was his behavior that needed the labeling!

As the description of a "hyperactive" child continues, we see other possible diagnostic and labeling problems. Consider the child who is constantly fidgeting, with hands, feet, and fingers always in motion—one who can't play with a toy for more than a few seconds and often has his parents angry with him. Or perhaps a child who is described by the teacher as constantly fidgeting, not following directions, excitable, fighting, and most of all, inattentive. If we examine any of these descriptions of a so-called hyperactive child, we can again easily see that any of these symptoms could very well depend on many other factors, including the school situation itself. This leads us to the same conclusion: the label of "hyperactive" is only that—a label. *It does not help us deal with individual behaviors.* And it certainly does not present us with a diagnosis!

Because of the popularity of this particular "diagnosis," especially in the schools, and the admitted confusion in accurately identifying the children involved, members of other disciplines such as teaching and psychology have often fallen back on the medical profession to help them identify these children. Some of the neurological signs and symptoms that are supposed to differentiate this type of child from other children with similar behaviors traditionally included perceptual problems, tremors, fine motor incoordination, muscle weaknesses, crossed eyes, poor finger movements, awkwardness, difficulty hopping, and many other signs that collectively have been labeled "soft neurological signs." These not widely agreed-upon signs are actually the type of thing one would see as being *normal* in a *much younger* child. In other words, a six-year-old should be able to hop on one foot. If he cannot do this well, it is considered to be a positive soft neurological sign. The same child at eight years of age may be able to hop very well. Therefore, he no longer exhibits this soft sign. Some physicians have developed entire sets of soft signs to help diagnose the neurologically hyperactive child, and have carried this even further into the entire area of so-called minimal brain dysfunction, which we shall speak of shortly.

This entire business of attaching signs of delayed development—signs that would be normal in a younger child—to hyperactivity or to any other diagnosis is pure nonsense. There are many children with all sorts of perceptual problems, coordination problems, and all of the other aforementioned neurological findings usually associated with this category who are not hyperactive at all. And conversely, there are many truly neurologically hyperactive children who have minimal or no associated neurological abnormalities or delays.

The logical conclusion to this type of thinking leads to some very important points that should be fully understood before proceeding further.

1.   The term *hyperactivity (hyperkinesis)* means nothing. It does not help identify a child's problem.

2.   There are some children who *do* exhibit many of the traits of the so-called hyperactive. But the only important thing to consider in these children is whether or not they have a short attention span.

3.   The hyperactive child will probably have no learning disability due to his overactivity alone, except if the short attention span interferes with his learning.

4.   There are many children who are *under*active and have short attention spans. These children may never move a muscle in the classroom and still have serious difficulties learning because of their inability to attend.

5. True physiological, organic, or neurological hyperactivity may be almost impossible to diagnose without the use of such aids as a trial of medication.

6. Some children with true neurological hyperactivity can have learning problems. Other children with various types of learning disorders also happen to be neurologically hyperactive. However, the two conditions may exist perfectly independently of each other. The accompanying diagram (Figure 2-1) illustrates this concept.

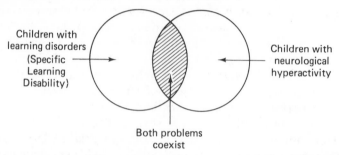

**Figure 2-1.** *Diagram of how children with neurological hyperactivity may have specific learning disabilities and vice-versa—or the two may exist apart from each other!*

If one can learn to appreciate the individual child with his own special problems, it will no longer be necessary to try to label a child as "hyperactive" except to say that he may be exhibiting certain behaviors that should be noted. If any of these behaviors is interfering with his educational, social, or familial relationships, it should be dealt with as necessary. A label is not necessary to do this.

### Minimal Brain Dysfunction or Minimal Cerebral Dysfunction (MBD: MCD)

As we have just seen, a very confusing state of affairs has arisen over terms such as *learning disability* and *hyperactivity*. Because of this confusion, the category Minimal Brain Dysfunction (MBD) has been suggested by many workers to supplant all of the previously used labels.* Some of the definitions applied to MBD include:

1. *Minimal brain dysfunction* is a term applied to a syndrome of deviations in neurologic, congenital, behavioral, social, and emotional functions.

*These definitions are excerpted from *Minimal Brain Dysfunction in Children, Terminology and Identification, Phase One of a Three-Part Project,* Sam D. Clements, ed. National Institute of Neurological Diseases and Blindness, Monograph No. 3. Washington D.C.: U.S. Department of Health, Education, and Welfare, Public Health Service Bulletin No. 1415, 1966.

2.   Minimal brain dysfunction applies to children who manifest varying disorders in learning and behavior that result from subtle dysfunction of the central nervous system.

3.   Minimal brain dysfunction refers to children of average intelligence with certain learning and/or behavioral disabilities associated with deviations of function of the central nervous system. These may manifest themselves by impairment in perception, conceptualization, language, and memory, and in control of attention, impulse, or motor function.

As we can see here, the MBD classification has grown to include almost any child who shows any or all of the manifestations we have been describing above. We can compile a long list of characteristics that would allow a child to be included in the category of MBD.

1.   Hyperactivity of the medical or neurological type (including all of the components such as short attention span, impulsive behavior, and distractibility).

2.   Emotional problems.

3.   Learning disorders.

4.   Visual-motor perceptual problems.

5.   Fine motor-coordination difficulty.

6.   Sleep disturbances.

7.   Behavior problems.

8.   Reading, writing, and arithmetic difficulties.

9.   Almost any neurological findings such as tics, abnormal reflexes, and unusual movements.

10.   Problems with right and left discrimination; mixed, split, and unestablished dominance.

11.   Speech disorders.

This type of list can go on and on. Each specialist has his own special characteristics or physical findings that he uses to describe a child with this label. There are checklists for parents, teachers, and doctors to use in identifying these children. These lists contain large numbers of behavioral descriptions, descriptions of characteristics that if present in certain quantities will identify the child as one of the MBD group.

There are many problems inherent in this whole attempt at creating a diagnosis or condition like MBD. As we have already mentioned, the condition is neither minimal nor necessarily associated with the brain. Any of the conditions listed under the diagnostic criteria can derive from many causes. The term is purely descriptive and does not help us at all in managing these children. The most devastating effect of such a term is the confusion it causes in the various disciplines who are exposed to it!

If we stop to examine some of the components of the MBD problem, we can readily see how fruitless it is to pursue such a cause with regard to the individual child. As we have already seen, many children who don't learn properly have absolutely no specific neurological, perceptual, or other problem except for the fact that they are not being educated; and many children with severe behavior disorders may exhibit no abnormal neurological signs. Also many children who are clumsy, awkward, and have visual perceptual problems have no real learning problems. Right here we would like to state that the entire area of perceptual problems has been blown totally out of proportion. Perceptual problems may have nothing to do with learning except that some children who don't learn properly also have perceptual problems.

We could go on and on through this entire maze of the MBD mess. Suffice it to say, the major function of this labeling has been to point out how much we really don't know about many children exhibiting these types of problems. What we do know is that there are large numbers of behavioral, educational, and neurological signs exhibited by many children—signs that can be identified and should be dealt with as necessary. However, it serves no purpose to try to legitimize a specific diagnosis when there are no common causes for it, no identifying tests to pinpoint it, nor any specific therapies associated with it. Most importantly, hanging a label, even if accurate, tells us very little about what to do from the point of diagnosis forward!

On the other hand, there are good reasons for identifying the various types of behaviors and abnormalities ascribed to the child who fits this category. First of all, the various educational, medical, social, and behavioral problems uncovered should certainly be corrected. Thus we might well be quite able to correct a child's poor nutrition, deal with his short attention span, be sure he doesn't have a convulsive disorder or brain tumor, help him with his family relationships, and teach him better word-attack skills—all without labeling him! If a better communication can exist between professionals in the field where terms such as *hyperactive* or *MBD* are used—great!—as long as we all are aware of what the terms don't include as well as what they do include! Remember—

we must describe what the child is doing and how he is functioning, but we do not have to put a name on it!

As one considers such labels as "learning disability," "hyperactivity" and "minimal brain dysfunction"—which we have just seen really mean very little in terms of helping a child—we must consider another term that is sometimes used, which could really be a very effective one, and that is *developmental delay* (also occasionally called *maturational lag*).

Most of the problems described in the symptom complexes of hyperactivity and MBD really belong in this category of developmental delay. Almost every symptom that people use to describe MBD is in reality a delay in the mastery of a particular function by a child. The child with this problem behaves like a normal younger child. This concept is quite important because it is the overwhelming cause or contributor to learning disabilities at almost any age. Therefore, if a child has not been able to master a particular skill by a certain age, if we just keep him under control emotionally until he *does* mature in that particular area, that special function may eventually be mastered. This kind of reasoning can be applied to most of the coordination, perceptual, and motor skills we can measure in developing children.

This concept of developmental delay or maturational lag has its greatest application in the case of the five- or six-year-old child who shows some signs of educational dysfunction. Oftentimes a physician, psychologist, or even teacher may try to label this child as one with hyperactivity, brain dysfunction, or a learning problem, when in reality he is just not ready to adapt to the school situation at this particular time. If we give this particular child emotional support and careful guidance and make sure he is properly placed, we often find that in 6 to 18 months he no longer is showing the same signs of delayed function— thus no more educational dysfunction!

## LANGUAGE DISORDERS AND APHASIA

Delayed language and/or speech development is one of the early indications of a child who might have a learning disorder. There may be many reasons for this, including hearing loss. The particular aspect we are dealing with is not the ability to hear, but the ability to discriminate, appreciate, and utilize sounds. The child who has normal hearing but who for some reason cannot receive or transmit language properly is likely to have learning problems. The term *aphasia* has been commonly associated with children in this particular category. This is a misnomer itself, since aphasia really means the disturbance of language functions due to brain damage in a person who already has fully developed language facilities. Thus we should not even use the term *aphasia* in children. *Severe oral language disorder* is more appropriate! This designation is commonly meant to denote a central nervous system or brain dysfunction that interferes with the development of the proper reception, interpretation, or expression of speech, not due to auditory impairment, mental retardation, autism, or a physical problem of articulation.

There is certainly no quarrel with the fact that a problem in this area can be quite devastating to a child. There are many auditory functions that can go wrong, including sound synthesis, processing, discrimination, memory, and others. And even if the reception and interpretation are intact, problems in the expressive areas may interfere with language development and learning.

The big problem here is not that these problems exist, but that they are often mislabeled. For example, the young child of five who has poor language development may be emotionally disturbed or may just have an extremely poor attention span, and either problem may seriously interfere with his learning. The diagnosis of aphasia may be made, and this automatically stamps a diagnosis of some kind of brain damage on the child. Although the diagnosis of aphasia certainly may be accurate in some children with language disorders, we should refrain from making a specific diagnosis based only on observational data. The child may well be best *treated* as a so-called aphasic, but all of the other components of his neurological and emotional states must be kept in mind as he is being observed.

There are many tests used to help identify this kind of child, including the Illinois Test of Psycho-Linguistic Abilities (ITPA), the Porch Index of Communication Abilities in Children (PICAC), the Wepman Auditory Discrimination Test, and the Mecham Verbal Language Development Scale. By using the various subtests in these evaluations, we can often identify just where the defect is most likely to be and plan our teaching strategy around these findings.

As we have noted previously, the diagnosis of aphasia does not really fit most children with language problems, except as a descriptive exercise. Therefore, we should discard a term like *aphasia* and again describe what we are seeing in a child. The child with language dysfunction certainly may well prove to have some type of brain dysfunction in an area of auditory processing that really is his basic problem. However, many times as he develops and grows in his other skills, we may see that the language disability was only a presenting facade—and the real problem may be something quite different. Remember—we must describe *what* the child is *doing,* not what we *think* is going on in his brain!

## EMOTIONAL DISORDERS

The last label we must consider here is that of an "emotional" or "psychological disturbance." This may well be the most widely used and loosely applied of all the labels. When we say a child is "emotionally disturbed", it can include anything from bed-wetting to fire-setting, or thumb-sucking to drug abuse. The entire gamut of psychiatric terms such as *adjustment reaction, depression, neuroses, psychosis, schizophrenia, autism,* and many others can fit here.

When we stop to reconsider for a moment, we can clearly see that any child can become emotionally disturbed within a certain framework of time or circumstances. If a child is attacked by a stranger on a dark street and he runs away screaming, he is certainly emotionally disturbed at that time—for very evident reasons, of course. However, if a child runs around screaming *all the time,* he may be considered to be emotionally disturbed also, perhaps for reasons not so clear. The first child may not have a learning disorder because of the brief duration of the disturbance; the second may well be deeply involved in all kinds of school difficulties.

As we have previously stated, the child labeled "hyperactive" sometimes is one who is seriously emotionally bothered and exhibits wild, impulsive behavior because of his problems. On the other hand almost every child who is neurologically hyperactive with a short attention span will become emotionally upset to some degree, especially if he has had very little or no help with his problems.

The child who is not learning in school is certainly apt to show disturbances of behavior, especially as he gets older and things become more difficult for him. Like the "chicken and the egg," it is often very difficult to decide whether the learning or the emotional problem came first! However, what does it really matter, since we must deal with the *child and his problems?*

As one looks at a child in the classroom, it is very easy to list various behaviors that might add up to a diagnosis of an emotional disturbance of one type or another. Often psychological testing can help to establish certain criteria for a certain diagnosis. Certainly psychiatric evaluation and therapy are occasionally needed for some children who exhibit totally bizarre and atypical behavior. However again, just denoting a child as "disturbed" does nothing for him except if this is quickly followed up by proper evaluation and action.

One of the more common labels in this area we sometimes hear mentioned is "autism." This diagnostic category has been argued and defined in many different ways by many different people. The autistic child has been described as one who has completely withdrawn from contact with anyone, including his parents. People are regarded as objects to these children, and there is no meaningful communication. Other characteristics associated with autism are a desire for sameness, and a love of inanimate objects, especially those with spinning or circular motion such as cars, clothes dryers, and tops. There is also an almost total lack of meaningful language. These children occasionally appear to be severely retarded or deaf. They sometimes make grunting sounds and noises and may show signs of poor coordination. Above all, however, is the fact that these children show no eye contact and do not relate to humans. They are also sometimes self-destructive, and we occasionally see outbursts of wild temper in these children.

There have been many theories concerning the cause of autism, from poor maternal interaction to brain damage. It is most probable that these children do suffer from some type of dysfunction of their central nervous system, but many people still feel that there is quite a bit of family or interpersonal strife involved in the etiology. The important point is not so much what caused the problem, but to identify it where it exists and to develop strategies to deal with the child so afflicted.

In summary, then, it is perfectly all right to state that a child is having school problems along with some emotional difficulties, and to try to deal with all of the problems together. However, it could be harmful to diagnose an emotional disorder in a child and try to correct this without taking into account everything else that is happening to the child.

## NEUROLOGICAL HANDICAP (NH)

"Neurological handicap" is another label that has been affixed to many children with learning and/or behavior disorders. The term is not rooted in either the educational or medical areas however. There is no specific way to identify a child as NH except by using general descriptive behaviors. Any child who fits loosely into the categories of "specific learning disability," "hyperactivity," "language disorders," or "minimal brain dysfunction" as defined earlier would be considered neurologically handicapped. This label could also be used for children showing any type of developmental delay, as well as for more severe neurological disorders such as seizures. The term has been widely adapted by various groups both inside and outside of educational and medical circles and now is used in a very general way to describe many different types of children.

Since NH includes almost any type of behavior or learning dysfunction, it can be used in a very general descriptive way but has no specific therapeutic implications. It probably should be regarded in much the same light as MBD, as far as being of no help with the specific remediation of a child. The label is very popular and all-inclusive and is used by many different disciplines, and therefore should be used only in a very general manner. However, it must be stressed again that children placed in this category often have no real proven neurological abnormality and often have no real handicap if their development is taken into account. Again we have a label that most people are familiar with and use, but one they really means very little in the individual child. Thus, we should not handicap ourselves with the term NH, except when we specify what it means to all parties concerned with a particular child.

## MISUSE OF LABELS FOR
## REMEDIATION PURPOSES

The labeling problem is not limited to the *recognition* of a child with learning problems. Quite often we are faced with the same type of difficulty when it comes to the *remediation* of this particular child. Various methods, techniques, groupings, and systems have evolved that were developed to serve one particular label, and sometimes they have very little in common with the type of child or problems they really should be serving.

Thus, we may see any or all of the following remediation labels used in a particular educational setting:

| | |
|---|---|
| Mentally retarded | Opportunity program |
| Educationally retarded | Educationally handicapped |
| Limited learner | Learning-disabilities group |
| Emotionally disturbed | Oral language program |
| Educationally immature | Aphasia class |
| Hard-of-hearing program | Orthopedically handicapped |
| Perceptually handicapped     training program | program |
| Multihandicapped program | Visually handicapped program |

There are many more that could be added to this list, but the main point to consider is the fact that there *are* so many programs. It is, therefore, at times quite difficult to figure out where to place a child even if we can identify his problems fairly well. Just because he is placed in one class or another does not automatically label him as unfit for some other program. And it is possible for a child with one kind of label to fit in a program with a different label because it is *better for that child.* This will be considered later (Chapter 8), but suffice it to say that it is perhaps just as dangerous to solidify our focus on remediation labels as it is on diagnostic labels.

A very cogent example of the entire problem may be best illustrated by the following case study:

> Billy D. is a four-year-old who has been a problem to his parents since birth. He has always been a wild, uncontrollable child who cannot sit still for one minute when his mother is around. He is better behaved for his father however. Billy speaks only four or five words and cannot jump, dress himself, or hold a crayon very well. He does understand complicated instructions that he will follow when he wants to. He loves television and can watch for long hours, humming all of the commercials—syllable by syllable. He has been thrown out of three preschools and his parents are at their wit's end with him!

Is Billy retarded, autistic, aphasic, or brain-damaged—or any combination thereof? Does he belong in a class for retardates, a language program, educationally handicapped class, or a psychiatric program? Labels are meaningless for a child like Billy. Educational intervention might change several times a year. Therefore, in order to get anywhere with a problem of this magnitude, there must be total cooperation between all corners of the educational triangle. Billy's type of problem will be discussed more fully in the remediation sections of the book, but it is used here to show the folly of labeling if we do it blindly. (See section on Global Atypical Child in Chapter 4.)

In running any type of program where we are dealing with many children with diverse problems, it is obvious that a certain amount of labeling will be necessary for bookkeeping purposes. However, we must keep in mind the fact that we should not try to fit square pegs into round holes, e.g., make educational categories for medical or psychological problems and vice versa. We should consider each child as an individual with his own individual problems. If we also keep in mind the fact that labels should be able to be peeled off, erased, changed, individualized, and even relabeled—and are unique for each child—we might just be able to get somewhere in our battle to help the child learn to his potential.

# CHAPTER 3

# Educational Dysfunction —What To Look For

Most children with learning problems are first identified when they enter school. The whole scope of the problem may not be clearly delineated at once, but within the first several years it is usually quite clear just how much of a deficiency really exists. To be sure, there are a small group of children who, because of severe physical or mental disability, will be identified at a much younger age. However, the large bulk of children will be sent to school with full expectations that they will take part in the regular learning process.

Since the bulk of identification *does* take place after the child is already enrolled in school, it is obvious that a large portion of this process falls within the domain of the teacher. It becomes extremely important, therefore, for the teacher to be able to develop some type of approach to this problem. It should not be expected on the one hand that the teacher become an expert psychological tester or medical evaluator. On the other hand, it would be quite helpful and proper for the teacher not only to be able to recognize the fact that a child *is* having a problem, but perhaps also to be able to sort out some of the possible causes for his problem in a fairly systematic manner.

In previous chapters we spoke of the problem of categories and labels as they pertain to children with learning problems. The various causes of these problems can be subdivided into many subgroups such as cultural, hereditary, medical, and psychological. Then the various subgroups can be divided into diagnostic categories such as dyslexia, minimal brain dysfunction, and aphasia—none of which are really very helpful in our approach to the child in many cases. Furthermore, it often becomes very difficult to classify a child with a short attention span as hereditary, environmental, or psychological. In reality, he is really a little of all of these, and what difference would it make in our strategy for him?

Because of the immense problems that are inherent in the etiologic approach to the child with a classroom problem, the method must be as simple as possible in order to insure an orderly, well-understood, easy-to-use guide. The causes of learning problems certainly do not always lend themselves to simplified explanations or diagnoses, but we often do not need to make a detailed diagnosis. It makes quite a bit more sense to look for various problems in the child that may be hindering his learning ability, and then simply deal with the problem and the child, rather than with some type of superficial diagnosis.

As we look at all of the possible things that can go wrong to produce an educational problem, we should try to make some sort of arbitrary classification so that we can be somewhat systematic in our approach to any particular child. The most simple way of dividing the possible causes is into two categories:

1.  The child's own makeup (internal)

2.  The child's environment (external)

However, even when viewing the problems of educational dysfunction in this simplified manner, we must be very careful because of the *interaction* between a child and his environment. Each child, whatever his own innate endowment, responds to the stress, structure, and distractions of a classroom in his own unique style. Thus, we may see various behavioral symptoms including shyness, excessive activity, withdrawal, or even "sick" symptoms such as headaches and stomachaches. Other behaviors such as hostility, aggression, belligerence, and even class-clowning may result from various causes either in the child *or* his environment—or sometimes both.

Right away we can see that even a description of a certain trait or behavior might fit into either of our categories to start with. However, that is perfectly all right if an open mind is kept in our approach to the subject. Thus, if we *do* describe a child who *doesn't seem to be able to follow directions,* we might think of any of the following:

Hearing loss.

Short attention span (unable to focus on something for more than five minutes at a time).

Difficulty understanding words.

Behavior disturbance.

Defiance of authority.

Physical sickness.

Poor nutrition and hunger.

Language deficiency.

It is not important for the teacher to make a specific diagnosis. It is extremely difficult for even specialists in childrens' problems to differentiate many of the above problems. What *is* important is the fact that the teacher is able to find out—and then successfully communicate the important facts regarding the nature and extent of the deviations. The rest is up to the various specialists the teacher calls upon for help. These may include the psychologist, language specialist, physician, social worker, counselor, and others, including the parents.

In our approach to the causes of educational dysfunction, we will consider the etiologic or causal approach first and then attempt to fit various behaviors into these categories (see Table 3-1). The next step will be a description of behaviors and how they fit into the etiologies (see Table 3-2 at the end of this chapter). By using both approaches to the same child, the teacher can start the machinery of remediation rolling.

## CAUSES OF EDUCATIONAL DYSFUNCTION

### The Child's Own Makeup (Internal)

#### CONSTITUTIONAL PROBLEMS—PREDETERMINED OR PRESENT AT BIRTH

##### Hereditary Disorders

Hereditary disorders are inherited from parents, either by passage through genes or chromosomes. Each person normally has 46 chromosomes, and a disturbance in the amount or makeup of the chromosomes can produce mild to severe defects. Some chromosomal defects are passed from parent to child, and others arise on their own in the developing child.

##### Genetic Disorders

Each chromosome has many genes on it, which control the physical and mental attributes of a person. Many of the diseases we know are passed on as genetic disorders; others are suspected to be genetic disorders but as yet are unproven. Many problems seen in children can have *some* genetic basis, and there are many well-defined diseases in this group that can produce specific defects leading to the learning disorders.

**Table 3-1**
**CAUSES OF EDUCATIONAL DYSFUNCTION**

---

The Child's Own Makeup (Internal)

---

A.  Constitutional problems (predetermined or present at birth).
    1.  Hereditary
    2.  Genetic
    3.  Congenital

B.  Constitutional problems (acquired *after* birth).
    1.  Perinatal problems (This refers to events in the time period immediately preceding, during, and just following birth.)
    2.  Infection
    3.  Toxins and poisoning
    4.  Nutritional
    5.  Injury
    6.  Emotional (may also be external—see below)
    7.  Other severe illness
    8.  Miscellaneous (idiopathic—no specific cause identified)

C.  Description of "specific" categories (which can be related to one or more of the above causes and are often combinations of several or many of these etiologies).
    1.  "Diagnostic" categories
        a.  Subnormal intelligence
        b.  Physical deformities
        c.  Growth problems
        d.  Disorders of special senses (hearing, vision)
        e.  Language disabilities
        f.  Convulsive or seizure disorders
        g.  Specific neurological categories or disorders
            (1)  Cerebral palsy
            (2)  Neurological "hyperkinetic" disorder
            (3)  Specific learning disability ("dyslexia")
            (4)  "Perceptual" handicaps
        h.  Maturational delay (developmental lag)
        i.  Severe emotional illness
    2.  "Symptomatic" categories
        Groups of behaviors or symptoms that seem to occur in clusters in various children. (These are explained in Table 3-2 at the end of this chapter.)

The Child's Environment (External)

---

A.  The school
B.  Cultural and environmental difficulties
C.  Emotional disorders (can also be internal)
D.  Illness
E.  Miscellaneous

---

### Congenital Disorders

Congenital conditions are those with which a child is born. They can be caused by genetic abnormalities, chromosomal aberrations, or maternal (prenatal) trauma, disease, or disability. Many congenital defects are mixtures of genetic *and* environmental causes; an example is an allergy, where the predisposition to allergy is genetic, but it will not surface unless the person is exposed to a certain environment. Many illnesses affecting pregnant women can cause congenital defects. Congenital defects can also be a result of maternal nutritional problems, drugs, X-rays, emotional disorders, and environmental hazards.

The important thing to understand here is that almost every disease or problem afflicting a child can ultimately affect his constitutional makeup. Even if a specific disorder is not fully obvious, the predisposition may be there. Thus, in a stressful situation a certain constitutional trait or disorder will manifest itself, whereas if the stress never appears, the condition remains undiscovered. Most disorders we see probably fit into this situation!

## CONSTITUTIONAL PROBLEMS ACQUIRED AFTER BIRTH

There are many harmful stimuli that can attack a child after he is born as a "normal" individual. These may begin right at birth and continue through the child's developing years. Any problems produced by these attacks on the child are then incorporated into the constitutional structure of the child and never change. Therefore, a static condition is produced that is no longer dependent on the stimulus that produced it. The most important of these factors include perinatal problems, infections, toxins and poisoning, nutritional disorders, injury after birth, emotional stress, and illness other than infection.

### Perinatal Problems

Any problem that causes loss of oxygen to the baby's brain at birth may cause a permanent disability. This may include problems in labor and delivery, compression of the umbilical cord, obstruction to the infant's airway, any damage to the skull that produces bleeding in the baby's head, or conditions that interfere with the initial respiratory effort of the baby. The extent of damage to the brain can vary, and the results may be quite different depending on the extent of the injury.

Infants who are born earlier than the normal time (prematurity) or with a much lower birth weight than normal (dysmaturity) also will have a higher incidence of difficulties relating to the brain and its functions. The smaller the baby, the more involved the problems are likely to be. These difficulties may be due to many different factors, but the very fact that the baby is smaller than normal or more immature than normal makes him even more vulnerable to stress and subsequent disability.

There are also other events that can affect a baby around the birth period that can have lifelong effects. Thus, a high level of bilirubin (yellow jaundice) or a low level of oxygen (cyanosis or blueness) might have a detrimental effect. Any severe problems or extreme changes in an infant's environment can also cause future damage. In short, this period of life is really the most vulnerable period a human being ever faces, and may condition the rest of his life.

### Infection

Invasion of the child's body by organisms such as bacteria, viruses, fungi, and various parasites may cause permanent problems at any age. The earlier the infection, the greater the likelihood of damage. Obviously along this line, infection acquired before birth (congenital) will wreak the greatest havoc. Infections of the central nervous system such as encephalitis and meningitis are the most dangerous and will often cause permanent damage at any age—they certainly are especially dangerous to the younger child who has not yet fully developed in the affected areas.

### Toxins and Poisoning

There are numerous substances that can cause permanent damage to a developing child. These include common household items such as aspirin, iron pills, vitamins, and many medications and cleansing agents, as well as things such as lead poisoning. Again the result will depend on the toxicity and amount of exposure of the substance as well as the time of exposure—the earlier, the more likelihood of a permanent problem.

### Nutritional Disorders

Severe undernutrition at any age can interfere with learning. However, because of the rapid growth of the brain during the first year of life, most of the lasting effects of poor nutrition are seen when it occurs in the first year of life. Severe intellectual retardation is known to result from general malnutrition. Specific vitamin deficiencies may also lead to permanent damage when they occur early in life. Besides general undernutrition, specific deficiencies such as protein lack may cause problems. Certain children who have a genetic predisposition to nutritional abnormalities may develop *permanent* change if subjected to improper nutrition. Here, too, the young infant is considerably more at risk than the older, more fully developed child or adult.

### Injury After Birth

Any trauma to the developing child can cause permanent changes in the constitution of that child. The most important injuries are those to the central nervous system that cause extensive damage, bleeding, or actual destruction of brain tissue. As before, the age of the child and the extent of the damage would be the most important factors in the actual result produced.

### Emotional Stress

Although it is usually thought that emotional problems are external causes of learning problems, there are conditions where early and excessive emotional abuse of a child can lead to permanent (internal) disability. The result of severe psychological stress may be quite difficult to differentiate from brain damage when we observe the child at a later age. Therefore, this category certainly belongs in *this* group of etiologies *as well as* in the *external* category of causes.

### Illness Other than Infection

This category is in the same general range as emotional stress—and will be discussed more extensively as an external category. However, there are certain illnesses not already covered in the genetic or infectious categories that can produce a *changed state* in the child. For example, severe heart disease, certain degenerative nervous system conditions, and illnesses that affect many different body systems such as rheumatoid arthritis can change a child's structure if they occur at an early age. It has been postulated that high fever of approximately 106°F or above, especially of long duration, can also cause lasting problems. This, however, is extremely controversial and difficult to prove.

### Miscellaneous or Idiopathic

Most of the illnesses or disorders that can affect the developing infant and child and that can cause a lasting constitutional defect are covered by the above categories. However, there are always children who can be identified as having major disorders of their mental or physical processes that seem to have arisen for no apparent reason. Thus, we may see a child with a major learning disorder, and no history of any congenital, perinatal, infectious, traumatic, or other reason for this. This represents a rather large group of children, and we can only classify them as constitutionally different for no apparent reason. Many of the cases of so-called hyperactivity or minimal brain damage would be classified in this group—or at least overlap with this category and several others listed above.

## DESCRIPTIVE OR SPECIFIC DISORDERS THAT CAN BE IDENTIFIED AS RELATING TO THE INTERNAL CAUSES OF EDUCATIONAL DYSFUNCTION

In the preceding paragraphs we have identified what can go wrong in the developing infant from conception, through birth, into childhood. We will now show how various conditions and symptomatology can be related to the above categories. All of the following may have something to do with one or more of the categories listed above in the two sections on constitutional problems. The causes of these descriptive or specific disorders can usually be found to overlap several of the internal etiologies. See Chapters 4 and 5 for a more complete description of these disorders.

### *"Diagnostic" Categories*

**Subnormal Intelligence (Mental Retardation):** Although the specific identification and labeling of subnormal intelligence are complex as previously noted (Chapter 2), retardation is a prominent cause of *major* learning disabilities. The intellectual problem itself can be caused by any of the above categories including congenital problems, hereditary factors, birth injury, infections, emotional disability, and others. The child with lower than normal intellectual functioning also may have other abnormalities such as physical defects, disorders of speech and language, convulsive disorders, and emotional problems. The symptoms used to identify these children may show up anywhere from early developmental delay to poor reading in school, and may include almost anything from extreme activity to poor motor coordination, to aggressive behavior, to facial and physical abnormalities.

**Physical Deformities:** The list of abnormal or deviant physical characteristics is endless. The more severe the defect, the earlier it is likely to be identified, with the most extensive ones showing up at birth. It might help for the teacher to be able to recognize some of the more common deformities and to know how these might relate to learning problems. It is important to note the following important facts about physical defects.

1.  They may be caused by any of the above categories.

2.  The more there are, the more likely the child is to have major problems in other areas—such as learning.

3.  The same defect can have various and different causes.

4.  The symptoms the child shows from his defect(s) depend on how early he developed the problem, how many other problems he has, and the severity of the disorder.

**Growth Disorders:** Any child who is more than two standard deviations below the norm for age in his growth pattern may be a candidate for learning problems also. Causes of growth dysfunction are multiple and can occur in any of the categories as listed under the two previous sections on constitutional problems. Because of the presence of growth disability along with other physical defects, it is certainly common to see learning problems associated with this group.

**Disorders of the Special Senses:** Hearing and vision abnormalities are the most common causes of concern in this area. There are multiple causes for both of these problems. If we just stop to consider a child who cannot hear (true hearing loss as opposed to attention or emotional cause), we may observe the following:

### POOR HEARING

| Type | Cause |
|------|-------|
| Nerve deafness | Congenital |
| Conduction deafness | Infection |
| Central (brain) deafness | Trauma |
| | General illness |

Any type in Column 1 can be caused by any cause in Column 2. The results may be the same as far as the child's behavior, but the treatment will vary widely.

The same type of thinking applies to visual defects. We may see disorders in any part of the visual system from the eye itself, to the eye muscles, to the brain area that controls visual function. Any of these areas can be affected by almost any problem from prenatal and genetic disorders to trauma and infection later in life. Again, the behaviors we see resulting from such problems will vary greatly with the age at onset and the extent of the disability.

**Language Disabilities:** Language disabilities may include everything from the reception of language through the comprehension of same to the production of meaningful language in return. Deficiencies in many different areas may cause this type of problem. Genetic, hereditary, infectious, traumatic, nutritional, and emotional causes have all been implicated in this category. Children with language disorders can exhibit almost any sign or symptom of disordered function in a classroom situation. It is important to consider this category when evaluating a child who shows such behaviors as inattention, excessive activity, poor reading, general learning difficulties, problems following instructions, noise making, shyness, disruptiveness, and behavioral problems. Language disability can be a great masquerader and is often missed in the search for remediation of the educationally disabled child.

**Convulsive or Seizure Disorders:** Any insult to the central nervous system can cause some type of seizure disorder. This may vary from an alarming total body "shaking" event and loss of consciousness to a brief staring spell. Seizures may be inherited or caused by many different things such as infections, poisons, metabolic problems (low blood sugar), or injury. Many different types of behavior may be seen in children with convulsive disorders depending on the type of seizure. Certainly uncontrolled seizures will be a major detriment to a child's learning process.

**Specific Neurological Disorders:**

    1. *Cerebral Palsy (CP):* CP is a nonprogressive motor deficit resulting from any insult to the motor control areas of the central nervous system from the prenatal to early infancy periods. There are many different types of CP, but the majority of these children show some involvement of their motor coordination or control, and many have a spastic type of paralysis or weakness. The resultant problems will depend on the amount of associated damage as well as on the extent of the muscular involvement.

    2. *Neurological "hyperkinetic" disorder:* Neurological disorder has been previously discussed (see Chapter 2), and we have shown how "hyperactive" behavior can be associated with many different conditions or situations. The type we are talking about here is that thought to be due to a specific defect in the central nervous system whereby the mechanism for screening impulses and sustaining attention is in some way disordered (neurological hyperactivity). This type of condition may result from almost any insult to the central nervous system from trauma, infection, and perinatal distress to nutritional deficiencies. It may be genetic or hereditary in many cases. We often do not know the cause at all. Neurological hyperkinesis may or may not be associated with learning problems and other deficiencies such as behavior disorders, perceptual handicaps, and coordination disability. These children generally have short attention spans, are easily distracted, and have poor impulse control—but not in all situations. It is one of the more baffling conditions to differentiate, identify, and treat, but certainly *does exist* and often causes learning problems.

    3. *Specific learning disability:* Specific learning disability has also been previously discussed (Chapter 2) and is presented here as another of the disorders that can result from various causes and may be quite different to identify and treat. Again, we are referring to certain children who seem to have no obvious physical, intellectual, sensory, or psychological abnormality but for some unknown reason cannot learn to read or grasp some other specific concepts such as spelling or mathematics. These children seem to have some defect within their central nervous system that is interfering with their ability to learn in specific areas. This may often be a hereditary problem. There may be associated problems of hyperactivity, poor perception, and poor coordination. The problem

may resolve itself as the child matures (developmental delay). In any case it is real, and very frustrating for the child, parent, teacher, and physician. It should be reemphasized here that every child with a specific learning disorder should be considered individually, and should not be lumped together into diagnoses such as "minimal brain dysfunction" or other such "catchall" categories.

4. *Perceptual handicaps:* Perceptual handicaps are a large group of descriptive phenomena often classified as visual or auditory perceptual motor disabilities. It is one of the most poorly understood and confusing categories we have to deal with. There has been a great deal of research, speculation, and experimentation in this area. As of the present time, there is very little agreement as to the proper place of this category in the field of learning disorders. The term *perception* refers to "having a knowledge, recognition, sensation, or awareness of anything through the senses," that is, "perceiving." Therefore, a handicap in this area can refer to any of the special sense areas. The most common areas referred to are the visual and auditory. The person who has a visual perception problem does not see or appreciate various things in his environment as he should. The auditory perceptual handicap relates to sounds in the environment. People with perceptual handicaps can see and hear quite properly. The things they are seeing and hearing, however, are in some way distorted or not decoded properly somewhere from the point of production of the stimulus to the point of comprehension in the person's brain. If we add to the visual or auditory *reception*—a problem in *reproducing* either what a person sees or hears—we have a visual-motor perception problem.

These types of problems have been historically associated with learning disability, hyperactivity, maturational delay, and brain disorder of one type or another. They can be caused by an insult to the brain from pregnancy to adulthood. They may be associated with almost every type of behavior in children. The question is whether or not they *cause* any of these behaviors! The following facts must be understood so as not to be mystified and inundated by this whole concept. Visual-motor and auditory problems may *coexist* with learning problems; however, there is no proven cause and effect. The correction of perceptual problems will help the child's self-image, but it is questionable if his reading will improve just because of this. Auditory perceptual problems are probably much more important to learning and reading problems than are visual; however, therapy in this area does not insure educational progress either. The most important thing to know about these problems is to appreciate their existence, but don't get immersed in them, especially the terminology!

**Maturational Delay (Developmental Lag):** The concept of maturational delay has been mentioned previously (see Chapter 2) and will be repeated here since it is so very important to an understanding of learning disorders. Every child is preprogrammed to develop at his or her own rate of speed in various areas of development, including intellectual, physical, social, motor, and hormonal. The rate of development is predetermined for each child and usually follows hereditary and other genetic lines. It is important to remember that a child's progress in school is almost totally dependent on his *own* rate of development. It follows that if a child is not ready to participate in certain academic areas at a certain time, there is very little that can be done to hasten this process along.

School success depends on the proper intellectual, physical, social, and motor (neurological) maturity. A child who is not at age level for all of these indicators, if pushed beyond his limit, may well show varying degrees of educational difficulties along with hyperactivity, behavior disturbances, perceptual problems, and other signs often misconstrued as belonging to some kind of neurological diagnosis.

Almost any sign of neurological dysfunction, reading disorder, hyperactivity, or behavior disturbance can be produced by a child with a developmental delay. It is often quite difficult to distinguish between a real learning disorder or just a delay in development, especially in the four- to six-year-old group. It is, therefore, a wise thing to always keep the concept of maturity lag in mind when evaluating a child's behavior in the classroom. All of his signs of deviant behavior may be caused simply by the fact that he is not in the right place at the right maturational time!

**The Severely Emotionally Disturbed Child:**   Most emotional problems in children are not in the "major" category. The majority of the disturbances we see are due to environmental stresses on the child and result in minor symptoms such as anxiety, minimal behavior problems, and perhaps some psychosomatic symptoms such as headaches and abdominal pains. Most of the causes for these minor disturbances are usually fairly easy to deal with and are not of long duration, so that the child can be helped in the majority of cases.

An occasional child will develop a severe emotional disturbance due to some inner neurological disability or perhaps a long-lasting and deep traumatic episode in his life. The infant who is abandoned by his mother either in spirit, body, or both might fit into this category, as well as the child who is subject to physical abuse. Any type of severe maternal deprivation can cause these more serious disturbances. Severe emotional disturbances may result in permanent changes in the emotional set of the child, so that no matter what kind of remediation is attempted, the child will *remain* disturbed. Children with severe psychiatric disorders such as autism, schizophrenia, and various psychoses fit into this category. These children may be wild and unmanageable or totally withdrawn and un-responsive. Most of them have communication disorders. No matter what symptoms they present, the majority of them will exhibit severe learning problems that for the most part are extremely difficult to deal with.

## Symptomatic Categories

There are various types of children who present certain familiarly grouped "sets" of signs or symptoms. Since many of the characteristics in this group of children will relate both to internal and external causes of educational dysfunction, we will discuss this group of children after listing the external causes of educational dysfunction.

## The Child's Environment (External)

### THE SCHOOL AS A CAUSE OF EDUCATIONAL DYSFUNCTION

Whenever we have a child who fails to progress properly in school, we must first look at the environment in which the failure is taking place. There are many reasons why a poor classroom situation can be at the root of the problem. The child might be placed in an open-type classroom or in a regular classroom with many distractions. This may not be the best situation for some children who have problems sitting still and paying attention. Also, the type of children in the class may be the wrong mix for a certain individual. Even the physical setup of the class-room or school may not fit in with what may be best for the child. Things such as the way the seats are placed or where he sits may be inappropriate for him.

However, the main area of difficulty in most cases is probably in the area of the teacher-child relations. Some teachers just do better with certain children and vice versa. Most teachers are enthusiastic and start out with good intentions toward working satisfactorily with every child. However, very soon it becomes evident that some of the children have problems that make it difficult for the teacher to reach them. After a few weeks, no matter how hard the teacher tries, there are winners and losers among the students. The sullen, withdrawn, or disruptive children often start to fade quickly from the learning process.

There are teachers who also have problems of their own in per-sonality, training, desires, or abilities—problems that make it difficult for them to reach certain children under any circumstances. This can be acceptable if the teacher can recognize her own liabilities and drawbacks and ask for and/or accept help.

It is not the teacher's job to totally judge the child or make a complete diagnosis—only to identify the child with educational dysfunction. Then she should either try to discover the reason for the difficulty, correct it if possible, or refer the child to the appropriate person or agency for remediation.

It would be helpful if the teacher remained *on the same side* as the parent, child, and physician at all times during this process so that the child is operating on a basis of total support. There should be no sides drawn—no winners and losers chosen. Only in this way can the poor classroom situation be eliminated or ameliorated as a cause of educational dysfunction.

Finally, it is well to remember that a child who is placed in the wrong classroom situation for him can show almost any emotional or physical sign or symptom described for almost any ailment. Therefore it is wise to correct *this situation* before we start to climb the diagnostic tree!

## CULTURAL AND ENVIRONMENTAL DIFFICULTIES

Very basic to the evaluation of learning disorders is a knowledge of the social and family background from which the child comes. The teacher is not expected to be a social worker or to pry into the child's private life. However, she is sometimes the only one who does know what is really going on in the child's home. Problems such as lack of sleep, transiency, improper nutrition, child abuse, parental strife, and similar situations are sometimes imparted to the teacher by the child's words or actions. It is often quite difficult for the teacher to know exactly how to handle this type of information. Occasionally confidential communication with the physician and/or psychologist would be helpful in matters like this.

There are many things going on in the child's background that can cause poor school performance. Unstable home situations, financial difficulties, poor housing, deaths, divorce, and remarriage—all can and often do take their toll. Again, the communication of this type of information should be very confidential and guarded. Refer to Chapter 7 for the team approach in handling this problem of communication.

Cultural causes are also quite often evident. The obvious ones include minority and underprivileged groups with all of their built-in problems. Included here are the associated difficulties of the scarcity or lack of medical services, poor employment opportunities, and certainly familial instability. The matter of minority bias or prejudice is sometimes an important factor. Lack of early stimulation and insufficient attention to educational-type activities from early in life are also part of this problem and may lead not only to educational problems but also to developmental and psychological-emotional disabilities.

On the other hand, we must strongly consider the opposite end of the cultural seesaw where we have the upper and upper-middle class with educational and vocational expectations exceeding the ability of the child. This disparity between the child's resources and his parents' aspirations is often one of the main causes of school failure among this group.

We must also consider cultural *differences* as well as cultural *disturbances.* Language unfamiliarity, lack of the same interests, and an entirely different philosophy of life and living may cause a child to have quite a few classroom problems.

A child who attempts to enter the educational process with any of these environmental or cultural difficulties will often show problem behavior characteristic of many other categories, including hyperactivity, short attention span, disruptiveness, fighting, and general poor classroom attitude. And most important, the child won't learn to his full potential.

## EMOTIONAL DISORDERS

Emotional disorders as a group of possible causes of educational dysfunction are very loosely defined and cross into many other categories. In the internal category we mentioned the child who showed signs of a severe emotional disturbance that seemed to be part of the child's own makeup—a disorder that is totally independent of any outside influences. It is really difficult to separate all of the factors that make up the profile of a disturbed child. Therefore we must consider both internal *and* external factors when speaking of any child with such a problem.

There are many children who exhibit problems in school that seem to be caused by external factors and that have made these children emotionally upset. Almost anything a child comes into contact with for a long enough time can cause emotional problems—problems that will affect his learning, behavior, and future outlook on life if he is unable to effectively deal with the situation. The big difference in this category from internal emotional disorders is that when the problem areas are removed from the child's life and his feelings are openly dealt with, he can usually resume an orderly and productive life. A poor family situation, frequent moves, unusual or harsh punishment, poor parental relationships, bad choice of friends, financial instability, and almost any other event in the daily life of a child can result in symptoms of various emotional disturbances such as anxiety, personality disorders, depression, acting-out behavior, phobias, and many other psychological and emotional disorders. In addition, "physical" symptoms such as chronic abdominal pain, headaches, nail-biting, and dizzy spells can occur.

It is often difficult to ascertain exactly what the real causes of a child's problems are, and sometimes it becomes a problem simply to identify whether a child really *is* emotionally disturbed or not. The important thing for the teacher to remember is that she does not have to make a diagnosis—but just has to *describe* what she sees. We often have to watch a child for quite a while to see how much of a problem he really *does* have.

A good rule of thumb to at least get an idea of what is going on is to see whether the child is happy more than he is unhappy. No matter what the *basic* cause of his problems, if he is a sad child most of the time, that child *is* probably emotionally disturbed and must be identified and helped before it is too late.

The types of behaviors we may see in this group of children can run the entire gamut—from hyperactivity to total inactivity and depression. Poor attention span and impulsive behavior may be just as common to this group as to the hyperkinetic category. We may see almost any behavior associated with a classroom situation, a fact that makes our evaluations of these children so challenging and exasperating.

## ILLNESS AS A CAUSE OF EDUCATIONAL DYSFUNCTION

In the internal group of disorders we discussed the problems that may make a child *permanently* disabled and thus often lead to some degree of educational dysfunction. However, the more common situation is one where a child is relatively healthy and then becomes a victim of some type of illness or disease that causes him to miss school and fall behind in the learning process.

Most of these illnesses are of the short-lived variety such as respiratory infections, gastrointestinal upsets, temporary orthopedic problems (broken bones, sprains, injuries), infectious diseases such as chicken pox, and other common maladies.

Some children develop more serious and long-lasting problems such as malnutrition, rheumatic fever, cystic fibrosis, crippling injuries, untreatable anemias, meningitis, and other chronic disorders. This group is the one that causes the major learning problems, although a child who has *many minor short-lived* illnesses may have just as much trouble as one with *one long-lasting serious* disorder, because of the amount of school he misses.

Medical illnesses will be more fully explored in a later chapter (Chapter 5) where the more common diseases will be briefly explained in terms of what they mean to the child, his parents, and the school.

## MISCELLANEOUS (MOTIVATION, ATTITUDE, ETC.) CAUSES

There are many factors that have been cited as a cause of learning disability that do not neatly fit into one of the above categories, or perhaps cross the lines into several of the above. Thus, concepts such as motivation, environmental stimulation, and attitude may be considered by some people as basic causes for educational dysfunction. However, if any of these are really looked at closely, and are broken down into their component parts, it can usually be seen that one or more problems exist in the child himself or in his environment that are leading to the particular problems. A child may be poorly motivated because he doesn't feel well, because his parents are fighting, because he is not stimulated by his teacher, or because of many other factors.

## SUMMARY OF CAUSES OF EDUCATIONAL DYSFUNCTION

We have noted that there are many causes of educational dysfunction, both internal and external. However, it is important to point out that children exhibit *symptoms* and *behavior,* not *diagnoses.*

We feel that it might be helpful to develop a method of dealing with this symptomatic approach so as to correlate certain behaviors with some of the more common diagnoses. We have previously mentioned this approach in category C-2 in Table 3-1.

In order to try to correlate common behaviors seen in the classroom with certain specific diagnostic categories, we have developed a table that shows some of the common relationships in this regard (see Table 3-2).

If the table is followed, it is easy to see that there is no one pure category. Children with one type of problem often have the same group of signs or symptoms as children with a different so-called diagnosis. And in the same vein, two different children who exhibit a certain group of behaviors may have completely different reasons for a certain type of behavior.

Again, we can use the often quoted and abused term of *hyperactivity* as an example. We know that first of all, this may be an observation by a teacher or parent with a very low threshold of tolerance for boisterous behavior. Some children will become hyperactive if they cannot see or hear well. An anemic or chronically ill child might be overactive. Occasionally a nutritional problem such as low blood sugar or sensitivity to certain food substances can cause these symptoms. Toxins such as lead poisoning may be the culprit at times. Children with an allergy may exhibit this type of behavior. If we stop and look at the family and domestic problems a child is having, we sometimes can see why the child is behaving as he is. Children with low intelligence may be hyperactive if stressed beyond their ability—others with superior intelligence if not stimulated enough. Or of course, the child may be a true neurologically hyperactive child with a short attention span that is the source of his problem. The list could go on and on. The point is

**Table 3-2    SYMPTOMATIC CLASSIFICATION OF EDUCATIONAL DYSFUNCTION**

Etiological Categories

| Observations | Retardation (Subnormal intelligence) | Nutritional and Health Problems | Neurological Dysfunction Including "Hyperactivity" | Emotional Disorder | Cultural and Environmental Difficulties | Developmental Delay | Specific Learning Disorder | Communication Disorders |
|---|---|---|---|---|---|---|---|---|
| Small, immature | +++ | +++ | + | ++ | ++ | ++++ | + | + |
| Clumsy, awkward, poor coordination | ++ | +++ | +++ | 0 | + | +++ | ++ | ++ |
| Aggressive, defiant, destructive, fighting | ++ | ++ | +++ | ++++ | ++ | 0 | + | ++ |
| Hyperactive, poor attention span, distractible, impulsive | ++ | +++ | ++++ | ++ | ++ | + | ++ | +++ |
| Poor self-image, easily frustrated | +++ | + | +++ | +++ | ++ | + | +++ | + |
| Heavy absence from school | 0 | ++++ | 0 | +++ | ++++ | 0 | +++ | + |
| Shy, introverted, isolated | ++ | + | ++ | +++ | +++ | ++ | ++ | ++ |
| Pale, sickly looking, withdrawn | + | ++++ | + | ++ | ++ | + | 0 | + |
| Excitable, falls apart with stress, oversensitive | + | ++ | +++ | ++++ | ++ | ++ | ++ | ++ |
| Serious, sad, depressed | + | ++ | + | ++++ | ++ | + | + | ++ |
| Stealing, lying, temper tantrums | + | ++ | +++ | ++++ | ++ | 0 | + | + |
| Overdemanding, over-anxious to please | + | 0 | ++ | +++ | ++ | 0 | + | + |
| Visual-motor perceptual problem | +++ | ++ | +++ | + | + | ++++ | ++ | + |
| Not learning | ++++ | ++ | +++ | +++ | +++ | ++++ | ++++ | ++++ |

For the sake of brevity and clarity many of the etiological categories are lumped together into more easily utilizable groupings.

Explanation of Symbols:
++++ Almost always seen, high correlation, often causative.
+++ Often seen, fair correlation.
++ Sometimes seen—not much causal correlation.
+ Probably just a casual relationship—only rarely causally associated.
0 No real association or correlation.

clear—we are looking at *symptoms* for the most part, and we should try to deal with *children* and not diagnoses or categories.

When we observe a child who is exhibiting difficulty in the classroom, we should try to describe the types of problems he is showing first, and then move on to a possible etiology. Often this will be quite difficult or perhaps impossible to do, and we might have to deal with remediation only. We must be very certain to remember our educational triangle here also, since any approach to the educationally dysfunctioning child must include parent, school, physician when appropriate, and certainly the child himself.

*Perhaps the easiest way to understand this entire business of educational dysfunction is to picture the child as a separate and complete organism with all of his built-in systems. Some of these systems may not be in the best working order—due to various causes. The child then becomes a risk, or vulnerable, in that area when he is placed in a situation of stress. Since the most stressful situation any child is exposed to is school and its educational demands, it stands to reason that the breakdown probably will occur here. It is up to the three corners of the triangle to make sure that the sides do not collapse on the center— the child!*

# CHAPTER 4

# The Medical Background of Educational Dysfunction

## Specific Disorders

As we stated in the previous chapter, many of the problems that cause a child not to learn properly are medical in nature, but the definition of a medical disorder is not necessarily a disease or illness. What we are referring to here is any adverse situation in the body whether it be infectious, nutritional, traumatic, or inherent in the child's physical or mental makeup.

Before proceeding further in this vein, we again reiterate that *we do not believe that the physician or other medical personnel are responsible for the educational remediation of learning disorders!* Rather the place of the medical consultant is to:

1. See if there *is* a disease process that is interfering with the proper functioning of the child.

2. Help define the scope of the problem.

3. Try to remediate any disorders that might be present by use of medication, preventive medicine, or by any other available means.

4. Work with the entire educational team and the parents to present a child as free of problems and disabilities as is possible to the school personnel.

There are two general areas we are going to discuss as far as the medical approach to the cause of learning problems:

1. The theoretical background.

2. Actual body disorders associated with identifiable causes.

## THE THEORETICAL BACKGROUND OF
## LEARNING DISABILITIES

As we have previously discussed (see Chapters 2 and 3), there are some children who manifest a certain difficulty in school that seems to be totally unassociated with any known cause. There are essentially three major well-known categories that should be considered here:

1.  Specific learning (reading, writing, etc.) disability.

2.  Hyperactivity.

3.  Language—communication disorders.

(As we previously noted, the first two of these are often erroneously lumped together into the unsuitable category of "minimal brain dysfunction".)

A child may fit into one, two, or all three of these groups. And, as we have seen, there may be many different causes for any of these three disabilities. What we are trying to focus on here is the child who exhibits a problem in one or more of these areas and *has no other known cause for this problem* (such as cultural, parental, or specific physical reason). Let us approach each of these areas and try to clarify some current thinking along these lines.

### Specific Learning Disabilities

The category of specific learning disabilities describes the child who shows an *unexpected* failure in learning in one or more areas as described in Chapter 2. This child may have signs of neurological or developmental delay such as excessive activity, poor coordination, and a short attention span, or he may show *none* of these symptoms. He has normal or above-normal intelligence. There is no known medical or physical history to support a cause for the problem. The disability may be in reading, spelling, writing, arithmetic, or any combination of these. The major point is that for some *unknown* reason the child cannot learn.

There have been many theories advanced concerning children with this type of problem. The subject has been discussed in books and monographs dating back hundreds of years. There have been labels associated with this group of children, such as "dyslexia," "dysgraphia," and "dyscalculia," etc.* However, with all that has been advanced concerning this problem, we are still not exactly sure of what the real problem is, in many cases.

---

*Dyslexia refers to difficulty in reading; dysgraphia refers to difficulty in writing; dyscalculia refers to difficulty with numbers or arithmetic.

In the child who fails to learn up to his potential, where there is no other known cause for this problem, most of the evidence points to the presence of some type of developmental delay of the particular area of the nervous system that the child needs to utilize to get on with reading or other such tasks. There are many operations involved in learning to read, including accurate discrimination of symbols, the proper spatial orientation of these symbols, sequencing, visual memory of those tasks, and then being able to reproduce the symbols. It is obvious that if any one of these functions has not fully developed in a child, he will run into problems. If we add to the above *visual* tasks a child needs to master, the *auditory* skills—such as perceiving certain sounds, breaking them into component parts, putting them together again, reproducing what he has heard, and then relating all of this to the visual requisites mentioned above—we can see that there are many different points of possible dysfunction or delay that can explain the child's inability to read. *Thus, we see there is really no one catchall we can use such as dyslexia—each child has his own unique brand of dyslexia!*

Quite a few theories on specific learning disabilities have included the concept of perceptual problems as part of, or all of, their explanation for the disability. Included in this approach would be all of the various subproblems such as right-left scanning, reversals, rotations, and others. Entire remediation programs have sprung up using this type of approach to the problem.

However, if we closely scrutinize this type of explanation, we find that there is really no solid proof that the perceptual problem predates the learning problem. True, the two often coexist, and certainly an immaturity of the nervous system that prevents a child from grasping a complicated task such as reading is quite likely to cause him to have trouble with other symbols and forms. However, we see many children with terrible "perceptual" problems who are excellent readers and certainly can find many poor readers who are able to copy and draw beautiful geometric designs! There is really no good evidence that the time-honored visual-perceptual theories have anything to do with the real *cause* of learning disorders, except as a sometimes coexistent factor. Most children with so-called perceptual problems that are supposed to be limiting their reading abilities actually possess much more complicated perceptual abilities, just to be able to exist in today's environmental jungle, than would be needed to learn to read!

As far as reversals are concerned, these are again mostly a mark of immaturity. Most children from four to seven or eight will reverse some letters and numbers. The more stress a child is under and the harder the word is for him, the more he is likely to reverse. Most children who reverse don't even know they are doing it. Most of the time they don't know *you* care about it either. The *form* is correct; *they* know what they mean; so why are *you* worried? We often see children who can read and write beautifully reverse letters right down the line. It is certainly a problem that eventually should be overcome, but obviously is not the basic *cause* of the reading disorder. An approach to finding a cause for a reading problem must not become bound down with such unproductive side issues as perceptual problems and reversals!

We cannot point to one particular process or dwell on one certain theory to explain a specific reading, writing, spelling, or arithmetic problem area. The best way to approach this matter is to understand that there are many rapid-action tasks that must be accomplished within a child's nervous system to master the art of reading or some other educational accomplishment. These tasks include recognition, understanding, encoding, decoding, synthesis, discrimination, auditory and visual memory, and reproduction. A child with a disturbance or delay in any one or more of these areas will have difficulties learning. Some of the problems will be caused by a short attention span—this will be covered in the next section. Other times, language dysfunction will be to blame—this will also be discussed later in this chapter. Often short attention span, and language problems may coexist.

It has been theorized that most of the problems in these children are somehow tied to poor functions in the cortex or cognitive area of the brain. It is thought that learning disabilities are perhaps a result of some type of inefficient functioning in the cortex. We feel, however, that these inefficiencies are more of an *imperfection* or *delay in normal function,* rather than a *type of injury* to the brain. At the present time there is really no physical way we can *measure* the actual areas of imperfection. We can only define the specific *functions* or *processes* that seem to be lacking in the child's approach to learning, by the use of educational-psychological evaluation.

If we attempt to subdivide the inefficiencies of the brain into their component parts, we can see how some children might have problems in auditory discrimination or analyses, or experience difficulties in the visual memory or discrimination system, or be unable to change auditory signals into the proper equivalents for speech or reading. Perhaps some children may learn what letters sound like but not what sounds look like when written. These types of inefficiencies vary from child to child and must be closely analyzed before attempting to teach the child. Each child's problem is quite distinct and cannot be covered by blanket approaches.

In the group of children who exhibit the above types of problems we are faced with our so-called specific learning disabilities. A number of these children have only a delay of the function; others never do develop properly and thus have lifelong problems. In many children with this type of problem there is a hereditary disposition, and often older brothers, fathers, and uncles have shown the same problem. It is generally accepted that there is a definite preponderance of males showing this problem, again probably due to some type of genetic predisposition. The result of all of this is a child who is exhibiting a type of educational dysfunction. As we have stressed previously, the cause is really not as important as what we are going to do about it. We must find out where the imperfections and delays are in the particular child's *own* version of *his own* learning disability and try to compensate for them by properly selected teaching methods.

## Hyperactivity

As we have discussed in previous chapters, the term *hyperactivity* is one of the most misused and misunderstood in this entire field of educational dysfunction. In this particular section we are referring to the group of children who exhibit either medical or neurological hyperactivity (see Chapter 2). As was previously noted, the most important common denominator in this group of children is the presence of a shorter than normal attention span with an associated lack of impulse control. All of the other signs and symptoms shown in this group of children can probably be attributed to the short attention span. This disorder may be associated with learning problems, but in many cases the children have no difficulty at all except in behavior.

There are also some children with a short attention span who may have a difficult time learning but may not exhibit overactivity. This subgroup of the nonhyperactive hyperactive is interesting and challenging since these children are not initially identified because of their behavior but because of their attention span and learning difficulty. This particular subgroup will be discussed later.

In this section we will concern ourselves with the theories that have been advanced to explain the short attention span in hyperactive children. There have been many attempts to approach this group of children, and in order to understand the problem better, let us briefly outline a model of brain organization and function that might clarify things a bit. We will simplify this explanation as much as possible since we are not concerned with neuroanatomy or neurophysiology as such in this book.

In essence the entire nervous system can be divided into three functional tasks: input, integration, and output. The input system collects and transmits information from the environment utilizing all of the special senses. The integrative system is the most complex, existing at all levels of the nervous system. This system is responsible for complex thinking, memory, formulation of motor activity, and general awareness—

both internal and external. The output system is connected with muscle movement or internal processes such as sweating, heart rate, and blood pressure.

Any action we are responsible for is obviously dependent on the smooth independent functioning of all three systems as well as the success-ful interrelationship of the three systems. It is obvious that any dysfunc-tions in one or more of these systems will lead to altered function some-where in the body or brain. It is also quite clear that there must be many connections or circuits working in harmony to produce a desired effect. In the brain alone, the transmission of a particular message or the response to a given stimulus depends on the smooth functioning of all of these circuits, much like a computer.

All of the signals that are received by the input system, assimilated by the integrative system, and finally utilized by the output system are dependent on the electrical transmission of impulses from one set of nerve cells to another. The actual transmission of these nerve impulses is dependent on some form of chemical reaction at the nerve ending to keep the impulses flowing. It therefore becomes obvious that a blockage or interruption of one or more of these nerve impulses as they travel through the various input-integrative-output circuits can produce problems.

It has been theorized that, in the true neurologically hyperactive children, there are specific blocks in certain of the integrative nerve circuits. Because of these blocks, there is a lack of stimulation of the nerves in the affected area, and the end result is a loss of function some-where between input and output. This leads to a loss of function of the arousal system. This loss of function can be manifested as the absence of concentrating power for a specific event. If this blockage is widespread, a generalized lack of concentration will be the result, due to the lack of stimulation of the nerves in the integrative system which controls the concentrating ability of the output system. On the other hand, if there is an interruption of the stimulation of the arousal system needed to block out environmental distractions, the person may lose his power to effec-tively screen out unwanted impulses. Hence the lack of concentration may be input *or* output. If both mechanisms are interrupted simulta-neously, the result is loss of both concentration and distractibility. This concept may be more easily followed if we refer to Figures 4-1, 4-2, and 4-3.

As we see on these very simplified schemata, if there is a block or interruption to the output areas, a loss of concentration for that event will take place. On the other hand, if there is ineffective screening of stimuli from the environment, a generalized assault on the senses will take place, and the result will be distractibility. Either of these events may often lead to a driven, impulsive type of behavior that is called

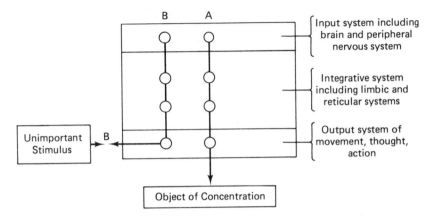

A    Stimulation of train of events to concentrate properly

B    Stimulation of train of events to block out unimportant
     stimulus at Point B

*Figure 4-1.*

*hyperactivity* or *hyperkinesis.* Certainly these types of defects in the various areas of the nervous system can be a prime cause of educational dysfunction. A child who cannot concentrate does not learn. A child who is totally distracted by his environment will have similar difficulties.

The next step in our discussion of medical or neurological hyperactivity is to find out what causes it. There have been many theories advanced in this area, and we will try to briefly list, discuss, and evaluate some of the more popular ones.

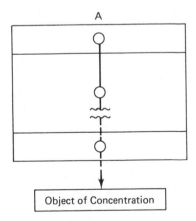

*Figure 4-2.*

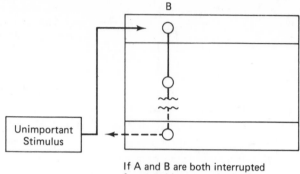

If A and B are both interrupted
from working properly, both poor
concentration and distractibility result.

*Figure 4-3.*

Before we go further it would be well to reiterate that we are referring here to children who demonstrate this particular syndrome associated with no other commonly identifiable cause. As we stated in Chapter 3, it is well known that children who are exposed to insults such as birth injury, prematurity, central nervous system infections, and poisoning can have a resulting neurological disturbance such as hyperactivity, with similar signs and symptoms. To be sure, the result might be the same as the problem we are talking about—perhaps the treatment also. But what we are referring to is the child with *no known* or easily identifiable *cause* for his symptoms. The children we are discussing here belong to groups 5 and 6 of the hyperactivity syndrome discussed in Chapter 2. They are the true neurological hyperactives and the medical hyperactives, both of whom often are interwoven in actual practice. These are the children who have a block of the arousal or stimulating systems necessary for concentration or screening out unproductive environmental stimuli. These blocks may occur for no known reason (perhaps genetic) or may be in some way related to various parts of a child's environment including foods or low blood sugar (medical hyperactivity). In the latter cases, it is theorized that the "medical" condition in some way causes or is related to the same attention span problems seen in the true neurological or genetic type.

## HEREDITARY (GENETIC) HYPERACTIVITY

A large number of neurologically hyperactive children have inherited the problem as a result of some inborn dysfunction of their central nervous systems. These children have a short attention span, are distractible, often have many other behavioral and learning problems, and are probably the largest group of true hyperactive children we deal with. It is this group of children who are often lumped into the category of "minimal brain dysfunction," which is a mistake, as we have mentioned. There are no sure-fire ways to differentiate this hereditary group from some of the other true, neurological hyperactive children—or occasionally from some of the nonneurologically hyperactive ones. Many times a trial of stimulant medication is the one specific factor that may help to identify this group. It is again important to note that it seems that there is a definite genetic disorder in the male that makes the problem appear much more commonly in boys, perhaps on a five- or ten-to-one ratio over girls. This may in some way be related to the XY chromosome combination.

## NUTRITIONAL HYPERACTIVITY

### Food Additives, Preservatives, Artificial Coloring, and Salicylates

A recently popularized theory holds that certain children have a sensitivity to various substances in their diets that cause them to become hyperactive and also can lead to various behavioral and learning disorders. There are two main groups of foods in this category.

1. Foods containing salicylate, which is the main constituent of aspirin. The foods in this group include almost all of the common fruits. Medication containing aspirin in any form would also be included in this group.

2. Foods containing various forms of artificial coloring, flavoring, and preservatives. This theory maintains that many children will improve their behavior, lessen their activity, and often learn better if placed on a diet excluding these products. Some of the children may not have to be completely kept away from all of these food groups—perhaps only one or two of them—for the diet to be effective.

The proponents of this theory feel that these particular food substances cause some type of dysfunction or irritation in the central nervous system in people who are sensitive to them—perhaps acting as a blocking agent such as we discussed in the neurological group. It takes anywhere from three to six weeks to see if such a diet works on a particular individual, and if a child is exposed to a "forbidden" food after the diet is underway and effective, there supposedly will be an adverse effect shown in the child's behavior in a very short time. The results of this approach will be discussed in Chapter 11.

### Food Allergy

It has always been popular to blame foods for various body ills including sneezing, asthma, rashes, and now learning problems. Some workers in the field have purportedly documented the dramatic improvement in a child's hyperactive behavior when certain foods were removed from his diet. The most commonly incriminated foods are in the milk and dairy-food category, with eggs, chocolate, shell fish, and others following closely behind.

This is certainly an extremely difficult field to evaluate. The intensity and beliefs of the physician or parent may be just as important to the reported result as the food elimination itself. The theory behind this is of course quite simple—if a food can cause a reaction in the skin or respiratory tract, why can't it cause a similar adverse reaction in the nervous system? Hence, could food allergy lead to hyperactivity and learning problems?

It is difficult to know the true answer. Obviously, if a child is constantly sneezing and feels badly because of a stuffy nose or congested chest—and if the milk is causing this congestion—he will feel and act better just because his congestion is gone, aside from any effect of the milk on his nervous system! It is probable that there are some children who have major allergic disease with food sensitivity who will behave and learn better if those foods are removed. Whether the food itself caused the disturbance in the brain is anyone's guess. Children with chronic fatigue, aches and pains, dark circles under their eyes, and repeated respiratory infections have been grouped together under the "tension-fatigue" syndrome. The cause of this is purported to be pasteurized-homogenized cow's milk. Learning problems are often associated with this syndrome. The therapy of such children will be discussed in Chapter 11.

### Sugar—Too Much and Too Little

**Too Little Sugar:** Hypoglycemia is low blood sugar resulting from an overabundance of insulin (a hormone produced in the pancreas) in response to sugar ingestion or various abnormalities of the pancreas or other glands. When the level of sugar (glucose) in the blood falls significantly, some people may respond with signs and symptoms such as restlessness, depression, withdrawal, tremors, nervousness, or fright. Others may show physical signs such as headaches, stomachache, hay fever, or asthma. Occasionally some people become mean and antisocial. In rare cases a person can develop convulsions or loss of consciousness from hypoglycemia. Not everyone responds to a low blood sugar with symptoms, so that many people could have quite a low level of blood sugar and not know it.

Hypoglycemia is usually caused by an abnormal release of insulin and other hormones lowering the level of sugar in the blood. There are many causes for this condition, including tumors, enzyme defects, drug poisoning, and hormonal dysfunctions. Because of these conditions, at various times and under various circumstances, the blood sugar will drop to extremely low levels and the above-mentioned adverse signs and symptoms may occur. In children the most common form of this disease is called "ketotic hypoglycemia" and usually follows prolonged fasting or episodes of illness or vomiting. Another form is called "reactive hypoglycemia," in which the blood sugar drops to abnormally low levels three to six hours after a meal consisting of mostly sugars or carbohydrates.

Some children with educational dysfunction become restless or have other symptoms that resemble those caused by hypoglycemia. Many of these children seem to exhibit the symptoms after they eat large amounts of quick or pure carbohydrates, which theoretically could be due to a rapidly dropping blood sugar after such a stimulus. It is often suggested that children who do show this type of reaction be placed on a special diet excluding the foods in the sugar or starch group to see if perhaps this type of hypoglycemia might be a factor in the child's problems.

The documentation of the actual levels of blood sugar would be quite helpful in order to know exactly whom to place on such a diet. However, the attempt to prove hypoglycemia by laboratory tests is usually fruitless. It is often helpful to try to take a blood sugar determination at the height of a child's adverse behavior reaction, but rarely do we see low sugar levels in these children. Because of this it may help to note that the type of child who might develop such a condition is more likely to be a sensitive, touchy child who has cravings for sugary or starchy foods such as candy bars, ice cream, cereal, and desserts. These children also might show a "Jekyll and Hyde" type of personality, with sweet, loving behavior suddenly turning into anxious, mean, depressed, and hyperactive behavior. Many of these children have a history of sleep disturbances, colic, bed-wetting, allergies, respiratory infections, and fear of new situations. In all of these situations, however, a high degree of stress is also involved, so that the relationship of the symptoms to sugar metabolism might be questioned in some cases. The family history of this type of child might show diabetes, obesity, and alcoholism in some cases, as a further aid in diagnosis.

Children who show this type of metabolic response to sugar ingestion may actually belong to the neurologically hyperactive group—a group who are already under stress due to their inability to handle all of the incoming stimuli presented to them by the classroom situation. The fall in blood sugar after the sugar and starch meals may be just enough to prevent the child from functioning optimally. Perhaps when the theoretical blood sugar fluctuations are controlled by diet, the neurological components become easier to control also. The therapeutic approach to this type of child will be mentioned in Chapter 11.

**Too Much Sugar:**   Many parents indicate that their child becomes quite wild as soon as a candy bar or other type of "junk food" is consumed (as opposed to *somewhat later* as with hypoglycemia). At holiday times this becomes a real problem. Some workers in the field and many parents feel that the behavior of these children is actually disturbed by consuming these sweets. As we noted in the section on hypoglycemia, this might be related to a rapidly dropping blood sugar after these foods are eaten. In some cases, however, it seems to be the food itself that causes the problem.

This observation is too common to be dismissed as sheer nonsense. There are probably some very good reasons why it is valid in a great many cases. Any of the following reasons might explain this.

1.   The child is one of those who is sensitive to food additives or preservatives, so that it is not the candy itself that is the problem.

2.   Dairy or milk allergy may be present to cause a symptomatic change.

3.   The time of day or season of the year when these types of snacks are more available is usually a wilder, more excitable time; thus, bedtime or Christmas or Thanksgiving is filled with so many other stimuli that it is hard to differentiate the food from the other causes of excessive activity.

4.   It would be difficult to do any real scientific documentation on such an observation. However, we must state here that if the parent or teacher feels strongly enough that the absence of sweets is a positive behavior determiner, it would be wise to experiment. Remember, though, we must not make the child into a *different* species from the other children because of our biases. The best thing would be to get *all* of the children eating less nonnutritious foods, and the problem would cease to exist as a diagnostic dilemma.

## Vitamins

Vitamins are compounds or chemicals that are required in tiny amounts for the metabolism of our bodies, including the central nervous system. There are many different vitamins known to be needed by the human body, and all of them must be supplied by our outside food sources—the body does not make its own vitamins. Most people receive enough vitamins from the foods they eat to satisfy their demands, although in some cases for various reasons, vitamin supplements may be suggested (such as in young infants or children where the diet is not as well-rounded as it should be).

There are certain diseases that are caused by vitamin deficiencies such as rickets (vitamin D), scurvy (vitamin C), and blindness (vitamin A).

Most of the vitamin deficiency diseases are due to chronic illness, poor nutrition, abnormal diets, or very poor living conditions. In the United States there are very few children with overt vitamin deficiency disease.

However, in the past several years it has been postulated by certain workers that some people need *more than* the average daily requirement of vitamins to function properly. They further theorize that if large amounts of certain vitamins are not present, a derangement of the cells and tissues of the brain can take place, and thus may lead to disorders such as mental illness, schizophrenia, learning disorders, and hyperactivity. This theory, popularly named "orthomolecularity," holds that some people with these particular disorders will be helped, or even cured, if given large doses of vitamins, especially of the B complex, along with extra minerals such as calcium and magnesium. This type of treatment has become known as "megavitamin therapy."

We do know that vitamins are essential for body enzymes to function optimally. B-complex vitamins are essential for carbohydrate metabolism. We can theorize that if a person is eating a large amount of carbohydrate foods without sufficient B vitamins ("empty calories"), the body will rob the brain and other tissues of B vitamins in order to metabolize the ingested sugars. Thus, theoretically the brain could be depleted of its B vitamins and be unable to manufacture certain brain chemicals (such as norepinephrine) that are necessary for proper academic performance. We also know that vitamin B6 is related to memory functions and other B-complex vitamins are essential for the manufacture of cortisone by the adrenal glands. Therefore, an improvement in memory skills and other body functions might theoretically be seen with a modest increase in these various vitamins. The role of vitamin therapy in educational dysfunction will be discussed in Chapter 11.

### Other Nutritional Theories

It has been postulated that if there is less than the required amounts of various metals such as magnesium, zinc, or copper in our diets, this can cause behavior and learning disorders. Since most of these metals are difficult to measure and are present in almost all foods, it is very difficult to properly assess their importance in this matter. It may well be that in the future a more specific recommendation will become available as our measuring techniques becomes more sophisticated. The role of mineral therapy will be discussed in Chapter 11.

## HYPERACTIVITY CAUSED BY THE ENVIRONMENT

There have been many theories advanced over the past several years concerning the possible effect of our environment on the central nervous system. Almost anything we see around us has been blamed for the adverse behavior of our children. Some of these adverse stimuli include:

Fluorescent lighting.

Smog.

Fluoride in water.

Nonionizing radiation (radio beams, microwaves).

Auditory pollution.

Aerosols.

To date, no proof exists that any of the above are causally related to behavioral or neurological problems.

In this section we have reviewed the group of children who fit into the classification of neurologically hyperactive. We see that most of them have some sort of brain dysfunction that shows up as a block of the arousal or stimulation system of the nerves that are necessary to concentrate on something or to screen out undesirable stimuli. This block may sometimes be associated with or made worse by various nutritional or environmental causes, but most often occurs for no known reason. It may be seen in families, and often is associated with other disorders of the nervous system such as learning disabilities, perceptual problems, and various other difficulties.

## Language Disorders

The third common area of disability that we must mention comprises language or communication disorders. There are certain children who have a central nervous system dysfunction that may coexist with specific learning disabilities and hyperactivity, but may also occur independently.

The term *aphasia* has been connected with this group of disorders, but it is really a poor term to use since it describes a disorder that is the result of some type of *brain damage* in a *fully developed individual;* whereas here we are referring to children who have as yet *failed* to *completely develop* in these areas.

The type of disorder we refer to is similar to some of the problems we discussed in the section on learning disabilities. Children with language disorders are defined as having some type of dysfunction in the various mechanisms necessary for the understanding, processing, or expression of language. These children have no hearing or physical speech defect, but because of some type of inborn impairment in the language centers that are located in the brain, the language functions are not able to be properly utilized. The defect may be in the receptive, associative, or expressive areas of language.

Every sound we hear must be properly received and analyzed by our brain for us to understand it. And likewise in order to produce speech, we must use many mechanisms to get the words out of the memory banks and ready to use. There are nerve centers in our brain that control all of the mechanisms necessary to language development and subsequently to learning. These mechanisms include auditory discrimination, analysis, synthesis, and sequential memory. In addition, the brain must prepare for reauditorization and articulation. Many children have inborn impairments in one or more of these functions and will thus have language problems.

It is useful to think of these auditory perceptual problems as follows:

> A person who has receptive disability is listening to a foreign language program. He hears the words, but they don't make sense.
>
> A person who has associative problems receives the words in the foreign language all right, but has lost his translation dictionary.
>
> A person who has expressive dysfunction knows what he wants to say, but when asked to do so in the foreign language, he cannot express himself.

This is a rather crude and simplistic explanation, but may help in the comprehension of this rather complex subject.

Most children with learning disorders also have one or more auditory perceptual problems, especially in the functions of auditory discrimination and memory. It is often difficult to differentiate a child with a pure learning disorder from one who has an auditory perceptual or language disability. Another problem often faced is the differentiation of a child with an auditory perceptual problem from one who has a neurological attention span disability. Even our testing may be difficult since we may have a hard time measuring auditory memory or discrimination in a child who cannot pay attention properly.

In summary, most of the auditory perceptual or language disability problems we see do not exist alone, and especially in younger children are likely to be associated with behavior and learning difficulties. The probable causes of these language disabilities are very much the same as we have discussed for the specific learning disabilities. It is felt that most of the children with this type of problem have either an inherited disorder, or the cause is unknown. The most important thing to remember is that special testing must be done by psychologists and language specialists to ascertain just where the specific blocks in the child's neurological learning process are located in order to be able to form the proper strategy to assist him to learn.

## Combination Dysfunctions

As we have just stressed, many children with educational dysfunction will not give evidence of a pure disorder. Most of them will have various combinations of specific areas of learning handicaps, such as attention span problems, perhaps language disabilities of one degree or another, and usually some type of emotional or psychological stress. It is therefore a more useful exercise to specify the problems or behaviors in need of remediation rather than to try to categorize or make a specific diagnosis.

Nowhere is this more obvious than in the case of the descriptive category we shall call the *global-atypical child*. This term refers to any of a group of children ranging in age from approximately two to five who show some or all of the following characteristics:

1.   Unmanageable behavior—often wild and impulsive.

2.   Extremely short attention span.

3.   Poorly developed, delayed, or often absent speech.

4.   Delayed developmental milestones.

5.   Often associated medical problems such as allergy, colic, and frequent infections.

6.   A desperate, often crumbling family situation.

These children are placed by various workers into many different diagnostic categories including mental retardation, hyperactivity, brain damage, aphasia, autism, and others. They are also treated in many different ways, both medically and psychologically. Because of the widespread behavioral deviations shown by these children, it is likely that they are exhibiting signs of some type of diffuse brain dysfunction. In a young child who is not fully developed neurologically, this may affect almost any area of function including language, coordination, perception, learning, and behavior. Thus, different workers see these children in different ways, often not realizing that they are dealing with a multiple-handicapped child who is exhibiting diffuse brain dysfunction affecting all areas of neurological function.

If diagnosis is so complex, can remediation be any simpler? The truth is that these children need to be looked at as possessing many major handicaps, and any program that they are to fit into must remain flexible and changeable. The term *global atypical child* is not as important to remember as the type of child it describes. Because of the large number of children who fit into this kind of situation, the teacher should be aware of the pressure and difficulty in handling this category of child.

Many other children may not be as severely affected as the "global" child, but could also present several types of dysfunctions and should also be considered part of this category. This is just another reminder of the importance of using descriptive terms and not labels in dealing with children with educational dysfunction.

This concludes the discussion of the medical-neurological conditions directly responsible for learning handicaps. In the following chapter we will present a summary of the medical conditions that may not specifically produce a learning problem by themselves but are often responsible for a child's absence from school, which in turn causes educational problems. We feel that a familiarity with some of the more common medical conditions, terms, and illnesses is of benefit to the teacher who must deal with large numbers of children on a day-to-day basis.

There are some workers who have developed a somewhat different approach to the diagnosis and treatment of learning disabilities, hyperactivity, and behavior disorders.* This group has postulated that some children who have these problems are actually suffering from a psychiatric disorder very much like the adult form of manic-depressive disease.

These workers feel that some children who show signs and symptoms of extreme mood changes, sadness, loneliness, and feelings of poor self-worth, as well as other similar emotions, fit into this category. The workers believe that children in this category have an inherited biochemical defect, and they treat the children with some of the very potent antidepressant medications (see Chapter 11).

It must be emphasized that a very distinct minority of workers follows this approach at the present time. However it is another example of the real problem that exists in the diagnosis and treatment of children with educational dysfunction.

*Weinberg, Warren; Joel Rutman; Leo Sullivan; Elizabeth C. Penick; and Susan Dietz. "Depression in Children Referred to an Educational Diagnostic Center: Diagnosis and Treatment," *Journal of Pediatrics,* 83, No. 6 (Dec. 1973), pp. 1065-1072.

# CHAPTER 5

# The Medical Background of Learning Problems

## General Disorders

This chapter deals with the medical problems that might interfere with learning or classroom behavior. There are many diseases that may affect children, both on a short-term basis and occasionally on a more chronic basis. Any loss of classroom time can be a detriment to learning. The child who is present but not feeling well may also have problems with the learning process. We are not attempting to present a complete compendium of childhood diseases at this time, nor do we expect the teacher to become a diagnostician. What we will present in this chapter is a brief, concise glossary of some of the more common illnesses a teacher may face in her classroom. For a more complete description of the various illnesses, we suggest any of the references listed at the end of this book.

It is imperative that teachers and other school personnel have a working knowledge of the various disorders listed in this chapter, including their possible effects on a child's learning. Very often, school personnel will be the first to notice behaviors symptomatic of a medical problem. By recognizing some neurological, pathological, or physiological problems that may be a potential contributor to the learning problem, the teacher can perform an invaluable service to the child and his family. Timely and proper referrals can often play a large part in the remediation process.

## GENERAL HEALTH PROBLEMS

### Nutrition

A child must be well nourished to succeed optimally in school. Nutritional problems refer to both under- and overnutrition. In the United States today we are faced with many more problems caused by the latter rather than by the former condition. Obesity must be dealt with in the young child before he develops a lifelong problem. The child who suffers from overweight may also have secondary problems from his obesity, such as peer group rejection or ridicule, as well as actually suffering some physical disability from his condition.

As far as nutrition is concerned, we may be dealing with deficiencies in calories, proteins, vitamins, minerals, or any combination of these. The child may show signs of weakness, paleness (pallor), fatigue, skin disorders, hair and nail problems, or almost any type of behavior disorder. The problem may be secondary to some other illness, or may be primary.

*A properly nourished child is essential for a proper classroom experience.* The teacher can be quite helpful, often working with the school nurse, to establish whether or not there *is* a problem and what can be done about it. No child can be helped optimally with a learning or behavior problem unless he is receiving the proper amount and type of nutrition.

### Infection and Immunization

Many different types of organisms can affect a growing child and may produce a variety of illnesses. We will mention some of the generalized infections affecting the entire body, and will review other more specific infections in the sections on the various organ systems.

Most infectious diseases are caused by microorganisms that are invisible to the human eye. The majority of these are either bacteria or viruses. *Bacteria* are organisms that are able to be seen with a regular microscope, can be grown as colonies on agar plates (cultures), and are usually killed or inactivated by antibiotics. *Viruses* are much smaller organisms that are seen only with the use of an electron microscope, cannot be cultured on agar plates, and usually do not respond to antibiotics.

Before mentioning some of the more common generalized infectious diseases, we might say a word about protection from disease, or *immunization.* We know that the body produces certain chemical substances called *antibodies* when any type of bacteria, virus, or other outside material is introduced. By introducing a nondangerous form of the particular offending agent, it is possible to encourage the production of these antibodies to provide a protective effect for long periods of time. This is called *active* immunization. There are two different types of products used for active immunization, vaccines and toxoids.

1. **Vaccine**—This is a preparation of the particular organism (virus or bacteria) against which we desire immunity—either killed, live attenuated (partially inactivated), or live (not attenuated).

2. **Toxoid**—This is a preparation of the poison (toxin) emitted by an organism. The toxin is inactivated chemically or physically before use as an immunizing agent.

There is also a form of immunization that involves the use of antibodies from another person or source. This is *passive* immunization and is involved mostly in the use of gamma globulin for diseases such as hepatitis, and when active immunization has not been utilized—for measles and polio.

## SPECIFIC FORMS OF ACTIVE IMMUNIZATION

The more common forms of active immunization we use today include DPT, tetanus, polio vaccine, measles vaccination, and vaccination for mumps.

### DPT

DPT includes diphtheria toxoid, tetanus toxoid, and pertussis (whooping cough) vaccine. It is given as three doses in the first 6 months of life with a booster at 18 months and another at five years of age.

### Tetanus

Following the preschool DPT, tetanus immunization should be given every ten years routinely, or at the time of a wound if it has been more than five years since the last tetanus shot.

### Polio

Polio immunization is given as a live (attenuated) vaccine in the first year of life and is repeated at 18 months of age and at five years. There is also a killed vaccine that is used in some circumstances.

### Measles Vaccination

Measles immunization is an attenuated live vaccine that is usually given when the child is 15 months old. It might have to be repeated in the teen-age years in the event of an epidemic. It is often given in conjunction with mumps and rubella (German measles) vaccines and is available in a triple-vaccine preparation (MMR).

### German Measles (Rubella) Vaccination

This viral illness will be discussed below. The vaccine to prevent rubella is a live, attenuated vaccine that is often combined with the measles and/or mumps vaccines.

### Mumps Vaccination

Mumps is also a viral illness which will be discussed in more detail later in this chapter. Mumps vaccine is another of the live, attenuated type vaccines.

There are other vaccines available such as for influenza, typhoid fever, yellow fever, and cholera. The most important and commonly used ones to remember are those listed above. Vaccination for influenza remains a very controversial and poorly agreed upon subject, with many supporters and many detractors.

## Common Childhood Diseases

Following is a discussion of some of the more common, generalized, infectious illnesses with a few important points listed after each. When the term *incubation period* is used, it refers to the time between a person's first exposure to the illness and the development of the first symptoms.

### CHICKEN POX (VARICELLA)

Chicken pox is a common contagious disease, caused by a virus, which almost all children get before they are ten years of age. There is no protection provided by the maternal antibodies, so a small baby can develop it. The contagious period is from one day before the rash breaks out to six days after onset, when the rash is crusted. The rash starts as red pimples (papules), and a clear "dewy" drop develops on the pimple that quickly becomes pus-filled (purulent). Following this the rash becomes crusty. The lesions are individual and usually start on the stomach, chest, and back, but may spread to any part of the body. There may be fever and respiratory symptoms present also. There is no treatment except for the itching, and no preventive measures are available in most children. The incubation period from time of exposure until the rash starts is generally two to three weeks. There is no active immunization for chicken pox, but there is usually lifelong immunity after one attack.

## MEASLES (RUBEOLA, RED MEASLES, HARD MEASLES, SEVEN-DAY MEASLES)

Measles is a viral disease that has become less common since we have developed a good vaccine for it. The incubation period is 10 to 12 days, and the illness begins with a high fever, cough, runny nose, and red eyes. This phase lasts for 3 to 4 days and is followed by the rash that is red, blotchy, and starts on the head and face and quickly covers the rest of the body. There are often tiny white spots on the inside of the child's cheeks as the rash is starting. The fever peaks in 4 days as the rash reaches its height. The rash lasts up to one week and often is associated with skin peeling. The contagious period is from the start of the cough and fever through most of the rash. There is no treatment except symptomatic relief. The disease should be prevented by measles vaccine. Babies are usually protected by their mother's immunity until one year of age. Immunity from having had measles is lifelong.

## GERMAN MEASLES (RUBELLA, THREE-DAY MEASLES)

German measles is also a viral disease. It is more important because of the complications than because of the disease itself. The incubation period is two to three weeks, and it usually starts with a slight fever and cold symptoms, followed by a blotchy red rash like the other type of measles. The rash starts on the head and face and spreads over the body to the feet in three days and then disappears. There are usually hard, large knots (lymph nodes) behind the ears. There is no treatment, and the contagious period is from one week before the rash breaks out until five to seven days afterward. The most dangerous thing about rubella is the fact that a pregnant woman who develops the illness in the first several months of her pregnancy may transmit it to her unborn baby, and this may result in serious birth defects in the child, such as blindness, deafness, retardation, heart and bone disorders, and other serious congenital anomalies. It is important that *all girls be immunized against rubella before puberty!*

## SCARLET FEVER (SCARLATINA)

Scarlet fever is caused by a form of bacteria (hemolytic streptococci), popularly known as "strep." It is moderately contagious and usually starts with a sore throat, fever, headache, and vomiting. The rash starts on the body, usually around the armpits and groin, and is bright red. The skin is usually rough under the rash, and the individual lesions usually run together so that the skin looks bright scarlet. The rash is not seen on the face, but the cheeks are often red. The child can be treated with antibodies (the most effective is penicillin), and he will lose his infectiousness in 48 hours. There is no vaccine for scarlet fever, and a person may incur the disease more than once. The incubation period is two to four days.

## MUMPS (EPIDEMIC PAROTITIS)

Mumps is a common viral disease that is not seen as much as previously because of the availability of immunization. The incubation period is three to four weeks, and the course of the disease is quite variable. Some children with mumps have no symptoms. Sometimes the child will have a slight fever and headache and then develop the characteristic swelling that is just in front of the ear and usually pushes the ear lobe up. The swelling is usually *not* on the neck. One or both sides may become swollen, and the swelling may last up to one week. The disease is communicable from one week before the swelling to ten days after the symptoms first appear. There is no treatment, but vaccination can prevent it. Second cases of mumps are rare.

## DIPHTHERIA, WHOOPING COUGH

Both diphtheria and whooping cough are dangerous diseases but are only rarely seen today except in small epidemic pockets, and therefore they will not be discussed here. Immunization is quite effective in the elimination of these diseases.

### Other Virus Diseases

## POLIOMYELITIS (POLIO)

Polio is a viral illness that is also uncommon today because of immunization procedures. However, it is wise for school personnel to have a nodding acquaintance with polio. This illness is one of the group of diseases known as "aseptic" meningitis. There are many other viruses that can cause symptoms similar to polio, but they do not usually result in paralysis. Polio usually has an incubation period of from several days to more than a week (usually seven to ten days). The illness is mostly "flu"-like, with fever, headache, sore throat, and gastrointestinal symptoms as well as muscle aches. Most of the polio cases stop here and cause no further problems. However, occasionally a viral meningitis with fever, headache, vomiting, and neck stiffness will occur. This phase might then proceed to full-blown paralysis of one or more muscle groups, including the respiratory muscles. The important thing to remember about polio is that it closely resembles so many other viral illnesses in its clinical manifestations, and more important, it can be prevented by immunization in infancy.

## OTHER VIRAL INFECTIOUS DISEASES WITH RASHES

Besides the more commonly known diseases that produce rashes such as chicken pox, measles, and German measles, there are numerous other illnesses that can be associated with rashes that are actually *more common* than the diseases mentioned above. For example, there are several groups of illnesses caused by viruses known as "Echo" and "coxsackie" (and occasionally others) that are extremely common in childhood and are often associated with rashes. Most of these illnesses are characterized by fevers, generalized weakness, occasional respiratory symptoms, and often have associated vomiting and diarrhea. Some illnesses may be part of the aseptic meningitis syndrome (mentioned with polio), and may produce headache, dizziness, and back and muscle stiffness. The rashes associated with these diseases may be red and blotchy like measles or German measles or papular like chicken pox. The rash may come on before, during, or after the fever.

It is extremely difficult to differentiate these illnesses by sight, and the only way to really know for sure which virus is the culprit is to do complicated blood and tissue viral studies. *Most of the rashes we commonly see probably fit into this group of diseases.* There are some we recognize more specifically such as the strain of coxsackie virus that produces a rash on the hands and feet and pimples (papules) in the mouth. We call this, very appropriately, the "hand-foot-mouth syndrome"! However, for the most part we just know that the majority of children who develop a fever, some other symptoms, and a rash probably have one of these "other" viral diseases.

## ROSEOLA (SIXTH DISEASE)

Roseola is an illness that is usually not seen in school-age children but should be mentioned here since it is often confused with other illnesses. The typical case of roseola occurs in a baby under two years of age—mostly between 6 and 12 months. It is caused by a virus and has an incubation period of around two weeks. The typical case of roseola exhibits a fever (often quite high) for three to four days, *followed* by a rash after the fever goes down. The rash is mostly on the trunk and neck. The important thing to remember is that the fever *precedes* the rash. There is no treatment for roseola and no real danger to the baby in most cases. Pregnant women exposed to roseola *do not* have to worry about harm to their unborn infant.

## TUBERCULOSIS

### Other Common Infections

Many people feel that since we do not hear about TB too much anymore, we should not worry about it. This is far from the truth. There are still many new cases of tuberculosis diagnosed each year, and school children are certainly fair game for this disease. Tuberculosis is caused by bacteria, and can affect almost any part of the body including the lungs, central nervous system, bones, and kidneys. In children we do not usually see the time-honored picture of the person who is constantly coughing and losing weight. Children may have many different presentations of this disease, but the most common is a very mild or symptomatic form, consisting of a positive skin test and perhaps a mild respiratory infection. The most important thing to remember is that there is a skin test that can be used to diagnose tuberculosis (Tine test, PPD, OT). This test should be given to all babies at one year of age or so, and repeated every several years—*especially at the time of school entrance.* The frequency of testing depends on the community or familial prevalence.

A positive tuberculin test identifies the child who has been exposed to TB and if followed through with the proper diagnostic and therapeutic measures, the child is in no danger of an on-going or worsening disease. Another important point for school personnel to know is that the child with active tuberculosis who is under treatment may promptly return to school since he is in no danger of spreading the disease. Any child who shows signs of chronic sickness, paleness, poor nutrition, and frequent respiratory infections might be a possible candidate for this ubiquitous disease, which is still in our midst although we sometimes try to deny its existence. However, as stated above, many children with tuberculosis may have no signs of illness at all.

### INFECTIOUS MONONUCLEOSIS (MONO)

Mono is one of the most poorly understood diseases as well as one of the most mis- and overdiagnosed. The reason for this is the fact that there are so many differences of opinion in the medical profession itself as to the diagnosis and proper treatment of infectious mono. Because of the variable signs and symptoms seen with mono, it is easily confused with strep throat, "flu"-like illnesses, various other viral infections with rashes, and even school-phobia.

It is probable that infectious mononucleosis is caused by a virus that has just recently been specifically identified. The incubation period may be anywhere from one to six weeks, but usually is only one to two weeks. The common picture is one of fever, sore throat (sometimes quite severe), and excessive fatigue. There is almost always enlargement of the glands of the neck, and often glands in other areas of the body also become enlarged. There is often a rash present sometime in the first week of the disease, which may resemble that of scarlet fever or rubella. Other problems may include liver involvement, neurological symptoms, and even joint and heart involvement. Diagnostic blood tests are not usually positive until the second or third week of the disease, which makes the diagnosis more difficult. The usual age of the child who gets mono is in the teen and early adult groups, although it occasionally occurs in a child as young as two years of age.

The big problem with this disease is that everyone thinks they have it, especially teen-agers. This is because of the very generalized type of symptoms that can be confused with so many other illnesses. Another misconception is the transmission ease of the illness. Even though it is called "infectious," the actual contagion risk is quite low, and it is even rare to see it in siblings. Thus, the label "kissing disease" is really a misnomer.

Mono may be quite severe in some children, necessitating absence from school for periods of a semester or more. The usual case, however, includes a period of several weeks at home and then *gradual* return to full activities. Relapses are common when the child tries to get back to the usual routine too rapidly. Some cases are so mild that the child misses almost no school at all.

There has always seemed to be a sort of mass hysteria concerning infectious mono, which has made it difficult for both parents and physicians to deal with it, especially since there is no specific cure. It should be stressed that (1) most suspected cases are in reality some other kind of illness, (2) the communicability is low, and (3) the usual result is rapid recovery. It is hoped that this book will help to eliminate some of the mono myth. The disease *is* real, and in some cases a cause for real concern. However, the vast majority of children thought to have mono are not actually afflicted with this illness, and most actual cases are quite mild.

## PARASITIC INFECTIONS (PINWORMS AND OTHERS)

There are many organisms besides viruses and bacteria that can invade our bodies and cause illness. Parasitic infections include worms, malaria, mites and ticks, amebas, and many others. By far the most common of all of these is the affliction so often seen in so many children— *pinworms.*

Pinworm infection is caused by a tiny, threadlike worm called *Enterobius vermicularis.* The most common symptoms of pinworm infestation occur as the female worms move around the child's rectal and anal areas, usually in the evening hours. The result of this is usually intense itching and discomfort, which awaken the child (and thus the rest of the family). Pinworms are also blamed for many other symptoms in children, some of which are difficult to corroborate. We do know that occasional attacks of appendicitis can be caused by infestation and blockage caused by the pinworms. Also bladder infections in girls sometimes follow invasion of the vaginal areas by the worm.

Some children who are heavily infested for long periods of time may exhibit loss of appetite, poor weight gain, and irritability. Occasionally a child's classroom behavior might be adversely affected by pinworms. Almost every symptom of childhood has been blamed on pinworms at one time or another. The danger is that other more important illnesses may be missed. The diagnosis can be made by actually observing the worms (usually about ½-inch long and threadlike) or by collecting the eggs on a piece of clear tape from the anal or vaginal areas (this should be done at night). Treatment involves medication and hygiene measures prescribed by the physician. We must always remember, though, that pinworms can be found in the "best of homes"!

## BIRTH OR PERINATAL PROBLEMS

Although birth problems are not something a teacher sees as part of the job, there are certainly many children who show some type of problem in class because of this type of difficulty. Therefore, it would make sense to briefly review some of the concepts relevant to perinatal problems. (*Perinatal* refers to that period of time just before, during, and after the birth process, including the first several days of life.)

The most common cause of some type of difficulty at birth is when the infant is too small, usually under 5 pounds, 8 ounces (some experts use 5 pounds). This may happen when the baby is either born too soon (*premature*) or when there was some nutritional or blood-supply problem during pregnancy, and although the baby was full-term, it was small (*dysmature*). Any baby who is too small at birth may exhibit problems in different body systems including the central nervous system. Therefore, it is not unusual to see children with learning problems, neurological dysfunction, and many other related difficulties with a history of low birth weight. Usually the lower the weight at birth, the more likelihood of problems occurring. Not all small babies end up with developmental difficulties, but enough do so to make low birth weight a consideration in the appraisal of children when they get to school.

The next most common problem occurring in the perinatal period is a loss or interference with the infant's oxygen supply. Any adverse condition such as strangulation from the umbilical cord, excess anesthesia, or fluid in the respiratory tract can cause a delay in respiration. This in turn leads to a loss of oxygen to the brain cells, which may cause any problem or combination of problems such as convulsions, chronic brain damage, cerebral palsy, or in some cases if severe enough, death of the infant. The longer the period of a lack of sufficient oxygen, the more severe the damage will be. Any child with this history must certainly be thought of as a good candidate for school problems.

Another cause for concern in the perinatal period is bleeding in the brain. Any number of adverse conditions may cause this, such as direct trauma at delivery, excess traction or pressure to the head, clotting disorders, or just immaturity and oxygen deficiency. Any type of neurological disorder could result from this type of insult to the newborn.

Besides the common conditions mentioned above, there are many other possible adversities facing the newborn infant. These include: (1) maternal disease (heart disease, diabetes, toxemia of pregnancy, high blood pressure, and poor nutrition); (2) infections (including meningitis); (3) chemical imbalance (such as low blood calcium or sugar levels); and (4) presence in the blood of a substance known as *bilirubin.* This is a chemical substance produced by the normal breakdown of blood cells and usually will be elevated in most babies in the first few days of life. In cases where the mother's blood type is O, or if she is Rh negative, there may be increased destruction of the baby's blood. The bilirubin will then elevate to higher levels and may cross into the brain and cause various neurological problems. Babies with an increase in bilirubin become yellow-tinged or jaundiced. Most of the time this is a mild condition and causes no difficulty, but if quite high or prolonged, there may be serious results.

In all of the perinatal conditions mentioned, the effects will be dependent on the extent of damage that occurred and the length of time over which the condition acted. It is impossible to predict exactly what the end result of any birth problem will actually be. What *is* important is the recognition of the fact that birth problems do occur and should be considered as possible contributing factors when evaluating a child with an educational dysfunction.

## *INHERITED DISORDERS*

There are hundreds of diseases that fit into the category of inherited disorders, and most of them are quite rare. What we will attempt to do here is to outline the types of problems a classroom observer might see so that an informed referral might be more easily forthcoming.

As we pointed out in a previous chapter (Chapter 3), inherited diseases can be caused by a problem in the child's chromosomes or the genes on the chromosomes. In the chromosomal disorders there are usually multiple-body defects (*dysmorphism*), and mental retardation is often present. The most common example of this type of problem is Down's syndrome (*mongolism*), which we will discuss below.

Genetic abnormalities can cause disorders of almost any magnitude— from unobservable body changes to generally devastating, crippling diseases. Many genetic disorders are due to inborn errors of metabolism whereby one or more of the body's chemical systems are not functioning. Other genetic disorders are associated with body change only; these may include disorders of both internal function *and* body structure. Most of these disorders are seen in a familial pattern. A great many of the children who are afflicted with genetic diseases show characteristics such as poor growth, delayed development, abnormal-looking facial characteristics, speech difficulty, body-structure defects (sometimes totally disfiguring), and certainly quite often, generalized poor health and learning problems.

A complete list of the disorders found in this category does not belong in a book of this type. The reader is referred to the references if a complete breakdown is desired.* To show how universal these disorders are, however, we shall mention some of the familiar inherited disorders at this time:

Phenylketonuria (PKU)

Some forms of hypothyroidism

Diabetes

Hypoglycemia

Hemophilia

Cystic fibrosis

Certain anemias, including sickle cell

Tay-Sachs disease

Many forms of kidney disease

Certain convulsive disorders

Osteogenesis imperfecta ("brittle bones")

The important thing to remember is that if a child exhibits a peculiar type of facial or body appearnce, seems to have generalized problems in his growth and/or development, and perhaps has a history of someone in his family showing the same types of characteristics, it

*\*Textbook of Pediatrics* by Waldo E. Nelson and *Inborn Errors of Metabolism* by David Yi-Yung Hsai.

would be well to think of the possibility of some type of inherited disorder being at the root of his problems.

## Down's Syndrome (Mongolism)

Down's syndrome is the most common of the chromosomal disorders and certainly represents one of the more common disorders seen in the special education classroom. The cause of this affliction is the presence of an extra small chromosome either existing by itself (whereby the person has 47 chromosomes) or being attached to one of the other chromosomes (so that the normal number of 46 will be present but aberrated).

Most people are familiar with the common characteristics of the Down's child: (1) the small skull, (2) flattened forehead, (3) lateral upward slope of the eyes, (4) extra skin folds on the inside of the lid, (5) occasional squint, (6) white dots on the iris, (7) tongue usually protruding, (8) nose small with a flat bridge, (9) delayed dentition, (10) usually a short neck, (11) prominent abdomen, (12) shortened extremities, (13) poor muscle tone, (14) hands and feet flattened and square, (15) fifth finger and toes often curved inward, (16) there may be one transverse line extending all the way across the palm instead of the usual two or three partial lines (simian crease), (17) usually there is an increased space between the first and second fingers and toes, (18) often afflicted with congenital heart defects, (19) usually has more respiratory infections than normal, and many other abnormalities.

Most of these children are moderately to severely retarded, although for the first few years of life they may develop in a close to normal range. The incidence of this disorder is about 1.5 per 1000 births, and it is much more frequent in children born to women over 35 years of age. Mongoloid children represent up to 10% of all retarded children.

There is a form of Down's syndrome known as *mosaicism,* in which the children do not have the full-blown clinical picture of this disorder. Many of the mosaic Down's children look very much like normal children, have near normal intelligence, and are quite difficult to diagnose. The cause of this form of mongolism is the presence of two types of cells in the person's makeup: some contain the chromosomal variant that causes the typical Down's symptoms, and some are normal cells with 46 chromosomes. Mosaic Down's syndrome is caused by some type of dysfunction in the first cell divisions of the developing embryo of the affected person.

There is no specific treatment for this disorder, although in recent years some individuals have formulated a type of therapy related to the orthomolecular approach used in children with schizophrenia and hyperactivity. This theory holds that with the proper chemicals and vitamins the mongoloid child will be able to undergo a restructuring of the body's cells so as to lose many of the physical and developmental characteristics of this syndrome. This type of approach is scorned by most experts in the field, although there is still work being done in this area.

The educational, emotional, social, and medical care of these children is a complicated matter, and all component parts of the educational triangle must be involved in this endeavor.

## COMMON RESPIRATORY PROBLEMS

Most of the illnesses seen in the classroom involving the respiratory tract are short, self-limited viral infections affecting the nose, throat, and upper bronchial tract—in brief, the common cold. Most children will develop somewhere between 50 and 100 acute respiratory infections before the age of ten. Most of these will hit the child somewhere between three and ten years of age—hence it often seems like the child "always has a cold." In some cases the cold will become complicated by such problems as ear infections, pneumonia, and croup, which may make the child quite a bit sicker. There are some important aspects of respiratory disease that are important to mention here because of the universal scope of the problem.

### The Common Cold

As stated above, most colds are caused by a virus, which means that there is no effective specific treatment. Some children will be ill for several hours with a fresh cold, whereas others will miss several days or even weeks of school. This is especially common in the kindergarten to fourth-grade group. Symptoms *usually* include running or stuffy nose, occasional fever, cough, and scratchy throat, as well as a generalized achy feeling. If a child develops shortness of breath, prolonged coughing spells, earache, or remains ill for more than several days, he is probably developing a secondary complication that should be treated by a doctor. The usual cold is highly communicable in its early stages, but by the time it is certain that a child is so afflicted, he has probably spread the virus throughout the classroom.

There are a variety of viruses that can cause respiratory diseases, and each child will normally be exposed to many of these in the first few years of school—hence it is not uncommon for any child to have some very bad years. Then there seem to be certain children who have a very vulnerable or sensitive respiratory tract. This means that instead of a cold lasting one day, it lasts seven days; instead of keeping to the nose and throat, it goes down to the lungs, and bronchitis results; instead of one cold every two months, there is one every month, or twice a month.

It is difficult to say why these particular children show this type of sensitivity. Some of them might have a form of respiratory allergy (which we will discuss later). Others are poorly nourished and thus more susceptible.

In some families a chronic stress situation caused by frequent moves, economic and financial problems, and parental difficulty is associated with an increase in illnesses. *In fact, stress is probably one of the more common denominators of all chronic illness!* In many children we find *no* cause for the recurring illness—they're just always sick! No matter what the cause, it is a common event and we do know that children with runny noses, eyes, and ears do not learn well.

## *Ear Infections*

Most ear infections are seen in children under six years of age (see Figure 5-1). The usual symptoms include earache, fever, and loss of hearing. The most common situation we see is an infection of the middle ear (behind the ear drum), called *otitis media.* This is usually caused by an accumulation of fluid behind the ear drum that develops because of a blockage of the Eustachian tube by a cold, allergy, or lymphoid tissue (adenoids). The fluid soon becomes infected by bacteria, and the resulting pressure of the expanding, infected fluid on the ear drum causes intense pain in most children. This is a treatable and potentially serious problem and should be brought to the attention of the school nurse and parents.

Middle-ear infections often follow a cold, and if they occur quite regularly, can definitely lead to a hearing loss. A child who has such a loss or diminution of hearing should be diagnosed and treated promptly. All earaches are not necessarily caused by infections, but certainly should be attended to promptly. Ear pain is a serious matter, and children with this symptom *must* be medically evaluated. Ear infections by themselves are *not* contagious. The hearing loss associated with ear infections is usually due to a collection of fluid in the middle ear. Therapy for this problem often involves some sort of surgery, often including the placement of tiny tubes in the ear drum for better ventilation, adenoid removal, or both. Occasionally allergies may be associated with this condition also. Whatever the cause, it is urgent to have children with ear problems receive medical attention in all cases.

Some children develop infections in the ear *canal,* which can also cause quite a bit of pain and discomfort (*otitis externa*). These infections are often associated with the irritation of the ear canal by water from swimming pools, lakes, or oceans—hence the term *swimmer's ear.* This condition must be treated promptly since hearing can be affected.

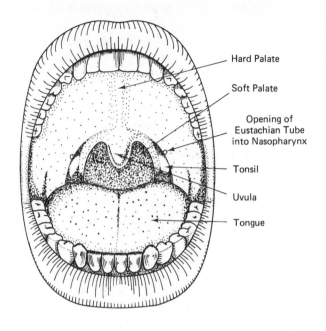

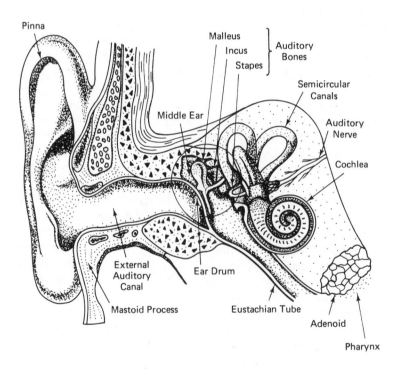

**Figure 5-1.** *(a) Frontal view of the oral cavity; (b) cross-section of the ear.*

## Throat Infections (Including "Strep")

The throat is usually not thought of as being a portion of the respiratory tract, but since a sore throat is commonly a part of a respiratory infection, it will be considered here. Most children with colds have a slight sore throat also. The only throat infection that we are really concerned with is that caused by the streptococcus type of bacteria. Most other throat infections are caused by one of the many viruses in our environment that are not treatable and are of no consequence except for the disability they produce. Some viruses can cause severe redness, ulcers in the throat, and high fever for up to seven days. They are untreatable and usually leave no lasting negative consequences.

The typical strep throat is usually associated with a beefy-red throat and tonsil area, a white membrane on the tonsils, tiny red dots on the palate, and enlarged painful glands in the neck. There is usually a fever and sometimes a headache and abdominal pain. These children can be treated with antibiotics (the best is penicillin) and can usually return to school after several days of treatment. The contagious period is during the first stages of symptoms until treatment is instituted, but the level of communicability is not nearly as high as with diseases such as measles or chicken pox. The most dangerous consequence of streptococcal infections is the damage that can follow because of toxins produced by the bacteria. The most common target areas of these toxins are the heart (rheumatic fever) and kidney (nephritis). If a child is suspected of having a streptococcal throat infection, seek the advice of the school nurse and/or notify the parents at once.

The scare of "strep" is a hysteria-producing problem in the classroom. Perhaps the fear can be lightened when we consider that most strep infections are: (1) really not streptococcal, but usually some type of viral infection that is self-limiting; (2) not highly contagious; (3) treatment is quite satisfactory, and (4) care can be given up to a week after diagnosis with practically no possibility of future rheumatic fever.

## Bronchitis and Pneumonia
## (Lower Respiratory Tract Problems)

Most children with disease of the lower respiratory tract are quite a bit sicker than those with simple colds. Children with pneumonia are often quite ill with a high fever, bad cough, and respiratory distress, and usually look quite ill. However, sometimes the illness causes nothing more than a slight cough or weakness and fatigue. The latter children are said to have "walking pneumonia."

Most cases of bronchitis are difficult to separate from either a very bad cold or early pneumonia. As a matter of fact, this diagnosis is often used by the physician as a "waste-basket" diagnosis when he doesn't know what else to call the process.

These diseases are usually caused by viruses, but since differentiation from bacterial causes is difficult, antibiotics are often used for treatment. Bronchitis or pneumonia is in itself not contagious, but the "bug" that caused it is. A child may show signs of chronic cough and general weakness for several weeks or even months after an infection of the lower respiratory tract.

## Croup

Croup is a descriptive term referring to a particular type of inspiratory noise and a barking cough. It occurs in any inflammation or infection occurring around the area of the voice box (larynx) and trachea. Many different viruses and bacteria can cause this syndrome (including diphtheria). It is not as common in school-age children as in the preschool group. Occasionally children with croup develop an obstruction of the respiratory tract, making this potentially an extremely dangerous disease.

## Sinusitis

Sinusitis is another one of those disorders that is blamed for many things such as headaches, visual problems, chronic coughs, dizziness, and other disabilities connected to the head. The sinuses are actually small empty spaces in the skull that are located around and connected to the nose and associated structures. Any condition that can cause inflammation of the respiratory tract may be associated with an outpouring of fluid into the normally empty-spaced sinuses. This can lead to symptoms of obstruction and increased pressure (headache) or chronic drainage (persistent cough). Sinuses can be affected by infection, allergy, or other noxious stimuli either acutely or chronically. Children with chronic sinus infections or allergic disturbances of the sinuses often have quite a bit of difficulty attending to their schoolwork. X-rays will disclose the presence of a problem, and medical treatment can often alleviate this annoying problem.

## The Tonsil and Adenoid Problem

There have been many myths perpetuated about the two groups of lymphoid tissue—the tonsils and adenoids—found in the back of the throat and near the Eustachian tubes (see Figure 5-1). Tonsils have been blamed for all sorts of things, and removal of the tonsils and adenoids has been given credit for such diverse phenomena as better appetite, improved learning, less colds, weight gain, and better behavior. We will not get into the controversy here, but for completeness sake we will present a few important facts.

1. The tonsils and adenoids will *usually* start to shrink by five or six years of age.

2. Routine removal of either or both is *not* good practice.

3. Indications for tonsil removal include chronic, recurrent, severe infections unresponsive to therapy (a condition that seems injurious to the child's general health); severe enlargement that blocks normal eating or proper breathing; large, chronically infected lymph glands in the neck; abscesses around the tonsils; and some other rare problems. *Enlargement alone* is not a valid indication for removal.

4. Adenoids should be removed because of a chronic obstruction to respiration leading to mouth breathing, repeated ear infections, hearing loss due to ear fluid, and some other less frequently found reasons.

Thus, the tonsils and adenoids are usually not to blame for most of a child's problems as some would have us believe, and their removal is usually not indicated except for the above reasons (items 3 and 4).

### Chronic Lung Disease

#### BRONCHIAL ASTHMA

There are certain conditions that cause a child to display breathing disturbances almost on a continuous basis, the most common disorder of which is *bronchial asthma.* This disease is quite common and is manifested by a breathing disorder associated with a whistling or wheezing sound that is caused by obstruction to the small bronchial tubes, especially during expiration. The cause of asthma is often uncertain, although it is generally a familial trait and is often ascribed to some form of allergy.

Many asthmatic children will be greatly affected by any number of environmental agents such as molds, dust, grass, pollen, trees, and animal hair. Others seem to be allergic to various types of foods. We often see a child develop a severe asthmatic attack when he is emotionally upset. Any form of stress seems to increase the entire problem. Asthmatic children should be carefully studied both medically and emotionally and a plan of action mapped out to decrease the causative factors, since long-recurring asthma attacks can lead to a significant loss of school time and poor attention when in school, and occasionally can become a severe threat to the child's life.

#### CYSTIC FIBROSIS (CF)

A less common chronic respiratory problem is a disease known as *cystic fibrosis* (CF). This is a genetic disorder that is associated with chronic respiratory disease, intestinal malfunction, nutritional disturbances, and many other problems. The cause is probably a malfunction of some of the secreting glands in the body, which leads to obstruction in many glandular areas and to subsequent infection and further malfunction. Any child with recurrent pneumonia must be investigated for CF. A child with this disease must be under a doctor's care continuously, but can often do quite well in the normal classroom when he is feeling well!

## *PROBLEMS OF THE GASTROINTESTINAL TRACT (DIGESTIVE TRACT)*

### *Abdominal Pain*

Abdominal pain is one of the most difficult symptoms to deal with in children. Most children can have a "tummy ache" with almost any acute illness. Often "strep" throats are associated with belly pain *before* throat pain. Some children complain of abdominal pain with almost every adversity, from acute infections anywhere in the body to failure to complete homework. If the pain is associated with nausea, vomiting, and diarrhea, the problem is usually localized to the gastrointestinal tract—a stomach "flu" or gastroenteritis. If the pain is associated with symptoms elsewhere, it is most commonly secondary to another disorder— so-called sympathetic or parenteral belly pain. The most worrisome thing for parents and teachers (and doctors) is whether a surgical problem such as appendicitis exists (this is not common in children and will be discussed below). Some children with abdominal pain have severe spasms of excruciating pain that are spasmodic and very hard to treat.

The child who *always* has abdominal pain even in the absence of other signs of illness is another problem entirely. The majority of these chronic "belly-achers" will be found to have no actual disease at all, even after prolonged and expensive medical evaluation. Chronic stress and anxiety are frequently associated with abdominal pain, and children with school-phobic tendencies show this symptom quite often. The child with chronic, recurrent abdominal pain must be evaluated for conditions such as urinary tract infections, bowel disorders, peptic ulcer (rare in children), and other less common problems, but the probability of a medical disorder is low. However, this child is telling us *something* with his pain, and the complaint must be respected and dealt with.

### *Acute Gastroenteritis*

Acute gastroenteritis is the "stomach flu" that people speak of and is usually due to a viral infection of the stomach and intestinal tract. It is usually quite contagious, and the child is sick for one to five days.

It is characterized by vomiting, diarrhea, and abdominal pain, which may be quite severe! There is no treatment other than diet and rest. Quite often a child will have disturbances of bowel function for weeks after an attack of this nature.

### Disorder of Elimination

Too frequent or too few bowel movements are very common in many children. Problems of this nature are extremely difficult to deal with because of the diverse diagnostic and therapeutic tools that must be utilized. We must also consider in this group those children who for one reason or another soil their pants (*encopresis*), a very disturbing classroom situation.

Children who manifest elimination disorders such as persistent diarrhea, chronic constipation, or encopresis must receive immediate medical intervention by someone well versed in these types of problems, since they are so difficult to deal with. In most cases these symptoms are but the tip of the iceberg, and often a very serious physical or emotional problem can be present that may harm the child's life if not intercepted.

### Hepatitis

Hepatitis is a disease caused by a virus that has various subtypes or strains. Some forms are passed through blood transfusions (*serum hepatitis*), others by direct contact with people who have the illness, or occasionally by contaminated food or water (*infectious hepatitis*). The incubation period varies from two to six weeks. The symptoms include fever, fatigue, cough, and nasal stuffiness at first; followed by loss of appetite, abdominal pain, vomiting; and then most often, *jaundice* (a yellow pigmentation of the skin and whites of the eyes). The illness may last for long periods of time (up to two to three months), and fatigue for several months after this is common. There may be many complications, but in most cases the child recovers completely. Infectious hepatitis is contagious for household contacts, and it is usually advised that these *close contacts* be innoculated with gamma globulin.

### Peptic Ulcers

Ulcers are not common in children, but are found on rare occasions. Most children with chronic abdominal pain do not have ulcers. The majority of children with ulcers *do not* evidence pain at all; instead they usually show signs of some of the complications of the ulcer such as bleeding, vomiting, and intestinal obstruction. Many children are subjected to X-rays to see if they have an ulcer, but the yield is minute. Ulcers are not a common classroom condition.

## *Appendicitis*

We mentioned above that most children with abdominal pain worry their parents and their doctor about the possibility of having appendicitis. As stated earlier, this is not a very common cause of belly discomfort, but it certainly does occur at all ages—even as young as one year of age. Young children under five are usually not diagnosed until the appendix has ruptured because of the difficulty of diagnosis and the problem younger children have in localizing the pain.

In the older child, appendicitis usually starts with pain around the navel, and it may stay there; in some children the pain moves to the lower right part of the abdomen. These children usually have a fever, nausea, and vomiting along with the pain—a pain that is *persistent* as opposed to the pain of gastroenteritis that comes and goes.

The child with suspected appendicitis should be seen medically as soon as possible. If an operation is done at the proper time, the child will often be back in school within ten days.

## *Chronic Bowel Disorders*

There are several inflammatory diseases of the bowel that can cause lifelong disability in children. The two most common are *ulcerative colitis* and *granulomatous colitis* or *Crohn's disease.* These diseases are marked by chronic diarrhea, abdominal pain, blood in the stool, nutritional and growth disturbances, and many other complications including emotional and learning disorders. Children with any of these disorders are often very difficult to deal with because of the severe physical discomfort they are faced with. Treatment of these disorders is at best only aimed at relief of symptoms (palliative type of treatment) and some children must undergo disfiguring bowel surgery in their teen-age years. A child with chronic bowel disease must often have a very special educational and emotional approach in order to complete his schooling.

## *HEART DISEASE*

### *Congenital Heart Disease*

There are many disorders that can affect the child's heart and circulatory system. The diagnosis of a congenital heart problem (one that the child is born with) is usually made in the first year of life by the presence of a heart murmur or signs of heart disease. On rare occasions, a child may escape early detection and may not be properly diagnosed until after he enters school. Some of the signs that may point to this type of problem include easy fatigue, poor growth, shortness of breath, a blue tinge to the lips and nails (cyanosis), or fainting spells. If a child is known to have some type of congenital heart defect, the school should be aware of the problem—including the child's limitations and what to look for when he is in trouble. Most children with congenital heart disease have no major problems, however, and are normally active children who should do well in the classroom.

### Rheumatic Fever (RF)

Rheumatic fever is another of those "diagnoses" that are made much too often. It used to be that every child with a prolonged fever of any type or chronic aches and pains in his legs would be labeled "rheumatic." Hopefully the trend is away from this mislabeling.

Rheumatic fever is actually not as common now as it was 20 years ago. The illness is thought to be an inflammation of certain tissues of the heart and joints as well as elsewhere following a streptococcal infection that was poorly treated or not treated at all. These children usually show the signs of RF about two to six weeks after the strep infection, which may include fever, joint swelling and tenderness, rashes, symptoms of neurological disorders, and inflammation of the heart (*carditis*) with mumurs.

The diagnosis of rheumatic fever should not be made casually; but it is most important to diagnose if present. Because of the early treatment of strep infections, we see very little RF today. Once a child gets it, he may recover completely, or he can go on to develop chronic heart disease. The classroom situation will depend on just how complicated the case gets.

### Hypertension

We mention hypertension at this time only to stress the point that children can have high blood pressure. Most of the time this is not diagnosed until some harm has occurred to the circulatory system, so it is urged that all children have their blood pressure measured at least yearly!

### Murmurs

Heart murmurs are extremely misunderstood both as to what they mean and what is to be done with them. A cardiac murmur is actually only a sound heard when listening to the heart. It is interposed between the normal first and second heart sounds or occasionally between the second sound and next first sound. Murmurs are very common in children and can often be heard up to 50% of the time at one time or another.

There are two types of murmurs: (1) those associated with some form of heart disease, and (2) innocent or functional murmurs. It is sometimes quite difficult to tell the difference between these two types, but the majority of innocent murmurs have a distinctive tone, pitch, and intensity, and are unassociated with any symptoms of heart disease. It is often necessary to obtain a chest X-ray and electrocardiogram to be sure there is not an associated heart defect.

The majority of murmurs in children will be innocent murmurs, with no cause for alarm, and represent *no danger or reason for the child to limit his physical activity!*

## BLOOD PROBLEMS
### Disorders of the Red Blood Cells

The most common blood problem is a low red blood cell count or *anemia.* There are many causes for anemia: hereditary, infectious, allergic, and nutritional. Children with anemia are often pale, chronically tired, do not learn well, and get sick quite often. The most common type of anemia is probably due to iron-deficiency, which is seen most often in children from one to three years of age. However, this type of anemia can be seen in any age group where a good nutritional source of iron is lacking, such as we find in children who are on specially strict diets, big milk drinkers, or where the economic situation precludes a good diet. Foods rich in iron include meats (especially liver), egg yolk, grains, nuts, and some green vegetables. The diagnosis and proper treatment of anemia should lead to better classroom performance.

### Disorders of the White Blood Cells

One of the most feared diagnoses any parent thinks of is *leukemia.* Any child who is sick for longer than one week is fair game for thoughts harboring on this dread disease. Leukemia is actually a disorder of the white blood cells. There is a malignant change in the cells, and they multiply rapidly causing anemia and many other disturbances that can be fatal if untreated. Within the past few years the treatment of leukemia has progressed to a point where some of the children are surviving for five years or longer, although the disease is still mostly incurable. Children with leukemia can attend school and do quite well when they are in remission, but when the disease is uncontrolled, they are sick and often need to be at home or hospitalized.

Leukemia cannot be diagnosed without the aid of blood counts and bone-marrow examinations. Once the diagnosis is made, the child and his parents must be extended the usual special consideration given to all children with potentially fatal diseases.

### Clotting Disorders

There are many children who have a defect in their ability to stop bleeding within the normal time. These children may bruise easily and excessively, or may actually lose large amounts of blood from inconsequential cuts or injuries. There are a variety of causes for this type of disorder, including deficiency of the platelet cells in the blood and genetic defects of the clotting proteins of the blood (hemophilia).

*Hemophilia* is a disorder that can occur in various forms, some of which are sex-linked and are only seen in males. Basically these individuals do not form the proper elements in their blood to clot normally, and insignificant injuries can be life-threatening. Any child who is noted to bruise or bleed easily, or has been diagnosed as having hemophilia, must be carefully watched, kept out of rough games, and referred for prompt medical aid if a problem arises. These children often have learning problems because of their frequent absences from school.

## *URINARY SYSTEM*

### *Infection*

Urinary tract infections are second only to respiratory infections in their frequency in childhood. Any part of the tract may be involved from the kidney, to the bladder, to the urethra. Symptoms may include problems with urinating such as pain, burning, frequency, or difficulty; also abdominal pain, back pain, and fever. At times the infections may produce no symptoms except a tired child who doesn't do well in school. Urinary infections are more frequent in girls than boys, probably because of the anatomical situation of the closeness of the bladder outlet tube (urethra) to the anal area. Urinary infections are a *very big problem* and can be easily diagnosed by urinalysis and bacterial culture. Treatment will often cause a great change in the child's attitudes and approach to life and learning.

### *Nephritis and Nephrosis*

Nephritis and nephrosis are uncommon diseases, and there are many different types and degrees. Basically they represent some type of disorder in the kidney microstructure that leads to generalized dysfunction such as swelling, chemical disorders, high blood pressure, heart disease, and often chronic kidney failure. The causes of these diseases are varied, some being an auto-immune type situation where the body becomes allergic to its own products. Children with nephritis or nephrosis may miss quite a bit of school and are often on medications that themselves cause disfiguration and swelling.

### *Enuresis (Bed-Wetting)*

The problem of bed-wetting is quite complicated, and there are almost as many theories on its cause and treatment as there are children who have the problem. We will try to make some general statements about this disorder in order to make the reader more familiar with the entire problem.

1.   It must first be determined exactly what the child's problem entails: day-wetting alone? night-wetting alone? or a combination of the two? It must also be established whether the child has other symptoms of urinary tract disease such as fevers, pain, or poor urinary stream. The cause and treatment will often differ according to which of these groups the child fits into.

2.   A child who is dry during the day, has no other urinary symptoms, and wets the bed at night up until the age of five may be perfectly normal—or he just may have immaturity of his control mechanisms.

3.   It is important to know whether the child has his problem continuously or was trained and then redeveloped the wetting after a dry period.

4.   It must also be determined if the child has any other physical, emotional, behavioral, or learning problems that may have something to do with the enuresis.

5.   A child who is over five, has no other physical symptoms of urinary tract trouble, is usually dry during the day, and *only wets at night* is considered by most people to fit the true definition of enuresis. The children in this group are often immature, sometimes have other behavior problems, usually have no physical defects of the urinary tract, and are a very difficult group to work with. Many neurologically hyperactive children fit in this group.

In this group there are many types of therapy that have been used, including bladder exercises, water deprivation, alarm systems, psychotherapy, and medications. The results range from very good to no change, according to the observer and his biases. The most important thing to remember is that usually the child *must really want to stop his wetting* before any mode of therapy will begin to work.

6.   A child who has enuresis should be thoroughly investigated by a physician with experience in the field, and who has the capability for compassion and understanding for the child and his problem. Surgical intervention or hospitalization in most cases is not necessary.

7.   If a child has this problem, especially if it occurs during school hours, a medical referral is essential in order to thoroughly investigate the whole child and his general life style and not just his problem.

## THE NERVOUS SYSTEM

We have already mentioned some of the more common neurological disorders associated with learning problems in previous chapters (see Chapters 3 and 4). Since the nervous system is the most closely allied to the learning process, any abnormality or disease in this area will be more likely to cause educational dysfunction than a defect in some other system. There are hundreds of disorders of neurological function that can affect the child and can cause various degrees of difficulty in the school setting. At this time we will review several of the more important categories that are commonly seen by school personnel.

### *Headaches*

Headaches are a disturbing symptom and are quite common in children. It is estimated that up to 30 or 40% of all children complain of headaches on a regular basis. Most of the headaches in these children are associated with acute illnesses (the common short-lived and self-limiting viral and bacterial illnesses which most children contract during the first 5 to 10 years of life), and the majority of these headaches are in some way connected to the presence of fever in the child. This is probably due to the dilation (enlargement) of the blood vessels around the scalp and head because of the fever.

The child who has chronic headaches that are not associated with a fever or acute illness usually may have some type of tension or vascular (blood vessel) headache—often associated with chronic stress. About 5% of children with recurrent headaches suffer from migraine, one of the vascular types of headaches.

Very few children with repeated headaches have a dangerous problem such as brain tumors or infections. Even the common idea that visual problems cause headaches is not really the case in most children. The best estimate is that the child with repeated complaints of this type has some type of tension, anxiety, or stress, and the headache is his body's way of expressing this.

Children who exhibit school-phobia also often complain of headaches on the days school is in session. When allowed to remain at home, the headache is "miraculously" gone by 10 o'clock. Most of the children with either "made-up" headaches or the common recurrent tension headaches have problems much more important than the headaches themselves. The child is telling us something is wrong, and we must find out what it is and take whatever steps are necessary to alleviate the situation. This will take the full cooperation of all points of the educational triangle!

## Convulsive Disorders (Seizures)

As we pointed out in Chapter 2, there are many different types of seizure disorders with many causes for each type. In this section we will mention only the more common types seen in children.

### FEBRILE (FEVER) SEIZURES

Febrile seizures are convulsions seen in a small percentage (about 7 to 8%) of children, and are usually associated with high fever. They occur primarily from six months to five years of age and are thought to be due to the rapidity of rise of the fever rather than the actual height of the temperature. Most children with febrile seizures do not have any problems with them after the age of five or six. Occasionally a child who has febrile seizures will go on to develop full-blown epilepsy later in life.

### EPILEPSY

Epilepsy refers to a type of seizure disorder that is recurrent, usually is associated with a total or partial loss of consciousness, and has some type of muscular spasms or abnormal behavior included in the picture. Some forms of epilepsy are unassociated with any known specific brain defect (*idiopathic epilepsy*). Other forms of epilepsy are secondary to brain injury, infections, poisons, and metabolic disorders. The latter group are called *organic epilepsy,* as distinct from the idiopathic form.

Idiopathic epilepsy (no known cause) is the most common type seen in most chldren. However, it is felt that there is some genetic defect in the central nervous system that causes this problem. This disorder is sometimes familial in nature and is quite varied in its effect on the child, according to the type of seizures he has. There are several categories of seizures that can be seen in either idiopathic or organic epilepsy.

### Grand Mal

Grand mal is the name given to a generalized convulsion that usually starts with some spasms (tonic movements) of the muscles and quickly moves into a loss of consciousness and generalized jerking of most muscle groups in a spasmodic manner (clonic movements). The child sometimes urinates and defecates during the attack. The convulsion may last from several seconds up to hours and is usually followed by a period of severe depression and sleep. The entire episode of a grand mal seizure is frightening, dangerous, and disruptive. It is imperative for the child with this type of problem to be promptly diagnosed and adequately treated to prevent this catastrophic occurrence.

### Petit Mal

The petit mal type of seizure consists of a momentary loss of consciousness often associated with other symptoms such as head nodding, staring spells, eye blinking, or slight movement of body muscles. The attacks usually last only a few seconds and may occur many times a day, and most of the children are not aware they have had a seizure. This disorder is more common in girls, especially in those from five to ten years of age.

### Psychomotor and Temporal Lobe Seizures

Psychomotor and temporal lobe seizures are difficult to document and categorize. They may consist of various combinations of strange and inappropriate motor acts, often associated with some type of behavioral outburst. The abnormal movements and behavior patterns are repetitive and similar, and this is what usually leads to a recognition of this type of seizure. Diagnosis and treatment are often difficult, even when the illness is recognized.

Occasionally children with learning and behavior problems in the classroom are suspected of having this disorder as a basis of their behavior aberrations. This is one of the reasons that an electroencephalogram is ordered on some of these children. This type of seizure is actually a very rare cause of the type of problem we usually see, but must always be considered when the behavioral outbursts are bizarre, seemingly uncontrollable, and paroxysmal (occur at specific intervals).

### Other Types of Seizures

There are several other decribed convulsive disorders including *focal, myoclonic,* and *dyskinetic.* Each of these is associated with various specific types of body movements and alterations of consciousness, and a specific diagnosis is often difficult to make. Any child with a suspected seizure disorder should certainly be evaluated by a physician conversant with all of the different types of convulsive disorders and who is experienced in their therapy. For the more difficult to diagnose and control types, a pediatric neurologist is often the person who should have the primary responsibility.

## The Electroencephalogram (EEG)

Before we leave the subject of seizures, we should say a word about the EEG. This is a diagnostic tool that is poorly understood by many people associated with children with learning disorders. Basically the EEG is a recording of the various electrical waves emitted by the brain. This is done through use of wires attached to the scalp. Injury and lack of stability of the central nervous system will produce abnormalities of these waves and will show as an abnormal EEG.

Most of the seizure disorders referred to above will have abnormal EEG tracings, and some will provide good diagnostic information about the disorder. Petit mal and often grand mal epilepsy are associated with specific EEG abnormalities. Many other seizure disorders will have EEG tracings that are not so characteristic or diagnostic. Children with brain injury due to any cause might have abnormal EEG's with no particular or specific characteristics.

The big problem arises in children with so-called minimal brain dysfunction or hyperactivity, where some workers feel the EEG is helpful in diagnosis. They state that children with these types of symptom complexes often have specific abnormalities on the EEG that can be helpful in diagnosis.

However, it is well known that if we were to examine large numbers of so-called normal children with no obvious learning or behavioral problems, about 15% of them would have some abnormalities on the EEG also. Hence, the EEG may be a waste of time and money, which is not really helpful to the child.

Most workers in the field feel that valid indications for an EEG include:

1. Suspicions of a seizure disorder, especially petit mal, including the observation of frequent daydreaming spells.

2. Repetitive, stereotyped episodes of abnormal behavior.

3. Neurological signs and symptoms that suggest a specific disorder of the brain such as a tumor, scar, or some other localized lesion; or some type of generalized brain disorder leading to a general deterioration in the child's learning.

We must remember that the EEG does not tell us anything other than the fact that the brain wave patterns are abnormal. Thus, a child who has a learning problem and an abnormal EEG that does not indicate a seizure disorder will not be helped by the EEG. However, in many cases, because of abnormal pressure from parents and/or other interested individuals, doctors are almost "forced" into ordering an EEG on a child to satisfy everyone. Where it helps to clear the air and leads to other more meaningful pursuits, the exercise may not be completely futile.

As a final footnote to the subject of the electroencephalogram, it should be noted that there is some current research being conducted on the isolation of some of the various components of the EEG as they refer to some individual neurological functions involved in learning dysfunction and developmental delay. If some of these activities prove to be helpful in the isolation of the component parts of a learning disorder, the future use of the EEG as a diagnostic tool may have to be reexamined.

## Cerebral Palsy (CP)

As outlined in Chapter 2, cerebral palsy has been defined as a non-progressive motor defect due to some type of problem occurring in the perinatal or neonatal period. Most children with this defect have symptoms referable to the control of their motor system that may be manifested in various ways. The most common forms are spastic paralysis (*plegia*) or weakness (partial paralysis or *paresis*). This may involve all four extremities (quadriplegia or *quadriparesis*), the legs only (*paraplegia/paresis*), one side of the body (*hemiplegia/paresis*), or one limb (*monoplegia/paresis*). Other forms of CP can cause various abnormal motor movements such as *choreoathetosis* or *dystonia* (abnormal posturing and/or writhing type movements) or occasionally coordination defects with loss of body tone or balance. There may be a mixture of the various types also. Some children with CP have normal intelligence, but obviously any damage to the nervous system severe enough to produce this type of problem could possibly be associated with other neurological disorders—including learning problems.

### Nervous System Infections

There are many organisms including viruses, bacteria, and fungi that can attack any part of the brain and cause disabilities. There are several particular forms of infection that are relatively common and should be mentioned.

### ENCEPHALITIS

Encephalitis is an infection or inflammation of the brain cells and supporting structures. It is most commonly caused by viruses, but may be caused by poisons such as lead, other chemicals, or waste products from elsewhere in the body (e.g., ammonia from liver disease). Encephalitis can also be caused by common procedures such as immunizations against diphtheria or whooping cough. Another common cause may be as an aftermath of common contagious diseases such as measles or chicken pox. Most cases of encephalitis are mild and produce little permanent damage. Others may be devastating and could lead to serious brain injury or death.

## MENINGITIS

Meningitis is an infection of the covering membranes (meninges) of the brain and spinal cord. The most common causes are bacterial, which are the most dangerous and will most often be fatal if untreated; and viral, which can be as dangerous as bacterial, or in some cases so mild as to go undetected. The complications of meningitis depend on the cause, rapidity of appropriate treatment, and extent of the disease.

There are other forms of infections in the nervous system such as *brain abscesses* and *spinal cord infections.* However, these are relatively rare and will not be discussed here for brevity's sake.

### *Tumors*

Brain tumors do occur in children, but are not a common cause of learning problems. The symptoms of growths in the brain are the result of increasing pressure inside the skull, so that any child who complains of chronic severe headaches, vomiting, loss of consciousness, decreased coordination, new seizures, change in behavior, deteriorating school performance, speech or visual defects, or other such signs should at least be checked for this problem. The diagnosis is often difficult to make and is often delayed because of the common occurrence of the same symptoms with many other disorders. The teacher should report these symptoms so that the physician can embark upon the diagnostic trail as quickly as possible.

### *Head Injuries*

Children constantly fall and bump into things, and quite often their head takes the brunt of the damage. Injuries of this nature are usually of no serious consequence but occasionally may lead to lasting problems. Any child who has hit his head sufficiently hard to cause him pain or discomfort, or where there are visible signs of injury such as bruising or swelling, should be at least reported to the nurse and the parents, which will often lead to a call to the physician. This is especially important when the symptoms prevail.

Minor head injuries will usually produce some headache, dizziness, nausea, occasional vomiting, and slight sleepiness. These children should be watched carefully at home for further signs of neurological dysfunctions, which might include difficulty arousing the child, persistent vomiting, difference in the size of the pupils, loss of consciousness, convulsions, or balance disturbances. These could all be signs of bleeding inside the head, and further medical aid is imperative.

A *concussion* refers to a head injury that is associated with a *temporary loss of consciousness.* A child who shows this type of response obviously must be medically evaluated immediately.

## METABOLIC AND ENDOCRINE DISORDERS

A teacher may observe many conditions arising from metabolic or endocrine disorders. However, the two most common ones that we will briefly discuss here are much more frequently seen than most of the others—these are diabetes mellitis and hypothyroidism.

### Diabetes Mellitis

Diabetes mellitis is a genetic hereditary disease that causes a disturbance in the sugar (glucose) metabolism. Children with diabetes may have symptoms from birth, or may develop the full-blown disease later on. The onset may be slow (over several months) or may occur within a week or so. These children usually show weakness, fatigue, frequent urination, and excessive thirst. Some children have a rapid progression of symptoms at the onset leading to severe deterioration. The diagnosis is made by finding sugar in the urine and an abnormal level of sugar in the blood by various types of tests. All children with diabetes must be on a special diet (which should be as close to a normal diet as possible) as well as on insulin therapy. Both the child and his parents should be fully acquainted with all aspects of the disease. These children will usually do just fine in the classroom once the disease is under control. If the child on the other hand shows severe behavioral abnormalities, a "drunk-type" behavior, loss of consciousness, or seizures, he may be having an insulin reaction.

The diabetic child should also be watched carefully after the diagnosis has first been made. He may show some signs of poor acceptance of the diagnosis and treatment, so his school work may suffer. The adolescent child will often show some school problems around this time due to heightening of the usual adolescent rebellion by this disease. For the most part, however, the diabetic child should be treated quite normally and be accepted as an integral part of the classroom.

### Hypothyroidism

Hypothyroidism is another one of those disorders for which a lot of people are treated, but very few really have the disease. There are various forms, and the manifestations may occur in infancy or any time later in life. Those cases present from birth have the congenital form that may be due to poor intrauterine development, genetic factors, or maternal difficulties. Cases that develop later are called "acquired" and may be due to disease, auto-immunity, or other causes.

All cases of true hypothyroidism are a result of the deficient production of thyroid hormone, no matter what the cause. Therefore, the diagnosis must depend on the measurement of thyroid hormone function, which is done by certain blood measurements. No one should be treated for hypothyroidism without first establishing the chemical diagnosis!

Symptoms of this disorder depend on the time the child developed the problem. Hypothyroidism present since birth and untreated will result in severe retardation of intellectual and physical growth. Most cases of hypothyroidism are diagnosed in infancy, and the children are under treatment by the time they reach school. Symptoms that may be seen in late-developing cases or poorly treated chronic cases may include poor growth; dry, coarse skin and hair; extreme sensitivity to cold; delayed dentition; swelling of some tissues around the head and neck; fatigue; muscle weakness; hoarseness; constipation; sleepiness; and a decline in school work.

Diagnosis and treatment of this disorder are urgent in order to prevent irreversible disabilities.

### Hypoglycemia

Hypoglycemia has been discussed in Chapter 4. It is also discussed in Chapter 11.

### Other Endocrine Disorders

There are many other entities that are the cause of endocrine or metabolic disorders. Most of these are rare and include *pituitary* and *adrenal disorders* and *gonadal dysfunctions* such as precocious puberty and sexual identification problems. These will not be included for the sake of brevity. The symptoms to watch for in the classroom are growth disorders, suspected hormonal inbalance, or other similar dysfunctions.

## IMMUNOLOGIC AND ALLERGIC DISORDERS

The entire field of immunologic and allergic disorders is quite new, and the information base is constantly changing. Basically we are referring to a group of illnesses that deal with the body's immune responses. This means the way in which the body reacts to certain stimuli. These stimuli may be from the outside such as viruses, bacteria, poisons (toxins), or chemicals, or from the inside such as various substances produced by our own body. The body's responses may include the production of certain protein bodies called *antibodies,* various types of cells, occasionally chemical reactants, and/or other types of substances. The major disease states that we consider here are the large group called *allergic disorders* (response to outside influences), *immune diseases* such as rheumatoid arthritis (internal responses), and the *lack of immune response* such as in hypogammaglobulinemia.

## *Allergy*

Allergy is another area of controversy and difference of opinion in the field of medicine. Some experts feel that almost all diseases we see are in some way associated with an allergic response, while others feel that there is really very little true allergic disease. The truth probably lies somewhere in between these extremes.

Most allergic disease refers to the body's response to a particular agent. The responding organ in most cases will be the skin, respiratory tract, or gastrointestinal tract. However, almost every organ system can be involved in allergic reactions at one time or another.

The most common classroom conditions are usually the respiratory allergies including "hay fever," runny and stuffy nose, recurrent infections, sinusitis, and asthma. Just how large a part of these conditions is related to a real allergic disorder and how much to other problems is difficult to say in many cases. Some children really *do* seem to have a sensitive respiratory tract that reacts overtly to many stimuli, and these children do have signs of chronic respiratory problems. Environmentally ingested and inhaled allergens are among the problems for these children.

Other allergic conditions may include hives, skin rashes like eczema, and digestive disturbances such as persistent diarrhea. Children with an uncontrolled allergy often have learning disabilities due to their poor physical condition—or perhaps as some say, due to allergy that affects the central nervous system. As we previously stated, it is wise to try to eliminate allergic disease if it is the *true* culprit. However, the overtreatment and overprotection of these children can often produce as much or more social and emotional deprivation as the untreated symptoms might cause. A specific entity often associated with allergy—especially food sensitivity—is the "tension-fatigue" syndrome that is characterized by signs of paleness, puffy eyes, aches and pains, stuffiness, fatigue, and many other signs of generalized disability.

## *Immune Diseases*

There are a group of illnesses that are characterized by an immune response in the body that seems to be a case of the body overreacting to some stimulus, either internal or external. Rheumatic fever was one of these diseases, where the stimulus was the streptococcal toxin. There are several other diseases in this category including rheumatoid arthritis, dermatomyositis, lupus, and scleroderma. The most common one is *rheumatoid arthritis.* This illness is seen at all ages, but often occurs in young children from three to five years of age. It may be associated with high fevers, joint swellings, rashes, and many other symptoms. Some children have one or two joints involved—others have many joints involved. Most children with this disease need treatment for their joint problems, often necessitating rest and physiotherapy as well as medication. The effect on school attendance and learning will depend on the number of joints involved, the severity of the problem, other systemic symptoms, and the response to therapy.

Most diseases in this group are rare, but can lead to crippling and often fatal results. Rheumatoid arthritis is usually not as severe as the others and will usually respond to proper therapy.

### Immune Deficiency Diseases

Immune deficiency diseases are another group of disorders often diagnosed and treated without proper laboratory verification. This group represents those usually inherited disorders that are associated with a deficiency of one or more of the usual body defense mechanisms for fighting disease. The most common disease in this group is *hypogamma-globulinemia.* This problem is a deficiency of one of the proteins (gamma globulin) that contains the antibodies necessary to combat many infectious diseases. There are many different forms of this disorder, and it is actually quite rare. Most children with repeated chronic infections have no deficit of gamma globulins, but occasionally one is found whose infections *are* explained by such a problem. The diagnosis must be confirmed by the laboratory, and the children will usually do well if proper treatment is utilized.

## MUSCLE AND BONE DISORDERS

There are many disorders of the body structure system (musculo-skeletal system), including ligaments, tendons, and other supporting structures. The most common problems seen in the classroom relate to injuries of the various parts of the body structure such as *fractures* (broken bones), *muscle bruises, sprains* (torn ligaments), and *strains* (stretched ligaments). Children with injuries of this sort do not usually miss school for more than a short period of time, except in the case of a severe fracture of the large bones of the leg (femur and tibia), which often necessitates surgery and/or hospitalization for proper healing. There are several conditions which are important to discuss more thoroughly here.

## Scoliosis

*Scoliosis* is a lateral curvature of the spine. This is commonly caused by muscular strains, unequal leg lengths, or other conditions not directly affecting the spine. Care of the other problem usually corrects the scoliosis. If the spinal curvature is caused by tumors, infections, or other conditions directly affecting the spine, it is more difficult to deal with. The type of scoliosis that is so often seen in school-age children is usually found in girls from 12 to 15 years of age, and there is no known cause. In these children the spine may show progressive curvature so that the posture becomes quite abnormal, affecting the entire skeletal system at times. This condition must be diagnosed early before substantial structural changes have taken place and while treatment can be of preventive help. Many schools have undertaken screening programs for scoliosis, which increases early diagnosis and treatment.

## Lordosis

*Lordosis* is a condition which is fairly common in children, especially in the prepubertal and pubertal periods; it is seen more commonly in girls. Lordosis refers to the anterior curving of the spine. This is usually noticed in the lower part of the spine, so that the child often looks as if he has a "potbelly;" the posterior lower spine often seems to curve forward quite a bit, making them look as if they are quite uncomfortable when they are standing up. However, most children with lordosis have no major problem except when it has been associated with a spinal or bone disease. When a disease state or symptoms such as gait disturbance, pains, or growth problems are associated with the lordosis, orthopedic help should be sought.

## Kyphosis

Kyphosis is essentially the opposite from lordosis. In this condition there is a "hump-back" with a posterior curvature of the spine. The convexity is backward as opposed to the forward convexity of lordosis. Kyphosis is usually secondary to disease processes which have caused destruction of the bones of the spine and is usually a very serious condition. Tuberculosis is one of the more common causes of kyphosis.

There are many other diseases of the bones and muscles that can cause both acute and chronic problems, but most of these are quite rare. One disorder that is uncommon, but has received quite a bit of publicity, is *muscular dystrophy.* This is an inherited problem that exists in various forms, and in its more severe types is associated with a progressive destruction of many muscles of the body with subsequent weakness and eventually paralysis and total incapacitation. Most children with muscular dystrophy need special programs for handicapped children and often get to the point where they cannot attend school at all.

For a more complete description of children's orthopedic problems, the reader is referred to a pediatric or orthopedic text.

## SKIN PROBLEMS

Almost any disease can have related skin manifestations as was discussed in the section on viruses and the various rashes produced. However, there are several common skin conditions seen in children that should be mentioned.

### Impetigo

Impetigo is an infection of the skin usually caused by either a streptococcus or staphylococcus bacterium. The typical lesions are blister-type (vesicles) that quickly become filled with pus (purulent). These soon rupture and form yellow crusts with a surrounding red area of the skin. Impetigo is highly contagious, and the child should be kept home from school until treatment is under way. If not treated, serious complications such as bone and joint infections and nephritis can result from impetigo.

### Acne

Acne is a universal problem in almost all teen-agers. The cases can be very mild or quite severe, and each individual case can show various shades of severity. Children with this disorder may have red pimples (papules), comedones (black heads), pustules (pimples filled with pus), or severe pitting and scarring. Medical and hygienic treatment is urgent in all serious cases because of the intense *physical* and *psychological* problems that acne can cause.

### Herpes Infections

The herpes virus produces the common "fever blister" that usually appears around the lips. The typical lesion is a group of clear blisters surrounded by a reddish area. After a few days the lesions become crusty and scabbed. This disorder is sometimes confused with impetigo, but it is due to a virus (herpes virus), not bacteria. It can be quite extensive, reaching into the mouth and gums, and can be associated with high fevers in young children. In older children it is localized and usually follows a mild illness or exposure to the sun or other elements. Herpes is minimally contagious, and there is no definitive treatment.

### Eczema

There are several conditions that fit into the category of eczema. Basically eczema describes a condition of the skin whereby the skin may be red, dry, or scaly with pimples or blisters. There may also be oozing of fluid in some cases. There are many causes of eczema from allergy, to contact sensitivity, to "nervous" eczema. The condition must be properly diagnosed and treated, but in many cases it is fairly difficult to do this, so most of these patients are treated uniformly with various creams and ointments that usually seem to work no matter what the cause.

### Ringworm

Ringworm is a fungus infection that may occur in many different areas of the body including the scalp, body, groin, and even on the foot, where it is called "athlete's foot." The fungi are microorganisms that are larger than bacteria but are quite similar in some respects. The fungi may cause infections in various parts of the body, but the ones that cause ringworm are quite specialized to specific areas of the skin. Ringworm is not always ring-shaped, is difficult to distinguish from many other skin infections, and is quite contagious, especially in the scalp. Children with this problem often have to miss school for varying periods until treatment is initiated.

## DISORDERS OF THE EYE

### Eye Infections

The most common eye problem seen (besides visual difficulty) is *conjunctivitis* or "pinkeye." The conjunctiva are the membranes covering the inside of the lids and also invisibly cover the white of the eye (sclera) (see Figure 5-2). Signs of conjunctivitis include redness, irritation, and often a mucus or yellow discharge that often causes the eyelids to stick together. The child often has sensitivity to light and pain as well as itching and some loss of vision. Conjunctivitis may occur as part of a generalized illness or may result from viral or bacterial infections of the eyes only. Many forms of conjunctivitis are extremely contagious, and children with this problem must be isolated until treatment is well under way.

### Refractive Errors

Some children are *hyperopic* (farsighted), which means they can see far-away objects better than close ones. A small number of children are *myopic* (nearsighted), which means that they have better vision for near objects than for distant ones. Myopia is often hereditary. Any child who shows one of these problems should be treated with corrective lenses as soon as possible. Testing of a child's vision is a necessity as early as he can understand the test, and is often possible at three and one-half to four years of age. Severe problems can often be picked up quite a bit earlier by various means of examination. Vision screening in school by the use of a wall chart should be considered marginal at best and is not really considered to be complete for most children. There are machines that do a much more thorough job, and most children should have at least one examination by this more comprehensive method every several years.

### Astigmatism

Astigmatism usually means that there is some distortion of the image the person sees, and it is often combined with myopia or hyperopia.

(By way of explanation, it might help to answer a common source of questions about vision acuity: 20/20 vision means that a person can see at 20 feet what the *normal* person can see at that distance; 20/50 means that he must move to 20 feet to see what is normally seen at 50 feet; and 20/12 means he can see at 20 feet what is normally seen at 12 feet.)

### Strabismus

Strabismus refers to a disorder of the eye muscles, so that the individual is cross-eyed or has a squint. It is usually caused by an imbalance of the muscles that control the eye movements. If this defect is significant enough, and lasts for a long enough time, it may produce poor vision from disuse of the affected eye (*amblyopia exanopsia*). Any child who is suspected of having strabismus must get an expert ophthalmological evaluation and treatment as early as six months of age for both visual and cosmetic reasons.

### Amblyopia

The term *amblyopia* simply refers to a diminution or dimness of vision, despite correction for refractive problems. It often occurs secondary to eye-muscle problems (strabismus), where one eye is not used properly. There may be many other causes of amblyopia, including disorders of either the structure or function of the eye. The condition must be properly diagnosed and treated when discovered, so as to prevent permanent loss of visual activity.

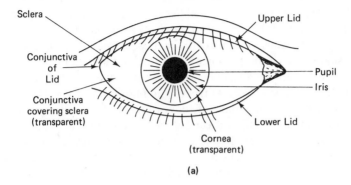

(a)

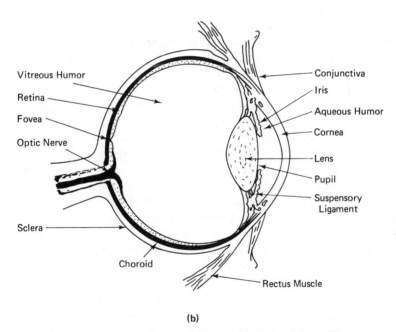

(b)

*Figure 5-2.    (a) Frontal view of the eye; (b) cross-section of the eye.*

## HEARING DISORDERS

Hearing disabilities may occur at any age from birth on; some of these problems are inherited as genetic defects, or they may be secondary to some type of maternal problems such as an infection (rubella). Hearing losses that are caused by disorders of the outer or the middle ear are called *conductive losses*. Abnormalities of the inner ear or the auditory nerve that goes to the brain are called *nerve losses* or *sensorineural defects* (see Figure 5-1). Conductive losses are the most common type in children and are usually due to the presence of fluid or adhesions in the middle ear after an infection or an allergic episode. Other causes of this type of hearing loss include abnormalities of the middle ear bones (ossicles), and/or obstruction in, or failure of, development of the external canal. Sensorineural defects usually reflect a greater handicap than conductive losses because they are less likely to respond to medical intervention. A sensorineural loss may be due to inherited defects, maternal disease, or medications such as streptomycin. It may also be the residual effect of diseases such as meningitis or mumps, and can be caused by various toxic substances such as lead.

Loss of hearing must be diagnosed as soon as possible in order to prevent long-lasting impairment of language development and learning. It is very difficult to diagnose minor hearing losses in young children. The definitive screening tests used are difficult to perform and to evaluate for children under the age of three or four. Generally the earlier a loss occurs, the more severe the disability will be. Parents must be questioned very carefully about the hearing of their infants since early diagnosis and prognosis are so important.

Hearing testing is usually able to be performed by standard methods by four years of age in most children—and in many by three. However, some of the three- and four-year-olds will fail the usual tests due to lack of attention or through misunderstanding, rather than poor hearing. The usual instrument used for screening is the audiometer, which presents pure tones and measures a loss in decibels or volume of sound. For children under three or four years, tests have been devised that are usually given by specialized centers devoted to hearing and language disorders in young children.

The audiometer (see Figure 5-3) presents a given frequency (pitch) and intensity (loudness) of sound. The frequency is calibrated in cycles per second (cps) and the intensity in decibels (db). The normal human ear can respond to frequencies from 20 to 20,000 cps, but normal speech and many of the environmental sounds are usually in the 250 to 4000 cps range. The normal person will hear sounds between 0 and 20 db. It is important to note here that the "0" reading on the audiometer is not the absence of sound, but rather the point at which the normal ear first perceives sound. If 20 to 40 db of volume are needed to hear the sound, it is a mild loss; if 40 to 60 db are needed, it is considered a moderate loss. Above 60 db is a severe loss, and above 90 db is considered deaf. With nerve losses, however, 20 db may be considered moderate to severe

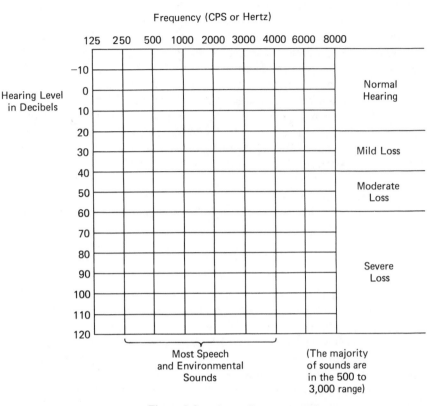

***Figure 5-3.*** *An audiometer graph.*

in most cases, as opposed to conductive losses. Not only volume is affected by a hearing loss; speech sounds are almost always distorted, and the reception of speech is unclear. Most hearing losses will contain elements of both intensity and distortion loss. In conductive disorders the main effect is usually one of reduction of loudness through all frequencies with no distortion of sounds, whereas sensorineural losses may show more of a frequency loss, especially in the very high ranges.

It must be stressed again that hearing losses must be diagnosed and treated as early as possible. If these are not picked up in infancy, a child's speech may not develop properly, or at all. At later ages a learning disability is frequently the first sign of a hearing problem. Some children may be able to compensate so thoroughly for mild losses—especially high-frequency losses—that it is a surprise when we *do* find a problem.

The typical pure tone audiological evaluation will usually be reported on a graph similar to that shown in Figure 5-3. The sound intensity necessary for hearing at each frequency is plotted on the graph so that a continuous curve is produced for each ear. If this does not produce a diagnostic picture, more sophisticated tests such as impedance or Bekesy audiometry are done.* These types of evaluations should be done by people trained in speech and language pathology, and may be necessary for a specific diagnosis in some cases.

As a final note, we must again stress the importance of both peripheral hearing and central processing for a total normal pattern. As we discussed previously, there are certain children who are able to hear sounds perfectly well at all frequencies and at normal intensity, but due to a central nervous system dysfunction cannot satisfactorily discriminate or process the sounds. (This is the group of children discussed in Chapter 4 in the "aphasia" category.) The proper evaluation of language and learning defects must take into consideration *both* peripheral and central hearing in order to properly diagnose and treat a child's learning problem.

## FINAL STATEMENTS: SCHOOL-PHOBIA, STRESS

Since a child spends a good part of his day in the classroom, it is natural that he often manifests signs and symptoms of many disease processes in this setting. It is also a fact that the average classroom will contain at least several children with some type of chronic illness or deformity—one that might interfere with their educational progress on a relatively permanent basis. Because of this, the teacher should have at least a nodding acquaintance with the more common afflictions of childhood, so as to be able to understand what problems the child with such a handicap faces. If the teacher is able to recognize that a disease or some other disorder may be causing a certain problem in one of her pupils, she will be able more quickly to refer the child to the physician or proper authority for definitive care. Since teachers are not expected to use medical textbooks on a daily basis, nor do we think it wise for them to become a medical diagnostician, we have provided a brief glossary in this chapter of some of the more important and common problems to be seen in the classroom.

Besides a nodding acquaintance with the disorders mentioned, the teacher should be acquainted with a very common masquerader of childhood diseases—school-phobia. Everyone knows about the child who becomes ill the morning of school, develops abdominal pain the day of a big test, or has headaches every Monday morning. These events are quite common and certainly are as important—and in some

---

*Impedance audiometry is a test of the middle ear system. It is the electric acoustic evaluation of the motility of the tympanic membrane, function of the conduction of the middle ear, and determination of the intraaural muscle reflex. Bekesy audiometry defines the difference between an auditory nerve or inner ear (cochlear) problem.

children more so—as the child who just screams, carries on, and tells
parents that he does not want to go to school. There are many su
children who tell us by their words, actions, or symptoms that school
represents a real or imagined danger to their well-being. It is often hard
to separate these children from those with *real* diseases, and the condition is extremely difficult to treat. The children should be kept in school
at almost all costs, but a good deal of detective work must go on while
they are attending. School-phobia is a real thing, and may represent a
major family problem. The symptoms can mimic many other diseases,
and can escalate those that already exist. It is in working with this group
of children that the educational triangle receives one of its most severe tests!

Finally, we must again mention one of the most familiar concepts
we are faced with. We have spoken of the word *stress* in connection with
various disorders in previous paragraphs. We know how the stress of
school itself might bring to the surface such problems as neurological
hyperactivity and borderline learning disorders. Stress—personal or
familial—is also a common denominator of many chronic and repeated
illnesses. We can also trace the development of many chemical disorders
in the body to the release of certain hormones from the adrenal glands
under stressful situations. These chemical reactions may affect brain function as in blood sugar changes or may affect other organs such as the
special senses. Thus, whole chains of reactions may be set into motion by
stressful situations, either acute or chronic. In many cases, the entire
direction of a child's disability can be changed by lifting the stress from
his environment or body. It is quite important that parents and teachers
work together actively to prevent the child from being placed in pressure-
filled situations and environments, and changing these if already present
whether at school, at home, or in extracurricular activities such as little
league or dancing. Finally, we emphatically remind all who assess the
medical condition and health situation of any child: *a child with a complicated problem will probably not recover unless a multifaceted approach
is used!*

# CHAPTER 6

# The Identification of a Child With Educational Dysfunction

As we previously mentioned, a child with a learning handicap may be discovered upon entering school, or in some cases might be suspected much earlier. It is obviously most important to identify a potential problem area before it actually becomes a full-blown crisis. Minor and freshly discovered difficulties are much easier to deal with than long-term problems. If we again refer to our educational triangle, we can see how the three cornerstones can work together to effect this type of approach.

The *parents* may be the first persons to identify a potential disorder in their child. The family history, pregnancy, and birth events, and development during infancy and early childhood are most familiar to the parent. Any suspicion of a problem in these areas should be initiated by the person who knows the child best—that is, the parent.

The *physician* also will have an excellent chance to identify and intervene in potential problem areas because of his knowledge of the child's background. A close working relationship between parent and physician during the early years of life is most productive in identifying children who might potentially be in trouble. The physician will further have the chance to diagnose and often correct any medical disorders before they cause major problems. If the doctor is able to work closely with the teacher, a smooth transition from home to school will be supported.

The *teacher's* role is an important one (principal, school nurse, or school psychologist could also fit here). In those children who attend a preschool, the teacher will have a special opportunity to recognize problems that may go unnoticed by the parents or by the physician.

If any type of remediation is called for at this time, the teacher could be quite influential in the initiation and continuation of such treatment. Thus it may be possible in some children to prevent certain problems before they get to be of major proportion. And as the child enters school, the teacher becomes the most important part of the triangle since so much of the child's day is spent in school.

A close working relationship between teachers, parents, and doctors is essential at all times, especially once a problem is identified.

## *EARLY IDENTIFICATION PROCESS*

There are specific historical events as well as certain signs and symptoms of aberrant behavior that can be identified by each part of the educational triangle. Some parts of the history will be known by the parent alone, some by the doctor, and often the information is shared. And certain behaviors will be more commonly seen by the teacher than by the parent or vice versa. The situations and stimuli at home as compared to those at school are entirely different, and it is important to note any variations in the child's behavior between home and school. It is also important to know who described the various behaviors in order to better evaluate their significance, but we should not ignore an observation because the observer represents a different discipline or presents a biased view.

We will attempt to outline some of the more important historical, developmental, and behavioral characteristics that may be seen in children with educational dysfunction in the following sections. Some parts of the background will be able to be utilized better by the parent, others by the teacher or by the physician. Some will be helpful to all. We have presented the material as a modified checklist, so that it will be more useful as a screening device. There could be many behaviors or events added to the list; however, as with any screening device, the more complex it becomes, the more difficult it is to follow and therefore the less helpful it is. We must also state here that a narrative account of a child's behaviors is often as helpful or sometimes more so than a list of behaviors. A person should utilize the format most comfortable to him.

The identification of a child with a possible problem may occur at any time in the child's life—often at birth, or sometimes before. Certain behaviors, signs, symptoms, or history may be quite helpful, as well as predictive, in many cases. There have been many instances of kindergarten and first-grade teachers being able to pick out which children will run into problems before any actual formal schooling really takes place. These very perceptive teachers have used certain characteristics found in the children that are often correlated with future learning problems to identify which students are at risk. *The correlation between the kinder-*

garten teacher's predictions and the actual course of the child's learning experience is often uncannily high!

In the identification process, there are several general descriptive areas that can be useful to the parent, teacher, and doctor. These include:

1. Developmental abnormalities

2. Educational difficulties

3. Medical problems

4. Behavioral characteristics

5. Personal and family history

Problems in any of these areas may be discovered by any part of the educational triangle, at any time. When we consider all of these factors including the history of the child and his family, we should be able to get a fairly good idea of what a particular child's chances of success in school may be. The following checklist might be useful for physician, parent, teacher, or other worker to use as a guideline in the early identification of the educationally disabled child.

### *History Checklist*

*FAMILY*

1. Retardation.

2. Behavioral disorders; delinquency.

3. Learning problems.

4. Neurological disease such as epilepsy, weakness, or paralysis.

5. Deafness or vision problems.

6. Financial or social difficulties.

7. Moves, separations, divorces.

*PREGNANCY AND BIRTH*
*(PERINATAL/ANTENATAL PERIODS)*

1. Bleeding, fevers, rashes, virus infections, injuries, smoking, medications, emotional problems.

2. Length of pregnancy.

3. Age of mother and father.

4. Problems in labor.

5. Type and difficulty of delivery (length of time).

6. Birth weight and condition at birth (breathing, color, abnormalities, illness).

7. Was treatment necessary at birth?

8. Problems in first several days (jaundice, cyanosis, breathing difficulty, jumpiness, sluggishness, illness, other abnormalities).

9. Feeding—type and problems.

10. Sex of the child (males are more suspect for learning disabilities).

## INFANCY

1. Was this a happy, pleasant baby?

2. Colic? Prolonged crying? Overly quiet?

3. Feeding difficulty?

4. Illness? Accidents? Hospitalizations?

## DEVELOPMENTAL HISTORY*

Normal time limits are shown in parentheses; some of the achievements will occur slightly later in boys. Children who show isolated developmental deficits usually have no real problems. When many delays are noted in several or all areas of development, the child should be investigated for future disabilities. It might be noted that a delay in the *language* area is usually the closest correlation with future intellectual and educational disorders.

### Gross Motor

Roll over (2 to 4 months).

Sit alone (5 to 8 months).

Stand alone (9 to 13 months).

Walk alone (11 to 18 months).

Jump (22 to 36 months).

Pedal tricycle (12 to 36 months).

Stand on one foot well (3 to 5 years).

---

*The format and some of the material in this section has been loosely adapted from "The Denver Developmental Screening Test" by William K. Frankenburg and Josiah B. Dodds, *Journal of Pediatrics,* 71, No. 2 (Aug. 1967), pp. 181–191.

Hop on one foot (3 to 5 years).

Heel-toe walk (3½ to 5½ years).

## Fine Motor

Follow object with eyes halfway across room (birth to 2 months).

Follow object with eyes completely across room (2 to 4 months).

Reach for object (3 to 5 months).

Transfer object from hand to hand (5 to 7 months).

Good pincerlike grasp with thumb and finger (9 to 14 months).

Scribble (12 to 18 months).

Build up four blocks (15 to 22 months).

Copy circle (2½ to 3½ years).

Copy square (4 to 5½ years).

Copy triangle (5 to 6 years).

Draw three-part human figure (3½ to 5 years).

Draw six-part human figure (4½ to 6 years).

Catch ball (bounced)(3½ to 5 years).

Catch ball (thrown)(4 to 6 years).

## Language Development

Laugh out loud ( 2 to 4 months).

Squeal (3 to 5 months).

Babble consonants (lalling) (6 to 9 months).

Imitate sounds (5 to 10 months).

Speak words (11 to 18 months).

Combine two words (15 to 24 months).

Use three-to-four-word phrase (2 to 3 years).

Follow directions (15 to 24 months).

Give complete name (2 to 3 years).

Know three colors (3 to 4 years).

Use good four-word sentence (3 to 3½ years).

Use longer sentences (4 years).

## Social Development

Social smile (1½ to 3 months).

Feed self cookie (4 to 7 months).

Peek-a-boo (6 to 9 months).

Cry with strangers (4 to 8 months).

Drink from cup (10 to 15 months).

Pat-a-cake (7 to 12 months).

Bye-bye (7 to 12 months).

Use spoon (13 to 24 months).

Remove article of clothing (14 to 22 months).

Put on article of clothing (22 to 30 months).

Separate from parent well (2 to 3 years).

Button (2½ to 3½ years).

Dress completely (3 to 4½ years).

Tie shoes (4 to 6 years).

Bowel and bladder training complete:
Daytime (3 years)
Nighttime (4 to 5 years)

## Miscellaneous

Eruption of second set of teeth—highly correlated with school-readiness development! This usually starts at six years of age.

## MEDICAL HISTORY

Include serious illnesses, hospitalizations, accidents, surgery. Especially look for:

1. Head injury.

2. Convulsions.

3. High fevers for prolonged period.

4. Loss of consciousness.

5. Long-lasting illnesses.

6. Poisoning.

7. Allergies.

8. Any handicaps such as orthopedic, muscular, or neurological.

9. Over- or underweight.

10. Neurological and coordination disorders.

11. Ear infections and hearing loss.

12. Abdominal pain, headache, constipation.

13. Anemia (low blood).

## NUTRITIONAL HISTORY

1. Overweight or underweight.

2. Loss of appetite.

3. Good nutritional diet (eating habits).

4. Food fads (including sweet cravings, high "junk food" consumption).

5. Type of breakfast eaten.

6. Milk consumption.

7. Vitamins or other food supplements.

## HOME BEHAVIORAL HISTORY

Any of these particular behaviors may be seen in almost any child at any time. They are significant when they are recurrent and present more than just occasionally.

It is important to note that a behavior should be reported as just that—and not indicated as a diagnosis. Thus, words like *depressed, hostile,* and *aggressive* do not specifically describe what the child is doing. Try to use specific, descriptive terms when possible. Thus: "Hits other children"—instead of "Aggressive"; "Sad more than happy"—instead of "Depressed."

### Signs and Symptoms

| | |
|---|---|
| Won't be disciplined | Daydreams |
| Can't follow directions | Worried, nervous |
| Hyper- or overactive | Thumb-sucking (Over age five) |

| | |
|---|---|
| Short attention span | Destructive of toys, materials |
| Makes odd noises | Facial grimaces |
| Easily frustrated | Bed- or pants-wetting |
| Excessive talking | Soiling pants |
| Underactive or passive | Always angry at others |
| Sleeping problems<br>  Restless<br>  Nightmares and terrors<br>  Insomnia | Defiant of authority<br><br>Lying and stealing |
| Disobedient | Tantrums |
| Severe mood changes | Sad more than happy |
| Head-banging and rocking | Stubborn |
| Nail-biting | Oversensitive, shy |

## PEER RELATIONS

Constant hitting and fighting with others.

Can't get along in large groups.

Can't keep friends.

Prefers younger or older children.

Hates to lose.

Disrupts games.

Must be the "boss" in games.

Leader? or follower?

Always touching other children.

## HABITS AND ROUTINES

Can't settle down for homework.

Must have parents' help with everything.

No hobbies or interests.

Puts off tasks.

Won't do tasks at all.

Television addict.

(There are many other items in this group that could be added for individual children.)

## SCHOOL BEHAVIORAL HISTORY

Any of the traits listed under Home Behavioral History on page 127 would apply here also. Some may be described both at home and in school; others may be seen only at school or only in the home situation. Behaviors indigenous to school include:

School-phobia (with attendant symptoms of various illnesses, abdominal pain, and headache).

Always handling objects.

Falls apart under stress.

*Distractible and disruptive.

*Short attention span.

Must always have teacher's attention.

Quarrels and "tattles."

No group participation; unaccepted by group.

Defiant toward authority.

Attendance problem.

Fighting, pushing, shoving, and hitting others (by far the most serious signs).

## EDUCATIONAL OBSERVATIONS

Obviously any of the behavior traits listed above or on page 127 might contribute to educational dysfunction. However, there are certain behaviors that a teacher can observe in the context of the classroom or learning process that might have a specific bearing on the identification of children with learning disabilities. These behaviors can be divided into strictly educational, neurophysiological, language-oriented, and medically oriented observations.

### Educational Behaviors*

Won't complete work.

Can't follow directions.

Difficulty with concepts for age level.

Work very uneven.

Work below expectancy.

*These observations must be correlated to age.

Previous school problems, special classes, retention.

### Neurophysiological Behaviors*

Poor coordination (especially fine motor).

Poor memory.

Distractible, short attention span, disruptive.

No hand preference or dominance shown by age five.

Reversals past age eight.

Poor balance.

Tics (abnormal facial or other body motions).

Weakness, sluggishness, or partial paralysis.

Poor hopping and/or skipping when older than seven.

Any type of sensory discrimination problem.

Problems distinguishing forms and shapes.

Auditory or visual perceptual difficulties, either receptive or expressive.

Fine motor difficulties.

Clumsiness and awkward walking and running.

Tremors.

Difficulty with repetitive movements.

Problem with right-left discrimination past age ten.

Jerking or nonsmooth movements of eye muscles (nystagmus).

Difficulty with tongue movements.

Actually, most of the above are what we call neurological "soft signs." These and many other similar indicators are usually brought out during a physical examination. Most examiners have their own favorite soft signs that are elicited by various maneuvers. The most important thing to know about the soft signs is that they are all a mark of developmental or neurological immaturity, and most of them will no longer be present as the child grows older. Another important thing to understand is that the presence of soft signs of neurological immaturity does not in any way indicate one-to-one precursors of educational dysfunction, but these soft signs often do *coexist* in a child who develops a learning disability. *The observer must remember that the description of a child with problems in these areas should not be taken synonymously as a description of a child with a learning disorder.*

## Language Behaviors

*Disorders of speech and language are often present in children with educational dysfunction, either as a cause or associated problem. Delay or deviation in language development is a more important factor in reading and writing and spelling disorders than delay in any other areas including that of visual perception. Problems in this area are often very closely correlated with the later development of learning problems.* Some of the important signs to be watched for include:

*Delayed speech at any age.*

Suspicion of a hearing problem; inattention to normal sounds.

Short attention span. (There's that very important observation once more!)

Immature speech.

Can't follow directions.

Substitutions of words and sounds.

Omitting syllables or words.

Can't be understood.

Poor or short-sentence structure by age five, especially omitting verbs, nouns, or pronouns, or scrambling the order of words.

Difficulty expressing self and frustration when not understood.

Lip reading.

Stuttering or other problems of rhythm.

Shyness and not speaking (may be indicator of poor skills).

Use of jargon (almost a different language).

## Medical-Physical Behaviors

Many of the observations of sickness or physical abnormalities and signs have been mentioned above. However, there are certain common observations that teachers or others may make that can be quite helpful to the other professionals evaluating the child. These include:

General weakness.

Paleness.

Falling asleep in class.

Staring spells.

Disorders of hearing or vision.

Respiratory symptoms (running nose, cough, constant sniffing, difficulty breathing).

Over- or underactivity.

Over- or undernutrition.

Skin problems, rashes.

Abnormal coloring such as circles under eyes.

Somatic complaints such as headache, belly pain.

Wetting or soiling pants.

Any observation of congenital physical abnormalities or abnormal physical characteristics.

## USE OF THE CHECKLISTS

The preceding checklists merely serve as a beginning in the long process of identifying and subsequently helping the child with educational dysfunction. Each corner of the triangle (teacher, parent, physician) is able to provide valuable input into one or more of these categories. As we stated above, in some cases the observations of one observer might disagree—often measurably—with those of another person. This should not lead to any divisiveness of effort in regard to the child. It *must* be understood that a child will often *perform quite differently* under different circumstances. Observations made by the teacher should be regarded perhaps as the *most* valid since many children are under the most stress in school. A vulnerable child will exhibit signs of tension and strain when he is placed in the most stressful situation, and this is school for most children. Thus a child will often sit at home quietly and play or watch television, but completely fall apart when asked to read in school. Even in the classroom situation, we may see differences according to the amount of stress the child is under. We may see a child perform quite well in a subject such as music or art—or even during dramatics—where there is no specific stress on an academic subject. But the same child may act completely different during the next period when he starts his arithmetic or spelling lesson.

It is important for school, parent, and doctor to add as much information as they can to the study of a particular child, and for all involved to freely share and evaluate these observations with one another.

It is self-defeating for one corner of our educational triangle to dismiss certain descriptions as invalid or biased because of a personal feeling or reserve toward another observer. All observations must be carefully studied in order to see which ones will be helpful in diagnosing and remediating the child's problem. Biases and points of view must be recognized and evaluated along with all of the other information.

The identification process is a continuous one starting at birth and lasting through the entire school career of each child. Some children will be recognized as having major physical or emotional problems quite early in life, and steps must be taken to prevent educational difficulties in these children also quite early in life. Thus, classes for orthopedically handicapped and language-disabled children should be utilized far before the "normal" school age of five is reached. Children with these types of problems should be identified by their parents and physicians at an early age and proper remediation sought as soon as possible.

In order to assist in following through with this type of help, however, the physician should be aware of the types of programs that *are* available in the community, since many parents are not well informed. In order to keep the parents, doctors, and others informed of available assistance, it might be necessary for the schools to publicize the types of programs available to the community. This is another way the educational triangle can interact even before any one specific child becomes a consideration. Publicity and communication are essential in each community so that the people living in the area are totally aware of all of the resources available. Methods of communicating this type of information may include commercial news media, community meetings, parent organizations, church groups, charitable and service clubs, and fraternal organizations among others.

### *Role of the Preschool*

There is one special category, however, that has a very important and urgent place in the early recognition and identification of potential problem children, and that is the nursery or preschool. A large number of urban children in this country attend some type of preschool before actual school entrance at age five or so. This may include the average preschool; a highly structured, special school; a day-care center; or just a loose, unstructured "baby-sitting" co-op. The one common denominator in all of these situations is that the child is taken out of his home and is placed in a situation that can cause him some stress or vulnerability. It is at least a *different* situation. Nursery-school experience generally begins at three or four years of age, but in many families children are thrust into this type of situation much earlier, often before one year of age.

There are some problems inherent in the reliability of observations made in this type of setting. The training, interest, and abilities of the teachers or caretakers in these settings are extremely varied. Some are highly trained professionals, while others are well-meaning but untrained mothers. Some settings are structured and geared to educational pursuits. Others are simply caretaking facilities for the children of working parents. Therefore, the type of observation we may receive from these sources will have to be closely scrutinized at times, but *should never be dismissed automatically.*

Another little cog in the machinery of identification is the fact that the child we are talking about—the one- to five-year-old—is in an unbelievably rapid period of growth and development during these years. Observations that are valid at one point in time may have changed drastically by the next reporting period. A child who is reported as having various characteristics of behavior may have matured greatly by the next reporting period, and therefore those particular observations may no longer be valid. Thus, it is somewhat difficult to get a good handle on what is really happening to a child in many cases, because of the differences in the child himself and because of the varied sophistication of the observers.

However, in spite of all of these shortcomings, children must be carefully observed during these years. Many problem areas will be able to be identified; others perhaps merely suggested. As we stated above, children with major problems such as physical handicaps, language disorders, and severe neurological and emotional difficulties should have already been singled out and started on their individual roads to remediation long before they enter school. However, there remains a large body of children who seem "suspicious" to many observers (that is, candidates who are likely to develop an educational problem), especially in the year or so before they are ready to start kindergarten. This is a group that is also important to identify so as to be ready for them when the time comes. It is very urgent to do so because it is such a very large group, probably as large as 15% or more of all school children.

## MOST IMPORTANT INDICATORS OF POSSIBLE EDUCATIONAL DYSFUNCTION

All of the characteristics in the lists presented earlier in the chapter may have some bearing on our index of suspicion, but there are certain clusters of historical and behavioral situations that should be *particularly carefully regarded.* These include:

1.  Family history of learning problems, especially in a male.

2.  Perinatal problems.

3.  Early illness and accidents, especially involving the central nervous system.

4.  Slow or uneven developmental milestones.

5.  Chronic illnesses.

6.  Poor home environment.

7.  Signs of neurological and developmental (maturational) lag or delay.

These types of observations, where present, should alert the people involved with the care of the particular child that there might be a problem on the way. Perhaps the school should be alerted, maybe the parents need some form of counseling, a special educational program might be looked into, or the child may need special medical care. Any appropriate recommendation we can feed into the educational or personal structure for this possible problem child is necessary and usually appreciated.

The most sophisticated task of identification belongs to the trained preschool teacher (the necessity for this type of person is *grossly underestimated*) and the kindergarten teacher. This is because many children who will go on to develop learning disabilities are not identified early enough, largely because they are not in the group who show obvious deviations of their medical history, and they do not have clearly recognizable handicaps. Therefore it is urgent that the observer of the three-, four-, five-, and sometimes six-year-old should have a solid idea of the *requisites necessary for a profitable learning experience.*

## SCHOOL READINESS

We should mention the most obvious problem first—that is, that many children are placed in an educational environment before they are *maturationally* ready for it. This is in itself a major cause of learning problems. We know that boys in particular are very often not ready by five years of age to assume the role of a student. This is why some educators stress the idea that *a boy who was born after September 1 (and many times after June 1) is often physically unable to become part of the school environment at age five.* Thus, many boys (and some girls) should be held out of school until they are well past their fifth birthday—and often their sixth!

Along these lines we must also mention the senseless American predilection for early education for all, even before school age. Too many children who are fed into the preschool educational mill will eventually be spit out as educational failures because they were not maturationally ready. The preschool experience should be a socially oriented process with the emphasis on *maturation* and *development* of *interactive* and *communication skills.* If this is done, the child who is unable to fit into this special type of environment will be identified early enough to initiate help. The four-year-old child who is referred for help because he cannot learn to read or add should be recognized as normal, and the referrer should be the one who gets helped—with the facts of child development.

It is important to be aware of the fact that three areas of development must be up to par in order for a child to enter into the educational process; these areas are: (1) intellectual, (2) neurological, and (3) social development. If any one of these is below age level, the child must be far ahead in the others in order to succeed in the learning process. If two are below, he most assuredly must be evaluated very carefully before school placement.

A parent, teacher, or other observer will often be able to identify a child who might be lagging in the readiness area by utilizing the various lists included earlier in this chapter. A child who presents many of these signs, symptoms, or historical factors would certainly be a likely candidate for educational dysfunction. Many physicians and educators have developed school-readiness screening exams that are given to children just before they are chronologically ready for school (see Appendix A at the end of this chapter). This type of screening device utilizes some of the more important facts that are correlated with intellectual, neurological, and social readiness for school. This is a rapid way of at least identifying a child who might develop problems, and can be quite useful in formulating educational strategies for some children.

The photographs that follow depict some interesting findings through the use of some neurodevelopmental tasks such as drawing simple forms like a circle, cross, square, and triangle, as well as drawing a picture of a person.

## Summary: Prerequisites for School Entry—Communication

In summary we see that there are a large number of behavioral, neurological, physical, and developmental prerequisites that are necessary for a satisfactory educational experience. We have reviewed many of the factors that when present might lead us to suspect a child to be "at risk." We have further shown how it is possible to use a short checklist at the time of school entry (usually four and one-half to five years) to bring our information up to date and help weed out some of the possible problem cases.

Finally, it might be helpful to develop a brief group of easy to use identifiers to help us establish whether a child who has no limiting major

ERIK

ALEX

square

circle

cross

Triangle

Man

**Figure 6-1.** *Erik was shown to be much less mature than his brother Alex through the use of these drawings. The drawings were done one year apart, when each boy was five, approximately four months before the boys were to start school. Mr. and Mrs. C. decided to start both boys at approximately five years of age. Alex did quite well, but Erik showed quite a bit of immaturity and had to repeat the year. The drawings turned out to be one of several predictors that could have been helpful in this instance.*

**_Figure 6-2._** *Kim, the child who drew this picture, was tested for school readiness for the first time at five years of age, but showed many signs of immaturity, including those demonstrated in these drawings. She was held back and was retested one year later. Kim was much more mature at that time, and she went on to have a successful year. Her later drawings exhibit her more complete neurodevelopmental maturity in 1976.*

**8/7/76**
**4 10/12 yrs.**

**8/22/77**
**Age 5 11/12 yrs.**

**Figure 6-3.** *At four years and ten months, Carol was not ready to start school, as demonstrated in part by her inability to copy or draw the basic figures. She was sent to school in spite of this, but did quite poorly. Testing one year later showed her maturity level to be much higher, as indicated by the later drawing. She has made a much more successful beginning in school the second time around!*

disabilities is otherwise ready to learn to read, write, and spell. This can be done by utilizing some of the most *important* factors in our *previous* checklists and *combining* them into the following group of prerequisites:

1.    The child must be free of nutritional, physical, or emotional disabilities that would interfere with classroom performance.

2.    The child must be able to sit fairly still and attend to incoming stimuli for at least ten minutes or thereabouts.

3.    The child must be able to verbally communicate with his teacher and classmates intelligibly.

4.    The child must be able to follow a three-part command.

5.    The child must be able to screen out unimportant visual, auditory, and tactile stimuli from the classroom environment.

6.    The child must be able to tolerate some frustrations and delayed gratification and should possess fairly well developed impulse control. He must also be able to accept limits.

7.    The child should be able to copy shapes such as a circle, square, and triangle; he should also be able to draw a six-part human figure.

8.    The child should be able to interact reasonably well with other children and should have learned to share and take turns.

If a child is identified as "at risk" by utilizing the above categories as screening devices, it might be necessary to either delay school entrance, or perhaps to start to develop different types of strategies for that particular child. It is much more desirable to know what to expect than to be surprised. We cannot emphasize this early identification process too much. The child's entire educational career may depend upon it!

In this chapter we have discussed the many diverse historical and observational characteristics that might alert the observer to a possible problem in a particular child. We have also taken a *closer* look at some of the more reliable observable predictors. We have noted that if a teacher describes what types of aberrant behaviors are being shown by the child in the classroom—whether these fit into the clusters of the historical and/or behavioral characteristics listed—a fairly high correlation of predictability can be reached.

The importance of these observations by and to all concerned with the child cannot be underestimated. We often find, however, that there is a communication gap concerning these matters between the professionals involved. We often find that teachers do not know how they should communicate with physicians, and the doctor in turn is not sure of his place in the school. Both may not be working properly with the parents. The reasons for these gaps may be professional insecurity, not caring, lack of time, poor trust, dishonesty, or just plain inexperience. We should not let the total communication process wither on the vine because of these, or any other reasons.

The form that the communication takes is not the important matter; the fact that it *takes place at all* is the real crux of the situation. It will certainly help if the physician makes himself more comfortable with the educational jargon and the teacher with medical terminology, and both should be able to converse freely and intelligently with parents. But the important thing is to let the other person know *what you see and think about the child.*

The doctor is usually interested in the child's daily academic performance and whether he is falling below the school's expectations for him. Discrepancies between daily performance and documented intelligence are important. Types of behavior, physical abnormalities, and just plain observations important to the teacher as a professional observer of children are all necessary for a total evaluation. It is also important to note the *immediate cause for the referral* if the school initiated such referral! If the parent initiated the referral, the teacher can be helpful if she points out whether the crisis was new or expected in view of past behavior and performance.

The teacher should not worry about making a *diagnosis*—either educational or medical. When all of the *descriptions* of the child's behavior are totaled, it is often necessary—and sometimes mandatory—that the diagnosis, or at least a working diagnosis, be made collectively by *all* disciplines involved. It is often difficult to spell out *exactly how* information is to be passed on from one part of the educational triangle to another. This will depend upon many variables such as who first noted the problem, how interested the various parties may be, the number of resources present in the school system, and the cooperation of all involved. Usually the teacher is the first person to note the presence of a learning problem, and ideally she would pass this information on to the parent. The physician would then become involved through contact with the family; and with the parents' permission, the teacher (or other school personnel involved) could then phone or write the physician to initiate that part of the communication. The possibilities are quite unlimited if the parties remain in close touch and cooperation prevails. Most children with learning disabilities will benefit greatly if this type of communication, no matter how initiated, prevails. Only by working together in a comfortable, open, and sharing situation can the ultimate goal of remediation of educational dysfunction be reached.

# School Readiness Checklist

*HISTORY*

1. Does child know first and last names?

2. Does child know age?

3. Can child be understood easily?

4. Does child play well with other children?

5. Does child separate easily from parents?

6. Does child have "accidents" in toilet habits?

7. Does child recognize letters?

8. How many colors does child know?

9. Can child button?_____ zip-up?_____ tie shoes?_____

10. Can child draw circle?_____ cross?_____ square?_____ triangle?_____

11. Can child follow three-stage command?

12. Has child established dominant hand usage?

13. Does child show interest in books, games, puzzles?

14. Can child color in lines?

15. Can child wash hands and face?

16. Can child run and skip?

17.   Can child dress himself alone?

18.   Can child hold pencil or crayon correctly?

19.   Can child share and take turns?

*Circle One On Each Question*

20.   Are child's drawings: scribble/fair shape/good detail?

21.   Does child finish projects: seldom/fairly often/always?

22.   Is child's memory: poor/average/very good?

23.   Attention span: very short (1–2 minutes)/fair (3–10 minutes)/ very good (over 10 minutes)?

24.   Distractibility: very easy/not too much/hardly at all?

25.   Number recognition: none/up to 5/up to 10/over 10?

26.   Counting: none/up to 5/up to 10/over 10?

27.   Letter recognition: none/few/some words/personal name?

*PERFORMANCE*

1.   Can child repeat a sequence of four numbers? (3–7–4–9)

2.   Can child repeat three numbers in reverse order? (2–8–5)

3.   Can child repeat B, D, G, C, in sequence?

4.   Can child identify colors? (red/green/blue/yellow)

5.   Can child name two animals?

6.   Can child tell where meat, milk, apples come from?

7.   Have child draw (or copy) circle, cross, square, triangle.

8.   Have child draw human figure.

9.   Can child recognize five numbers?

10.   Can child recognize five letters?

11.   Can child count to 10?

12.   Can child hop on one foot? (two to three hops)

13.   Can child stand on one foot? (5 to 10 seconds)

14.   Can child perform heel-toe walk?

15.   Has child established hand dominance—right or left?

### PART II

# *Remediation*

# CHAPTER 7

# *The Total Approach*

The first six chapters of this book have presented material that relates to the identification of the child with educational dysfunction. We have shown how a child might develop this particular type of disability for many reasons or combinations of causes. We have also pointed out the folly of trying to use labels in identifying or treating these children. The importance of considering each child's individual and unique problems and solution was stressed. Finally, in the previous chapter we pointed out why these children should be identified as early as possible, as well as the importance of the communication between the three parts of the educational triangle in dealing with these students.

We shall now approach the question of remediation—or the question of help of some sort for the child with learning disorders. In order to proceed it would seem logical to show how each corner of our educational triangle might achieve the best possible result for each child. We must remember that there are usually many questions that are asked by all of those concerned about each individual student. Then all parties must be able to communicate their feelings and suggestions to each other. This means that there must be some type of reproducible and easily utilizable methodology developed to expedite this type of communication. The form and format are not really important except for the following points:

1.   All information should be clearly presented and specifically related to the child in question.

2.   Explanations and descriptions should be in terms that can be easily understood by everyone working with the child.

3.   The information presented and recommendations made must be concise, easily readable, attainable for that child and his family, and most important—geared to that particular child's special problems.

4.   All information should be freely available to anyone interested in the child.

5.   Communication between all parties must be open, informative, freely available, and as nonbiased as is humanly possible.

6.   All parties involved must remember that the most important product of their job is the progress of the child, and personal needs, biases, and jealousies must be put aside.

| Remember: | Teacher vs. Parent | Will | Everyone |
|---|---|---|---|
|  | Teacher vs. Doctor | lead | vs. |
|  | Parent vs. Doctor | to | Child |

Help for each child with educational dysfunction usually falls into three general categories:

1.   Educational

2.   Psychological-emotional

3.   Medical

## EDUCATIONAL REMEDIATION

Educational remediation is certainly the most important area of intervention for each child. This category includes the diagnoses of what the real educational problems involve, and subsequent remediation based on this assessment. The various procedures involved here will be more completely outlined later in this chapter as well as in Chapters 8 and 9. Some of the components of this category include psychological and academic testing, language evaluation, special-education team review, counselor involvement, and in general, use of all of the personnel in the entire school "stable" in both diagnostic and educational approaches.

## PSYCHOLOGICAL-EMOTIONAL HELP

The category of psychological-emotional help includes some overlap with the school functions in the psychological testing, and is also oriented toward the student's emotional problems and needs. This approach deals with personality, emotional conditions, family stability, and in general with all aspects of the child's personal adjustment and feelings. A more complete review of this phase of intervention is presented in Chapter 10. The entire educational triangle will be involved in this undertaking since the emotional care of the child is dependent on the close, healthy interaction of teachers, family members, psychologists, counselors, school nurses, physicians, and any other persons involved with that particular child.

## MEDICAL INTERVENTION

The category of medical intervention involves the physician for the most part, although the teacher and school nurse are often intricately involved also. Here we are concerned with the proposition that the child should be presented to the school with the best possible health and receptivity, so that his education may proceed unimpeded. This category includes such things as nutritional care and advice; treatment of illnesses; prescriptions for special diets; medications for various disabilities, either physiological or neurological; and, in general, a close observation of the entire course the child is following. Very often the physician can act as a coordinator of other people involved with the child if his background, training, time, and interests lie in that direction. This type of approach will be discussed in more detail later in this chapter and in Chapter 11.

## THE COMMUNICATION GAP
## AND "FORM-PHOBIA"

Before we discuss some of the specific approaches of each part of the triangle in each of the three categories listed above, it would be wise to dwell again on one of our most important considerations—that of communication. We have already considered (see Chapter 6) some of the various forms and types of interdisciplinary communication. We have discussed how different disciplines—or even different persons within each discipline—might be comfortable with one type of communication or another. On certain occasions verbal interaction is necessary, while in other cases a written report is in order. Bilateral communication might suffice at times, or occasionally a meeting of all concerned might be necessary for proper decisions to be formulated. Simple phone calls, checklists, reports, and even video or audio tapes or movies all fit into this category. The important thing to remember is that whatever is necessary *for the child* should be done, after all parties feel that they have had proper input.

One of the most frustrating and seemingly counterproductive results of the attempt of one discipline to request or transmit information to another has been the creation and profusion of a never-ending number of forms. What started out to be a helping device often has turned into a major hindrance. Forms to cover almost every contingency—from diagnostic to therapeutic, to identification, to placement—have been devised. In our zeal to transmit and/or collect all of the possible information about a particular child we have committed ourselves to a never-ending amount of paperwork that is taking time away from the important task of working with the child himself. It has now gotten to the point in some instances where the clerical time involved in the transmission of information has become irksome, bothersome, and tiring. Many of the people asked to fill out the forms are completely turned off by the entire situation. Thus *no* information, or sketchy material at best, is communicated, and the *child* ends up suffering.

All persons who evaluate a child wish to convey as much information as they can about their findings and feelings on a child. This certainly is especially important when the communication is interdisciplinary—so that everyone knows what the other professionals are thinking. In our mania to be complete, however, we have perhaps gone too far. The checklists to convey our findings have become extremely complicated and lengthy, and the forms we send to other workers are cumbersome and taxing to finish. The result of all of this is often a failure to read any incoming information at all, as well as a reluctance to complete the request for outgoing information.

It certainly is necessary to report our findings to others. It is also important to request a summary of the findings of the other disciplines. However, the importance of including every known fact about the child, or breaking down behavior into lengthy, complicated checklists often doesn't really help our final decision that much. It is more important to *keep the attention* of the person we are communicating with, rather than trying to impress him with our knowledge and/or thoroughness. We should try to say what we mean in a short, concise format wherever possible, and aim for a complete understanding of the important factors by *all* parties—especially the parents (who are sometimes turned off and confused by long, wordy reports).

As we discussed in Chapter 6, the form that the communication takes is not as important as the fact that it does take place at all—and it must be meaningful. It is usually necessary to have *some* written corroboration of each discipline's observations and suggestions, but these should be as utilitarian as possible. The best way to discuss how this can be made easier is to again look at each corner of our triangle and see how it would work here.

Communication must certainly exist among the members of each separate group to begin with. Thus, the teacher, principal, school psychologist, school nurse, and counselor must each work out the best method to accomplish this. Each school district and probably every school will need its own unique methods, because no situation is exactly like any other. Most schools and teachers have already worked out this part satisfactorily, and there is really not a major problem in this area. Similarly, most medical personnel have some sort of built-in communication device that usually works quite well for them, although at times this process would seem to move more slowly than warranted.

The big problem arises when the school either gives or requests information from the doctor or vice versa. The unfortunate result of this is that the parent too often is completely shut out of the picture by both sources. Therefore, it would seem necessary and helpful to develop some type of approach, both in theory and in practice, to accomplish the goal of meaningful communication between all parts of our triangle. In the following paragraphs we will outline one possible way that this might be accomplished. We will also include some sample forms that might be used by the school and the doctor to accomplish the all-important interdisciplinary communication. (See Appendices A, B, C, and D at the end of this chapter.) We have developed two sets of forms. One set is a fairly inclusive and more complex one, while the second is briefer, easier to use, and probably just as informational.)

## SCHOOL-PARENT-DOCTOR COMMUNICATION

### The School Talks to the Doctor (With Parental Permission)

When it becomes necessary or beneficial for the teacher to communicate with the doctor, it would be helpful to consider the following approach. The type of questions the physician would consider important include:

Why is the child referred to the doctor at this time?

What is the child like in the classroom? (Short, narrative statements may be better than checklists, since respondents tend to "overcheck".)

What is the child's academic progress in relation to expectations?

Is there any family problem known to the school?

Is there a memory problem?

Do you see any physical disabilities?

Are there any language problems?

Has the child had psychological testing? If so, a brief summary of results should be included.

Is there any problem with writing or hand-finger movements?

How does the child get along with classmates?

Has there been any special educational intervention?

Are the parents aware of the problem and have they been cooperative?

Is the child's performance consistent?

How does he react to frustration?

Does he work by himself?

Does the child finish his work?

The above specific information may be followed by a brief description of various classroom activities and behaviors, which can often be coded for frequency of occurrence (see Appendixes A and B at end of chapter). These descriptions should include such behaviors as overactivity, excitability, attention span, finishing tasks, distractibility, disruptiveness, mood changes, aggressiveness, memory, work habits, academic progress, and work quality in general.

It is very important to state at this time that any communication on referrals from the school to the physician must be done with the *expressed consent of the parents in every case,* legally and so that a full degree of cooperation can be achieved. It is also stressed that the teacher might expect the physician to be helpful in physical, emotional, social, and community questions, but the doctor should not address the educational needs of the particular child *unless he is part of the planning team.* Too often the physician makes educational decisions and gives educational advice that he is ill-equipped to give.

### *The Doctor Talks to the School*
### *(With Parental Permission)*

The fact that a referral to see a physician has been made or information has been requested means that the teacher has specific concerns and questions about the child. Or perhaps in some cases the doctor has made the initial contact with the school before any communication from the latter. The physician should be able to report his findings to the school in the same manner that the school communicated to him. The amount and type of information imparted will vary as to the type of problem, but there should be some format that includes basic facts and findings from the educational and medical history, as well as a report of the physical and neurological examination. The physician should then summarize the entire case and present a capsule view of his medical plan and recommendations that can be utilized by all parties concerned—of course including most importantly the parents. The doctor's reply to the school should be general as far as a complete overview of the child's assessment, and specific in terms of replying to specific information being asked for by the teacher. A suggested, concise format is shown in Appendices C and D.

## TEACHER-DOCTOR COMMUNICATION

Information passed from teacher to physician and vice-versa can occur either before or after a medical evaluation. This will depend on the mode and timing of the referral. The format developed for this communication (Appendices A, B, C, and D) includes both possibilities. Ideally feedback of this type occurs right from the beginning of the first contact and hopefully continues on a productive basis from that time until the child is no longer in educational trouble.

## THE PARENTS ASK AND TALK

The most important part of all of this communication is the absolute necessity for the child's family to be totally involved in the entire process. This means that all plans for evaluation, referral, and remediation must be *understood and agreed upon by the parents*. It further must also be clear that the results of all of these contacts have to be totally explained to the parents by all parties involved so that the parents know what is proposed in regard to their child. The breakdown of this segment of communication by members of the evaluation team is the most common reason for noncompliance on the part of the parents. We cannot stress this function enough. If the child is to succeed through the plans the professionals make for him, his family *must* pave the way! The accomplishment of this endeavor is often difficult and time-consuming, but the results are worth the time and effort in every case.

## HOW THE TEAM FUNCTIONS
## (THE TRIANGLE AT WORK)

A child may be recognized as showing educational dysfunction at any time or in any situation. In most cases the initial identification will be made in the school or preschool. However, as we previously discussed (see Chapter 6), there are many opportunities for the parent and/or doctor to be the first to start the ball rolling in establishing help for the child. No matter which corner of the triangle initiates the process of identification and remediation, all must eventually become involved. In the following sections we will outline the type of approaches that should help this come about. As we have stated before, we can identify three general areas of remediation: educational, psychological, and medical. Each of these will be discussed in a separate chapter. However, it would be useful to briefly outline the components of each area and the personnel who might be involved.

### *Educational Remediation*

The assessment process leading to educational remediation begins with the preschool or regular classroom teacher. Whether the child is first identified in the classroom, or the teacher is prewarned of a problem, no one is in a better position than the teacher to let everyone know how the child actually performs in the classroom. The teacher is able to tell quite a bit about each child and will probably be the person who knows the child best except for the parents.

When the teacher (or other professionals who come into contact with the child) feels that some type of help is indicated for the child, the referral process begins. From that point on a whole series of events starts to occur. This may take many diffuse pathways, and there may be any or most or all of the following activities going on:

Educational history

Psychological evaluation (including potential, achievement, personality, adjustment, and/or sensory impairments as appropriate)

Language and speech evaluation

School nurse evaluation

School counselor evaluation

Other specialists as appropriate (audiologist, social worker, etc.)

The psychologist is usually in charge of the accumulation of data. He/she will coordinate the efforts of the other informants and will pull together the findings into a case-study folder. A most important factor in this process is parental involvement. The parents must know why their child is being studied and what educational options will most likely be offered. The parents also need to be brought up to date as information is gathered that either refutes or reinforces the original supposition. There should *never* be any surprises for the parents! Almost all problems that occur between home and school are the direct result of a lack of honest and forthright communication when a child is having difficulty.

After the evaluation procedures are completed, and input from other sources is considered, the remediation program for each child is planned. This may include anything from a few minutes a day in a resource center with a special teacher, to full-day placement in a special program—or private school—or home placement (see Chapter 8). Other parts of the total program of service might consist of involvement with the school psychologist, counselor or nurse, remedial speech specialist, remedial/ adaptive physical education teacher, physical and occupational therapist on an ongoing basis as the need arises. At times the situation may call for personnel outside of the particular school to become involved, and often includes activities or services from outside agencies. The important thing is the establishment of a special program for each child to meet the specific needs of *that* child.

The actual planning process itself may be done in many different ways. Often a meeting of the involved personnel (teacher, parents, special-education teacher, principal, psychologist, nurse, or others) on the local school level will suffice, although most school districts have a special committee to review the placement of each child in a special program, when needed. This committee usually consists of administrators, psychologists, classroom teachers, special-education teachers, nurses, physicians (where possible), and any other people who may be needed such as language specialists and private school personnel. The parents should always be invited to sit in on the discussion and offer any input that would be helpful in setting up the program for their child. This type of group planning for each child is a very essential part of the total programming, since everyone involved with the education and care of the child has a chance to help with the decision-making process. As the child then progresses through the programs set up for him, he is reevaluated by both the local school personnel and the total evaluation and planning team as often as necessary so that he remains in, or is changed to, the proper situation for him.

## Psychological Remediation

The psychological approach to educational dysfunction operates in two general areas. Every child with school problems should be evaluated by a competent educational psychologist so that a profile of his strengths, weaknesses, abilities, and problem areas can be clearly defined. Most school districts have a staff of psychologists who are familiar with the various tests that are available to assist in these areas. Psychological testing at this level can usually give us a general idea of the child's intellectual functioning and ability, his achievement in various educational areas, and whether there are any specific neurological or psychological pathways to learning that may be malfunctioning. Often personality disturbances will be found in the process. Sometimes specialized testing that is beyond the province of the actual school psychologist is needed, or in some cases the school may have no psychological help. In either case, there are well-trained psychologists who are available to do this type of evaluation in most communities. A more specific discussion of the usual tests performed will be presented in Chapter 10.

After a child is evaluated for educational or emotional disorders, the psychologist may then function in the remedial area. The school psychologist often is quite helpful to the teacher in the classroom in observing and working with the students with both their educational *and* emotional problems. This type of person can often serve as a go-between in the school-physician-parent triangle and usually performs very well in this capacity. Many children may benefit from some type of counseling or therapy in the emotional or personality areas, and this job is capably filled by the school psychologists with the help of the counselors. Another very important function may be the parent-education programs concerning behavior control, parent effectiveness, and educational aid that are offered in many communities by psychologists and/or teachers.

Sometimes the child will need more help than the school staff might be able to provide. This is where the community resources should be brought into play. It is quite important for someone in the school district (usually the administrator of special education, chief psychologist, or often the nurse or doctor) to be aware of the various programs available—including information as to who is eligible, who runs them, what the financial obligations are, and their "track record."

A very important question that is often asked by teachers and parents has to do with the type of person who should be providing psychological help and/or counseling to children. Professional resources in this area may include all of the following:

1.  Psychiatrist

2.  Child psychiatrist

3.  Clinical psychologist

4.  Psychologist

5.  Marriage and family counselor

6.  Psychiatric social worker

7.  Psychiatric aide

8.   Psychiatric technician

9.   Community mental health worker

The fields of interest and expertise of these professionals vary but also overlap in many cases. The child who is obviously seriously emotionally disturbed, or psychotic, should be treated by a child psychiatrist in most cases. Most of the children we see, however, are not in this category. It very often boils down to the proposition that the child should see the person whom he can best relate to and who has the most successful *experience with the particular type of problem,* no matter what the professional label or title. The professional who sees the child must then be able to recognize whether the child is more severely disturbed than first thought, and whether he (the child) should be referred to another professional with more appropriate training. However, this entire area remains quite nebulous, and individual circumstances and local availability are both important in this type of help.

The question of the mode of therapy—whether individual, group, family-oriented, or any other type—is also quite controversial and varies according to the needs of the child and his family. This will be more thoroughly investigated in Chapter 10.

## Medical Remediation

The *medical* approach to the child with educational dysfunction is fraught with confusion and lack of uniformity. As we have stated previously, the physicians, with the nurses and others acting as their extensions, have a definite role to play in both the identification and remediation process. The time-honored role of the doctor as far as the medical care of the child is well understood and will not be pursued here. The various medical and paramedical therapies of educational dysfunction will be more specifically covered in Chapter 11. This section will deal with two major points:

1.   What kind of physician should evaluate and treat these children?

2.   Does each child with this problem need a total medical and neurological evaluation?

### PHYSICIAN'S AREA OF SPECIALIZATION

There are many types of doctors currently diagnosing and treating children with school problems. These include family practitioners, general practitioners, pediatricians, pediatric neurologists, neurologists, psychiatrists, child psychiatrists, internists, ophthalmologists, optometrists, chiropractors, dermatologists, and others. Except for specialists in eye, skin, or similar problems, the type of medical specialist who cares for these children is not as important as the specialist's own training, experience, and understanding of the problem, as well as his *availability to the school and family,* his personal *interest,* and the amount of *time* he can allot to the case. It is a sad but true fact that most physicians who see children with educational dysfunction are deficient in one or more of these areas.

The two groups most likely to first be alerted to the child's problem are the pediatrician and the family or general practitioner. In many cases, because of their familiarity with the child and his family, they can be of tremendous help and influence. However, the fact is that most pediatricians and generalists do not have the time to devote to the history taking, examination, communication, and family explanation so badly needed in this area. It is also true that only a few physicians in these categories have the proper training and exposure to the educational world to be of real help with these problems. Therefore, because of the lack of time, interest, training, or a combination of these, the child is often referred to a neurologist or psychiatrist for evaluation. This may be quite appropriate if this particular specialist physician fits the above qualifications, but we often see that these medical practitioners are no more qualified than the referrer. For example, it is quite common for a physician to refer a child for placement in a special-education class when he (the physician) doesn't even have the vaguest notion of what goes on in that classroom!

The upshot of all of this is the fact that the medical care of children with these problems has become almost a specialty unto itself. As noted above, the particular specialty or background of the physician is not as important as his/her approach to the problem. The doctor who evaluates and becomes involved with these children *must* allocate large blocks of time to totally evaluate the entire situation, including the time to take the usual medical history and make a physical examination. In addition, he/she must develop a working knowledge of the educational systems and resources in his area and must be able to freely communicate with the school personnel. It is also desirable for the physician to personally visit the school and see exactly what types of activities are going on there so as to enhance his/her own knowledge and expertise in this area. Obviously very few physicians in the usual practice situations have the time or inclination for this type of approach. Thus the development of the educational specialist physician is now starting to evolve. When this type of physician is *not* available in a community, the parent or school must be sure the physician they are working with has at least some of the above attributes in order to work advantageously and effectively as part of the educational triangle.

## TYPE OF MEDICAL EXAMINATION NEEDED:
## THE NEUROLOGICAL EXAMINATION

Another medical consideration concerns the type of examination a child needs. A common situation is the referral of children to a neurologist by the school because someone suggested a neurological examination would be appropriate. However, this type of request and the attempt of the doctor to fulfill it usually result in mutual confusion and disappointment among all parties concerned—school, family, and physician. The problem arises because the school may feel that the child's educational dysfunction or behavior problem is secondary to a neurophysiologic disorder, and they (the school) expect the neurological examination to explain why the child is having trouble reading, writing, or adding. It may also be expected that the neurological examination will be able to show us why a child has a poor attention span or is easily distracted. *The truth is that a neurological examination cannot identify the reasons a child is not learning in school!*

It may be discovered by a routine neurological examination that a child has some major neurological disabilities. However, for the most part, these are usually conditions that are well known to the school and family already, and are not the cause of *unexpected* learning disorders. Such neurological findings might include obvious brain damage, cerebral palsy, paralysis, etc.

If we consider the type of neurological examination that tests for so-called soft signs, we again enter into a controversial area. As we have previously seen in Chapter 2, "soft" neurological signs are used by many physicians, psychologists, and educators as "proof" of a neurological deficit that leads to a learning disorder. Thus, most physicians and clinics have developed their own lists of these types of signs, most of which are related to immaturity and maturational lag, and not true disability.

There are many commonly described soft signs such as poor right-left discrimination (normal under ten years), overreactions, perceptual deficits, spatial discrimination problems, odd movements, tremors, poor hopping and skipping, abnormal eye movements, awkwardness, fine motor incoordination, and many, many others. However, we wish to reemphasize the fact that *these signs do not make a diagnosis of brain damage or learning disability.* They probably relate only to the maturation of the nervous system, and they change as the child grows. There is no relationship between the presence of soft signs and the child who does not learn, except that both the soft signs and the learning disability may be evidenced by the same child at various times. The only thing that we can really say is that the presence of these soft signs may tell us that a child is *vulnerable* to some types of pressures and may consequently develop a learning problem. The soft signs and neurological examination do *not* help us *teach* the child, and only rarely do they tell us new information that is in any way educationally valuable.

The medical evaluation should encompass a total approach to the entire problem. If the child has been carefully examined by his family physician, perhaps a good history may be the only thing needed. If there is a good history *and* a physical examination, a complete review of the problem with proper two-way school communication would be in order. If the entire history and communication areas are already accounted for, perhaps a short additional physical examination would suffice. If a child is referred for the first time with no real previous medical evaluation, a complete, total workup might be necessary. The physician should be able to assess what type of intervention is needed in each case and apprise the school and parents of the findings.

The physician's role starts with the initial evaluation and continues through the entire treatment program. The medical part of the treatment should be closely correlated with the psychological and educational areas, and the physician ought to be a continuing member of the evaluation team. The specific medical remediations, medications, and other forms of "therapy" in this field will be discussed in Chapter 11.

## SUMMARY

When the total evaluation and assessment of the child are finished, it is urgent for all parties concerned not only to communicate their findings and recommendations to each other and to the parents, but also to make sure everyone *understands* exactly what is going on. If disagreements arise, it is healthy for the parties involved to try to come to a meeting of the minds, so that the program can move ahead. This may involve even further phone calls and meetings, but the necessity for a united approach may make this unavoidable.

Again we want to emphasize that the classroom teacher should be aware of the types of help that are available for the child with educational dysfunction. It is even more urgent for the teacher to feel that she can freely exchange ideas and thoughts concerning the child during the identification, evaluation, and remediation periods. The input of the teacher during this entire process is an absolute necessity, and to proceed without her help is sheer folly. There are many methods available for the teacher to become involved in this process. Personal communication with team members is certainly always helpful. A series of meetings or seminars with other individuals on the "team" can also be valuable and should be arranged throughout the school year. If these types of meetings can be arranged with the parents present, they will be that much more valuable. In short—the total approach should be just that—*total*.

## PROPER CLASSROOM PLACEMENT

Before concluding this initial discussion of the educational, psychological, and medical roles in remediation of educational dysfunction, it would be useful to discuss one very common cause of educational problems—one that needs no remediation except proper classroom reassignment. This is the problem of *improper* classroom assignment. There are many children who do poorly in school because of being in the wrong class. We all have seen the child ill-suited to a particular teacher, and vice versa. Also the "chemistry" of a classroom can often be corrected by the removal or addition of certain students, which may reverse a potential problem before it gets under way—or at least keep it from going too far!

However, the most common cause of improper placement is the child who is too immature for the class he is in. As mentioned in Chapter 6, the chronological age of a child is often the wrong criterion for grade placement. A child may be chronologically, intellectually, and even neurologically ready to attend, but socially not quite up to par. Perhaps the social and intellectual levels are fine, but the developmental maturation is poor—and this can cause a big problem. Of course if the intellectual ability is below par, failure is almost guaranteed.

It is well known that many children are not ready for formal, academically oriented school at age five, especially if their birthday is in August, September, October, or November. This is especially true of boys, who are often much slower than girls to develop. We often see a young child placed in kindergarten to "see how he will do," and after a rather rocky start, the teachers and parents report that he is "making it." Thus nothing is done and he moves on to first grade. Another slow start in first grade is followed by fairly good progress, and the "I told you so's" are passed around. As this child then advances through the grades the pressures silently but persistently continue to build, and often not until fourth, fifth, or even sixth grade do we see the eruption of a full-blown problem. At this time the problem is usually a much more complex one, and retention becomes a poor option—certainly more difficult to accomplish at this age. Finally, it is those who raised the first questions who have the last "I told you so!"

This sort of thing should never happen! Parents *and* teachers should not be afraid to say that a child is too immature for his or her class situation. If intervention of this type is undertaken before school entrance, or at the latest at the end of kindergarten, a severe educational *and* emotional problem can often be prevented. Do not be afraid of hurting a six-year-old's feelings by retention. He will thank you by being more at ease, by progressing at a regular rate, and ultimately by being a happier, better adjusted human being.

If we keep this concept in mind, we can prevent one cause of educational dysfunction before it has a chance to occur. Proper placement at five years is vastly superior to total remediation at ten years. Finally, we stress the point that *any* remediation program must include the fact that the child is in the *right class for him.* At no time is this more important than on the first day of the first year of school! No one is comfortable or reacts favorably to continual frustration and failure. Do the child a favor by doing whatever you can to assure him of proper and successful placement.

# Forms Used in Communication Between School and Physician

School Report to the Physician (Long Form)

Birth Date_____

Grade_____

Name of Child_____ Type of Class_____

Teacher_____ Principal_____

Part I-Background

(Please use back of page when more space is desired)

Reason for referral at this time_____
_____

What questions would you like answered?_____
_____

How can doctor help?
Significant school history, including special classes_____
_____

What is child's current academic functioning?_____
_____

Has psychological testing been done? Important findings:_____
_____

Do you see any physical disabilities?_____
_____

Are there any problems with language?_____
_____

How is the child's writing, coordination, and perception?_____
_____

Does child get along with classmates?_____
_____

Has the family been involved?_____

Other comments:_____
_____

Name of child_____Observer_____

Dates of observation_____

| Behaviors and Achievements | How Noticeable | | | |
|---|---|---|---|---|
| Behavior | Not at All 0 | Few Times A Day 1 | Quite Often 2 | Almost All Day 3 |
| 1. RESTLESS OR OVERACTIVE | | | | |
| 2. EXCITABLE, IMPULSIVE | | | | |
| 3. SHORT ATTENTION SPAN | | | | |
| 4. FAILS TO FINISH WORK | | | | |
| 5. EASILY DISTRACTIBLE | | | | |
| 6. CONSTANT FIDGETING | | | | |
| 7. DISRUPTS CLASS | | | | |
| 8. EASILY FRUSTRATED | | | | |
| 9. DEMANDS MUST BE MET AT ONCE | | | | |
| 10. CRIES EASILY AND OFTEN | | | | |
| 11. FREQUENT QUICK MOOD CHANGES | | | | |
| 12. TEMPER OUTBURSTS | | | | |
| 13. DAYDREAMS | | | | |
| 14. QUALITY OF WORK VARIES | | | | |
| 15. POOR MEMORY | | | | |
| 16. CAN'T FOLLOW INSTRUCTIONS | | | | |
| 17. HITTING, FIGHTING | | | | |
| 18. READING PROBLEMS | | | | |
| 19. SPELLING PROBLEMS | | | | |
| 20. ARITHMETIC PROBLEMS | | | | |
| 21. GENERAL CLASSROOM PROBLEMS | | | | |

OTHER OBSERVATIONS_____

PHYSICIAN COMMENTS (NEW PROGRAMS, MEDICATIONS, ETC.)_____

SIGNATURE_____

This rating scale is loosely adapted from C. Keith Conners' "A Teacher Rating Scale for Use in Drug Studies with Children," *American Journal of Psychiatry*, 126, No. 6, Dec. 1969, 884-888.

## School Report to Physician
### (Short Form)

Name of Child_____ Date of Birth_____

School_____ Grade/Class_____

Teacher_____ Referred by_____

### Part I—Background
(Please use back of page if necessary for further description)

Reason for this referral_____
_____

What questions would you like answered?_____

Significant educational history_____

Current academic functioning_____

Any language, coordination, neurological problems?_____

Any physical disabilities?_____

Other comments_____

### Part II—Behavior
(Please add narrative on reverse side, if indicated or more comfortable)

Behavior and Achievement      How noticeable

| Behavior and Achievement | Not at All 0 | Few Times A Day 1 | Quite Often 2 | Almost All Day 3 |
|---|---|---|---|---|
| Restless, overactive | | | | |
| Short attention span | | | | |
| Distractible, disruptive | | | | |
| Easily frustrated | | | | |
| Frequent mood changes | | | | |
| Daydreams | | | | |
| Temper tantrums | | | | |
| Quality of work varies | | | | |
| Cannot follow directions | | | | |
| Hitting, fighting | | | | |
| Academic problems | | | | |
| General class problems | | | | |

Other observations_____

Physician comments (medications, etc.)_____

            Signature_____

Physician Report to the School
(Long Form)

History

Name of Child_____ Date of Birth_____ Date_____

Address_____ Parents' Names_____

School_____ Natural Parents_____

Grade_____ Teacher_____ Principal_____

Informant for history_____

Referred by_____

Reasons for evaluation_____
_____
_____
_____

Parents' main concerns_____
_____
_____

Does child like school?_____

## Past History

Birth: Age of parents at birth_____
  Pregnancy (Circle if present) Bleeding/Illness/Smoking
  Length_____ Weight gain_____ Other_____
  _____ Miscarriages_____
                                         Vaginal_____
  Delivery   Birth weight___ Labor difficulty___ Cesarean_____
  (Circle if present) Breathing problem/Jaundice/Cyanosis/Transfusion
  Illness/Feeding problem/Never cried/Overactive/Sluggish/Problem caring for baby/
  Home with mother
  Other_____

  Infancy   (Circle if present)  Sluggish/Breast/Bottle/Difficult/Colic/
            Feeding problems/Hard to care for/Illness
            Other_____

Illnesses, hospitalizations, injuries, allergies_____
_____
_____

Development   Do you think development was normal?_____
_____

When did child:
  Walk alone_____              Dress self_____
  Say words_____               Finish potty training_____
  Say sentences_____           Pedal bike_____
  Copy circle_____             Tie shoes_____
  Know letters_____            Use pencil correctly_____
  Know numbers and count_____  Know colors_____

Systemic compaints (Circle if present)
  Convulsions/Fainting/Dizzy/Headache/Abdominal pain/High fevers
  Bed wetting/Pants wetting/Soiling/Tics/Nervous habits/Weakness
  Generalized pains/Vomiting/Diarrhea/Constipation/Nail biting
  Other_____

Behavior (Circle if present)  Problems as toddler_____
  Hyperactive/Poor attention span/Impulsive/Distractible/Disruptive
  Temper tantrums/Breath holding/Aggressive/Fighting/Loner/Depressed/
  Lying/Stealing/Nervous/Leader/Follower/Clown/Perfectionist
  Doesn't listen/Sloppy/Won't follow directions/Easily frustrated/
  Doesn't finish tasks/Daydreams/Difficult to discipline/Cries easily
  Overreacts/Sibling rivalry/Head banging/Rocking
  Difficulty playing and sharing
  Other_____
_____

*166*

Body Functions (Circle if problem)

Sleep_____  Coordination_____
                                    Gross_____
Eating_____  Fine_____

Vision_____

Hearing_____

Speech_____  Hand preference _____

Other_____  _____

Habits_____

Family Discipline_____

Family
  Mother's age_____  Father's age_____

  Many moves?_____

  Occupations_____

  Previous divorce, remarriage_____

  Siblings (age, problems)_____

Family History of (Circle if present)

  School problems/Behavior problems/Retardation/Other disease
  _____
  _____

Does family have a diagnosis?_____
_____
_____

How can doctor help the child?_____
_____
_____

## Physical Examination

Name of Child_____ Age _____

Weight_____Height_____ Blood Pressure _____

Hearing (test)_____Vision (test)_____

Child's conduct during examination_____

General description _____
_____

Abnormalities in General Physical (Circle if present)

  Speech_____
  Head and face_____
  Neck_____
  Chest, lungs_____
  Heart_____
  Abdomen_____
  Extremeties_____
  Genitals: Sexual maturation_____
  Posture_____
  Nutrition_____
  Body defects_____
  Other_____

*167*

<u>Abnormalities in Neurological Examination</u>  (Circle if abnormal or present and describe)

Fund of knowledge/Gait/Weakness/Paralysis/Balance/Coordination/Awkward
Muscle strength/Sensory exam/Cranial nerves/Reflexes/Right-left discrimination
problem/Poor repetitive movements/Impulsive/Fidgety/Hyperactive/Can't follow directions/
Overflow movements/Sensory discrimination poor/Poor perception/Can't repeat letters,
numbers/Abnormal movements/Inattentive/Tremor/
Handwriting/Other "soft" signs for age. Describe or add to above._____
_____
_____

Other tests done including laboratory_____
_____
_____

Medical impression_____
_____
_____

Physician's recommendations to family and school_____
_____
_____
_____
_____
_____
_____
_____
_____
_____

Other comments_____
_____
_____
_____

Date_____          Signature_____
                                         Printed Name_____
                                         Address_____
                                         City_____
                                         Phone_____

Physician Report to the School
(Short Form)

<u>History</u>                              Date _____

Name of Child_____ Date of Birth _____

Informants_____

Are parents natural parents?_____

School _____ Grade _____ Teacher _____

Reason for evaluation_____
_____

Parents' main concerns_____

Educational, academic problems (including pre-school)_____
_____

<u>Past History</u> Birth weight_____ Length pregnancy_____

  <u>Birth</u>  Pregnancy problems_____
        Labor and delivery_____
        Difficulty at birth_____

  <u>Infancy</u>   Colic, feeding problems, activity, etc._____

  Previous illnesses, allergies, hospitalizations, injuries_____
_____

  <u>Development</u>  Any abnormalities?_____ Walk_____
             Sentences_____ Potty training_____

  <u>Systemic complaints</u>   Headache/Fevers/Abdominal pains/Others
_____

  <u>Behavior Problems</u>   Hyperactive/Short attention span/Temper
  Aggressive/Stealing/Other_____

  <u>Body Functions</u>   Sleep, vision, hearing, speech, coordination, eating
_____

  Family history of problems_____

  Does family have a diagnosis?_____

*169*

## Physical Examination

Name of Child_____

Weight_____ Height_____ Blood pressure_____

Hearing_____ Vision _____

General observations_____

Abnormalities in General Physical   (Circle and describe)

Speech _____
Head, face_____
Chest, lungs, heart_____
Abdomen_____
Extremities_____
Genitals (maturation)_____
Posture_____
Nutrition_____
Body defects_____
Other_____

Abnormalities in Neurological Exam   (Circle and describe if present or abnormal)

Fund of knowledge/Gait/Muscle strength/Sensory Exam/Cranial nerves
Reflexes/Attention span/Movement disorders/Perceptual problems/Right-left
discrimination/Fidgety/Hyperactive/Coordination/Other ''soft'' signs for age/
Describe or add to above_____
_____
_____

Other tests done_____

Medical impressions_____

Recommendations_____
_____

Date_____                    Signature_____

                                     Printed Name_____

                                          Address_____

                                             City_____

                                            Phone_____

*170*

# CHAPTER 8

# *Educational Remediation and Management— The Program*

In previous chapters we have shown how there are three main areas of remediation for a child with learning handicaps. These are the educational, psychological, and medical areas. The most important interventions are those that go on in the school. The following two chapters will deal with the educational program for the child with a learning handicap. This chapter will discuss the philosophy and types of programs that have been developed to deal with children manifesting educational dysfunction. Chapter 9 will be devoted to the child in the classroom, including educational plans, approaches by the teacher, and the activities in the classroom. We hope to make the field of educational remediation more clearly understood to the average teacher with this review of special educational theories and their implementation.

Before we discuss any type of program, however, we should address ourselves to a very important and all-encompassing new development: PL 94-142. As we have stated previously, this is the "Education for all Handicapped Children" Act that was passed by the U.S. Congress in 1975 and will be almost totally implemented in 1977. This significant legislation will have far-reaching effects, and final details are slow in coming. As of this writing, all challenges, legal interpretations, and lawsuits have not yet been resolved and specific guidelines in many areas are still in the process of being developed.

However PL 94-142 is the law and *all educational agencies must comply.* All public and private school personnel would be well advised to review the law in its entirety and become acquainted with its provisions. The authors will not attempt to treat this subject in its entirety since such a treatment would require a volume in itself; the reader is referred to the federal guidelines and registers and his own state plan for specifics.*

## PL 94-142—HOW IT RELATES TO CHILDREN'S SERVICES

In order to familiarize the reader with PL 94-142 as it relates to children's services, we will summarize some of the important global concepts before discussing specific programs of remediation. For a more complete list of the provisions of PL 94-142, refer to the Appendix at the end of this chapter.

### States' Responsibilities Under PL 94-142

Each state must develop an annual Master Plan for special education and must monitor the plans of local agencies. State facilities for the handicapped and all programs must be in compliance with the law. There must also be an advisory commission interested in handicapped students and all state activities must be legally tied into PL 94-142 through the state's Master Plan.

### Local Responsibilities Under PL 94-142

Each local agency must be capable of delivery of full services to all handicapped pupils, and must submit an annual Master Plan which is in compliance with PL 94-142. Each pupil must have an individual educational program, which must be developed with parent involvement. This plan must provide for education in the least restrictive environment (see pages 179 to 181). Local and state plans must include other public and private agencies when appropriate.

### Procedural Safeguards and Due Process Under PL 94-142

Parent or guardian consultation is required, and disagreements between parents and the school may be resolved by negotiation or by due process hearings. Parents must also be given prior notice in understandable language and terms of all matters relating to the child. Parental consent must be obtained on the basis of informed understanding and all records are to be open for examination.

## PROGRAMS FOR CHILDREN WITH EDUCATIONAL DYSFUNCTION

With the above introduction to some of the important provisions included in PL 94-142, we will now proceed to a discussion of special

*Department of Health, Education and Welfare, Office of Education, *Federal Register,* August 23, 1977, Part II.

education programs and how they may work under the new law. In all of the programs for children with an educational dysfunction, two programs should exist side by side—one aimed at remediation and the other at the child who needs a developmental program.

## Programs of Remediation

Programs of remediation are educational systems aimed at assisting each pupil to accelerate his individual learning curve (see Figure 8-1). The pupil should reach a higher ratio of performance/ability through remediation than he is now producing. The program will, we hope, move the child from where he is, will accelerate his pace, and will take him to where he could and should be. The youngsters at whom this program is aimed have what is hopefully considered to be temporary or largely ameliorable deficits.

Included in this group could be:

1. The child with a minor specific learning disability and no other major problems.

2. The child with a mild to moderate hearing loss, who has the potential to use oral language for communication.

3. The child with a speech disorder.

4. The child with a mild to moderate vision impairment, who can function satisfactorily among sighted students.

5. The child with a reading disability not due to retardation or sensory impairment.

6. The child with a mild aphasic-like communication disorder.

7. The child with a crippling condition, who needs special physical education and perhaps academic assistance.

8. The child with a mild to moderate behavior disorder, who is undergoing psychiatric or psychological counseling and who is responding to remediation techniques.

## Developmental Programs

Developmental programs are educational systems aimed at assisting each pupil with identified deficits to achieve at his highest potential, with the recognition that these deficits may be the result of intellectual subnormality, severe impairment of vision or hearing, or emotional/behavioral problems of long duration. It is also expected that the child's performance/ability ratio will probably remain fairly constant. These systems recognize the probability of these deficits being relatively permanent. Although we never stop trying for remediation, our end goals and objectives are geared to the recognition of the existence of these areas of dysfunction.

Included in this group could be:

1.  The child with mental retardation.

2.  The child with a moderate to severe hearing loss, who does not and probably will not communicate orally.

3.  The child with a severe vision impairment, who needs a specially oriented program of instruction.

4.  The child with a moderate to severe aphasoid or other probably organically based communication problem.

5.  The child with a crippling condition that requires a program and environment quite different from the regular classroom.

6.  The child with a moderate to severe behavior disorder or emotional disturbance.

7.  A moderately to severely involved multihandicapped child.

8.  A developmentally disabled child.

As can be seen from the above definitions, both remediation programs and developmental programs exist for most of the classic conventional categories of handicapping conditions. It must also be noted that students may move from a developmental program to a remedial program and vice versa. All of our educational programs and classes should be thought of as having swinging doors—easy access, both in and out.

## *PHILOSOPHIES*

### *Remediation Programs*

In remediation programs the school can promise effort, but cannot promise results. The goal here is to accelerate and remediate the youngster to the point where he can function in the regular classroom or in a class with a less restrictive environment (see Figure 8-2). These programs should offer progressive, successful integration into the regular classroom during the remediation process. Without the chance for the youngster to be slowly assimilated back into the regular class as he gains in proficiency, the program cannot meet its objectives.

One of the inherent problems with these programs is the nature of the youngster with whom we are working. He is often one who is "turned off" or poorly motivated, and yet according to our definition, we must accelerate his learning so that he learns at a faster rate than his contemporaries in a regular class. This *must* be done if he is to join his class somewhere along the continuum of learning. This pupil actually needs *more* time, effort, and learning in the educational process. This seems to be an enigma and a dichotomy that is very difficult to work around. This youngster needs more education than he is assimilating, has the potential for more, yet for some known or unknown reason either has refused to put forth the effort or has been unsuccessful. Perhaps he has tried to succeed, but the school has not been able to develop a program to suit *his particular needs*. As educators, we *must* recognize these individual learning needs and do all we can to meet them. This concept is discussed more in detail in Chapter 9.

Too often, the youngster who is turned off by school is rewarded in his own way for his noncompliance with the rules. For example, he is often sent home when he malfunctions or when he violates some of the more stringent rules placed upon him. In fact, all the child needs to do to leave the environment in which he is uncomfortable (the school) is to violate the rules. We then promptly reward him by sending him home, and thus give him less time in which to remediate those areas that need attention. (Of course, the student doesn't have to be in a special program in order to receive this bonus for misbehavior.) When he has less time in school, his performance/ability ratio gets worse, and the program intended to remediate him is indicted for not fulfilling its role.

There is one *best* solution for the student who misbehaves and is sent home or out of the class. This solution is perhaps the most difficult to achieve and yet is so beautiful when found and functioning—that is *motivation*. The motivated student is not a problem student. However, we also know that what motivates one student will turn off another. Therefore, a major effort of the teacher should be to find the best motivator for each pupil and then continually attempt to make it more effective. Quite often the parents and previous teachers can be very helpful in locating and implementing this most elusive teaching aid.

### Developmental Programs

The programs that fall into the developmental category usually have a total offering for children starting at a very young age and extending through the twelfth grade. The federal & state laws governing such programs are often written to include pupils between the ages of 3 and 21. A program is developmental in that it is a continuum of planned presentations, each one building on the last. The end result aims at a child who is functioning at *as high a level as is possible for THAT PARTICULAR STUDENT*. The program recognizes that the child has handicapping conditions that impair his general performance. Although we hope to increase his performance/ability ratio, this may not be a specific objective for every student. A particular pupil may have talents or skills that allow him to perform at near normal or even at normal levels in a particular area or areas. These would most likely be non-academic abilities and should be developed when present.

The end goals and objectives for developmental programs are necessarily somewhat different and below that for the regular curriculum, and therefore also different and below the end goals for the remedial program (see Figure 8-1). It is hoped that integration will take place *where success can be met*. We would not expect to see a progressively increasing program of integration among this group of pupils.

A good question for the assessment team, including the parents, is, "What will this child be doing as an adult?" If the answer includes a recognized lowered performance, chances are a developmental program is proper. Once the home, school, and the child are all geared to the diminished objectives, we can usually promise results in this program.

### TYPES OF PROGRAMS

Figure 8-1 is a graphic representation of the various types of programs that would be available to the student. The capital letters

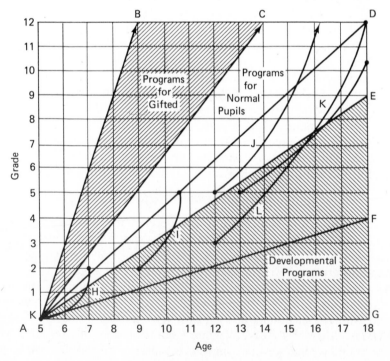

*Figure 8-1.  Learning curves and approximate program limits.*

represent some possible pathways through, and limits of, the educational systems. The text below will offer an explanation for this chart and will show how different types of students may progress through the various programs.

## Developmental Programs

Developmental programs are those explained earlier in the chapter. Figure 8-1 shows some examples of these types of programs.

1.  Line A-D is the route followed by the average pupil who starts kindergarten at age 5 and progresses through the grades until graduation at age 18.

2.  Lines A–C and A–E are the approximate limits of the regular educational program. A nonhandicapped pupil will generally progress on a relatively straight line from A to the point that represents his potential on the right side of the graph.

3.  Lines A–B and A–C represent the approximate limits of the programs for gifted pupils. The lines actually extend up and to the right, beyond the graph, representing a grade-level achievement expectancy above the twelfth grade.

4.  Lines A–E and A–F represent the approximate limits of the programs for the mildly or educable retarded, with IQs between 50 and 75. A pupil will progress on a relatively straight line from A to the point on the graph between E and F that represents his particular grade-level expectancy.

5.  Lines A–F and A–G outline the approximate boundaries of the programs for the trainable or moderately retarded. These pupils have IQs of approximately 25 to 50. A pupil will progress from point A to the point between F and G that represents his potential.

> *Note:* It must be recognized that none of these representations on the graph are inviolable or rigid. There is an overlap between all adjacent categories. As mentioned earlier, we must also think of all programs as having swinging doors. It must be recognized that children do not always fit these neat categorical definitions, and we must be ready to move students from one program to another easily, as we reassess and evaluate their needs and progress.

## Remedial Programs

These programs were described earlier in the chapter. The pupil who is in a remediation mode will not follow a straight line on the graph. As his performance/ability ratio improves, his learning curve will accelerate as shown by the arcs drawn on the model in Figure 8-1.

The following explanation of the lettered arcs in Figure 8-1 will help the reader to understand the philosophy and intent of the remediation process. The following examples can be seen in Figure 8-1.

**CHILD H—** Found in kindergarten to have an educational dysfunction. Remediated in two years to grade level after a slow start.

**CHILD I—** Found at age 9 doing second-grade work. Remediated in a little over one year to grade level.

**CHILD J—** Found with an educational dysfunction at age 12 in fifth grade. Remediated to above grade level by graduation.

**CHILD K—** Found at age 13 doing fifth-grade work. Remediated to expectancy (not grade level) by age 18.

**CHILD L—** Found at age 12 doing third-grade work in an EMR (educable mentally retarded) class. Remediated to grade level by graduation.

In remediation programs we expect the pupils to accelerate their learning out of the developmental programs area, and approach or exceed grade-level standards; whereas in developmental programs for the handicapped we expect the pupils to progress essentially on a straight line within that area.

The etiology of the problem(s) necessitating remediation may have a multiple base. Therefore, the process of remediation must often include other professionals representing the other disciplines that may be involved.

## CONCEPT OF THE LEAST RESTRICTIVE ENVIRONMENT

Largely as a result of PL 94-142, the trend nationally is to think of the various special-education programs as representing a continuum extending from very restrictive to unrestricted learning environments.

This concept of special-education services may be thought of as a continuum with no real clear-cut divisions or rigid categorical boundaries. This model (see Figure 8-2) can be adapted to any school system anywhere, by redefining the letter designations to match local services available.

The most restrictive educational environment is the lack of any planned learning activities. This includes the child who is so severely

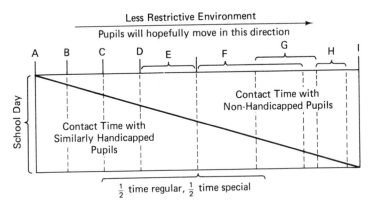

*Figure 8-2.   Continuum of special education services.*

involved that he receives no organized help. Also included is the handicapped child who has been officially excluded from school experience as being noneducable. Here we find the unknown and unserved handicapped children who are hidden by their parents. We must also recognize that there are geographical areas that have no programs for certain handicaps, and the compulsory education laws up until the advent of PL 94-142 have excluded them. This non-served category is not shown on the continuum in Figure 8-2.

The following list of educational settings can be envisioned by using the concept in Figure 8-2.

**POINT A—** Represents *24-hour care* in hospitals or institutions, or live-in private schools serving only handicapped pupils. These pupils may be in contact with nonhandicapped friends and/or siblings during vacations or visits. (This category would most likely include institutions for the severely emotionally disturbed and some state schools for the blind, deaf, or developmentally disabled.)

**POINT B—** These pupils are probably in daily contact with "normal" siblings or youngsters in the neighborhood. They also are in contact with nonhandicapped on weekends and during vacation periods.

1. *Special center, separate facility.* May include trainable mentally retarded, orthopedically handicapped, deaf, developmentally disabled, or severely emotionally disturbed.

2. *Private schools serving only handicapped* pupils. Same handicaps as in B 1.

3. *Home teaching* programs. Usually includes severely emotionally disturbed, behaviorally disabled, or physically handicapped.

**POINT C—** *Special center* adjacent to or part of a regular campus. These pupils usually will have some regularly scheduled activities with the regular students. Usually the same handicaps as in B 1.

**POINT D—** *Special day class* on a regular campus with *no planned integration* during the instructional day. These pupils will necessarily have daily contacts with the nonhandicapped population on the playground, at lunch, on the bus, etc. These pupils are generally less handicapped than C, but may have the same impairments. Some of the most severely communications handicapped and educable mentally retarded will be found here also.

**RANGE E—** *Special day class* with *planned integration.* The integration may be for academic and/or nonacademic subjects. Generally, the special day-class dategory will provide at least half-time help in the special class. Pupils will have approximately the same handicaps as in D and may also include some learning disabled youngsters. These pupils will be less severely involved than the previous categories.

**RANGE F—** *Regular class* with *regularly scheduled,* usually daily *comprehensive assistance* from a teacher specialist outside of the regular class. This is a take-out program and requires much coordination between the special and the regular teacher. This special assistance may be up to half-time. These pupils are usually learning disabled, have a mild communication problem, or a minor physical handicap.

**RANGE G—** *Regular class* with *regularly scheduled assistance* from a teacher specialist in a specific area of deficit. The schedule may be *daily or less frequent,* but is planned with specific educational objectives. This may include speech and language therapy, adaptive physical education, and assistance to visually handicapped or mildly hard of hearing pupils.

**RANGE H—** *Regular class* with *consultative help* to the teacher. This help may be in the form of intermittent help directly to the pupil, aide time to provide in-room assistance to the supervising regular teacher, curriculum modifications, or consultative help and support to the teacher. This may be one-time assistance or intermittent, ongoing. This assistance is for the minimally involved pupil—any type of problem.

**POINT I—** *Full time* in *regular class*—student needs no organized special-education assistance.

Several factors must also be considered in all types of special-education programs:

1. Generally the services will be available as needed, ages 3 to 21 or until graduation.

2. There may be assistance from school or outside agencies in addition to the educational program in any category. This aid may be medical, psychiatric, counseling, various therapies, psychological, etc.

3. There is an inherent need for regular, comprehensive evaluation of the pupil's progress. This assessment will show when it is appropriate to move a child to a less restrictive environment. In some cases, it will be necessary to move a child to a more restrictive environment when the assessment shows a need for more comprehensive educational interventions and a lack of progress or regression under the present program. This assessment should be at least annual or more often if indicated.

4. Generally, classes A, B, C, and D will provide a developmental approach to the education of the pupils. Category E may be developmental or remedial. Categories F through H will probably have a remedial orientation.

## PROGRAM COMPONENTS

In order for any program for the learning handicapped child to be successful, there must be certain tangible things inherent within the program itself.
1. The classroom and the physical plant.
2. Special equipment and materials.
3. Personnel.

### The Classroom and the Physical Plant

It would be virtually impossible to provide a master design for a plant, room or a portion of a building to serve any particular category of youngsters. This must be done by the personnel involved with that special group of youngsters within the social, financial, and availability structure of that district or building.

Generally, plans for the facilities provided for the handicapped child should be based on certain philosophical tenets, as noted below.

1.    The facilities should be on a regular campus.

2.    They should be as much like the facilities of the regular students on the same campus as possible.

3.    They should be as close to the centers of activity as possible (i.e., the sixth grade or upper-grade classes for the handicapped should not be in an unused kindergarten classroom). These pupils all need to associate with, develop rapport with, and become part of, the student body at their own age level.

4.    The physical size of the room is not nearly as important as its location. Physical size becomes important only to provide adequate space for a certain teacher's way of working with the youngsters. Some teachers prefer a smaller room than the standard 900 square feet. They feel that a smaller room automatically sets some environmental limits for the students. Other teachers like to work with a larger than normal room because of their particular way of working with interest centers and to allow for a pattern of movement within the classroom during the day. The actual size of the classroom is not nearly as important as whether or not the *teacher feels comfortable* with that size classroom.

5.    Generally, the room should be at least as desirable as the average classroom on that site whenever possible, (i.e., the special-education room should not be the noisiest, the only one without air conditioning, or the only portable classroom).

## Special Equipment and Materials

Physical equipment and materials are one area where these programs must differ from the regular program if any measure of success is to be expected. Most of these youngsters have already failed in some kind of a regular setting. To put them back into an unmodified setting with regular materials, regular techniques, and regular devices would be tantamount to having them face another session of failure. What we need to do is to recognize that these are "special" students and that they need "special" materials to assist them in getting where we want them to go.

The first thing that we need to be constantly aware of is the grade designation that is emblazoned on much of the material used in the public school setting. We should do away with graded materials and work with ungraded materials and systems that are sequential and developmental in scope and pace. The materials, although ungraded, *must be aimed at the pupil's level of current functioning*. Yet, the youngster, or anyone observing, should not feel this is "babyish" material. Unfortunately, it is difficult to find material written at primary-grade achievement levels that is not written in large type. This will turn off a sixth-grade student. What we need are materials with upper-grade interest, content, and form, but with low requirements for reading skill and comprehension.

Children are generally fascinated with gadgetry. We should take advantage of this phenomenon and use tape recorders, tachistoscopes, calculators, programmable devices, audiovisual machines, displays, models, and any other motivational device we can think of to present parts of the curriculum. As stated earlier, these are difficult students to teach. These are the ones who have already failed, and we need to do something *different,* something *unique,* something *dramatic* that will catch on where regular methods have not been successful.

Another big factor in material and equipment selection is durability. If it happens that, in heavy usage, it will be very easy to break a portion of the teaching aid or device, that item should be passed over in favor of something that is more durable. How frustrating it must be for a youngster to be unable to complete a particular assignment because a piece of the equipment is not usable.

One factor that is generally not considered to be important, but that seems to be recognized more and more by practitioners as being *very* important, is the packaging of a particular device or material. No matter how good the contents are, how practical they are, or how well developed they are from the standpoint of scope and sequence, if the box they are packaged in falls apart, the value is greatly diminished. We have all seen a $60 or $70 or perhaps even a more expensive set of educational materials packaged in a cardboard box that practically disintegrates at first use. When materials are comparable, choose the material that comes packaged in the most durable container. When the material in the inferior container is much more desirable, spend the few extra dollars to provide a container to protect the contents, even if this has to be individually or locally made. Whenever possible, get the material to use for a trial period before purchase. These problems will soon come to light when the inferior package is subjected to daily use.

Materials should afford flexible usage so that we can skip portions of the presentation when best suited for the particular child. If the *only* way to present a particular material with continuity is to go from page 1 to page 2 to page 3, etc., then we should put that material aside. There is no flexibility of use. We should choose material that provides lateral practice lessons and vertical learning of new concepts, but in a very flexible system. For example, an author who developed a workbook in Albuquerque, New Mexico, can't possibly know the exact sequence and proper amount of time to be spent on each level of skill development for

Johnny in your classroom in Texas or California. Only *you* know that, and *only after working* with Johnny. Any teacher of the handicapped who uses a bound workbook, and presents it to the students in its bound form, insisting that the students move sequentially from page to page, is certainly not fulfilling the requirements of individualizing the program for those students.

Students will often need several workbooks at the same level, on the same subject, jumping from one to another for a great deal of lateral movement before moving on to some higher sequential skill. Other pupils can move through a single workbook, work every third or fourth page, and still reap maximum benefit. This concept of individualizing instruction is discussed in greater detail in the chapter on the pupil in the classroom (see Chapter 9).

Whenever two or more special-education classrooms exist on the same campus, a great deal of saving can be accomplished by sharing materials. Only rarely would two teachers need exactly the same material at exactly the same time. By appropriate planning, the material can be used over a wide range of classrooms, and thus a much wider repertoire of materials and equipment would be available to several or many teachers.

There is no magic list of equipment and/or materials to serve any particular group or level of students. What really matters is what the teacher is comfortable with, and what seems to work with the youngsters in that particular class. If a teacher is enthused and "turned on" by a particular system or set of materials, chances are these materials will be presented with a lot of vigor, and the enthusiasm will be passed along to the students. By the same token, if a teacher is using a particular material because she must, or because it's standard for all classes of that "type," or because someone else thinks it's a good idea, the chances of its success are severely hampered.

When a teacher requests a particular set of materials costing perhaps several hundred dollars, a great deal of thought and research should have gone into making the selection. She should be able to justify the expense and explain the specific use as it applies to her classroom and her pupils. Too often, materials are bought at the whim of an individual who after using them determines that they are really not appropriate. Many thousands of dollars worth of equipment and materials are gathering dust on the shelves in all too many classrooms.

The care that is taken in the selection of materials and equipment is the important factor in assuring the appropriateness of the materials and equipment.

When equipment and materials are carefully chosen to serve *a particular range of abilities* with *a particular variety of handicaps,* and to serve *a particular goal* for *particular students,* then success is much more likely. Some excellent sources for information are:

1. Your local purchasing office.

2. Experts within your school or district (i.e., reading consultants, media specialists, librarians, etc.).

3. Other teachers.

4. Vendors. (Often a trial can be arranged.)

5. Your special-education supervisors. (They see effective and ineffective programs.)

6. Catalogues.

7. School-supply stores.

## *Personnel*

### *PRIMARY PERSONNEL*

The primary personnel in any program are the teacher and the immediate specially trained supervisor. These are the two persons who really set the stage, design and develop the program, and are actually responsible for the student's learning. Each state will have its own credential requirements, and these must be met before a teacher can work with a particular group of students. Assuming proper training and competency on the part of the teacher, we can go on and discuss some of the attributes that would be important in these individuals.

### *Pardon Me, Your Attitude is Showing*

One of the most important things that any teacher of any child can possess is the proper attitude. Attitude is even more important in the teacher of the youngster with a learning handicap.

At the time an individual graduates from high school, or perhaps shortly thereafter, he or she decides to be a teacher. Unfortunately, there is not a great deal of screening taking place between this point and the actual entry on the job market of a "trained individual" with diploma and credential in hand. The successful teacher of the handicapped pupil must be well trained and not only *like children* but also *like* her *job, people,* and *life.* The teacher who has personal, deep feelings for the pupil and a real desire to help has a much better chance to be successful in working with the handicapped. The teacher of the handicapped child starts work long before the regular school hours and goes on well into the evening. Activities will include plotting and charting, keeping

**Figure 8-3.** *A colorful welcome area for newcomers that has been cut and colored by the children. The puppets serve to overcome shyness.*

track of students' progress or lack of progress, calling parents, previewing materials, reviewing catalogues, reading journals, attending meetings, communicating with other professionals, and generally becoming better informed so as to better help the pupils. This does not imply that regular teachers are not as dedicated or are in any way doing an inferior job in their role as regular educators.

It's a good idea, sometimes, for the teacher of the handicapped who feels too much tension after awhile to spend a year or two teaching a regular class. This has a spin-off advantage of giving the teacher a new look at normalcy and a chance to get a grip on the regular curriculum.

### Personality

The person with positive attitudes will generally also be a "people" person; one who likes to be around others, and one who is comfortable initiating conversations with strangers. In the authors' experience, the best special-education teachers are sometimes a little "overcharged" or "supercharged" themselves. The most effective teachers are often bubbly or effervescent. These traits generally come across to the students and parents in a very positive way and help with the public relations aspects of the teacher's role.

The specially trained immediate supervisor will usually be the

*Figure 8-4.   This photo depicts familiar shapes and colors from the environment with auditory reinforcement in the listening center. A beanbag clown target is supplied to assist eye-hand and large muscle coordination.*

teacher of a particular group of handicapped students who has shown leadership ability, a good knowledge in the field, and has been promoted to this supervisory post. All of the things that have been said of the classroom teacher would necessarily be true of the first-line, specially trained supervisor.

## PERSONNEL—PROFESSIONAL OR ANCILLARY

The ancillary group of workers includes the psychologists, school nurses, regular teachers who work with the students on an integrated basis, principals, deans, counselors, and the students' physicians. All of these people can and should contribute greatly to the monitoring, the evaluation, the success, and the modification of the program as it goes along.

Some of the roles are well defined no matter where the program is located. For example, from coast to coast we would find general agreement as to what the school nurse's or psychologist's role is in working with these pupils. However, individually, we should tap these sources for whatever help they can give us, based on their individual training, expertise, and interests. Some of the people such as the regular staff on site will have to be constantly in-serviced by the specialists so that they

*Figure 8-5.    Here is a center where reading is fun and success is assured.*

have a better understanding of what we are trying to do with our special students.

As far as the medical people are concerned, unless we are fortunate enough to have a school doctor, we must rely on the parents' willingness to have the physician and school be in close contact with one another. In the case of the child with an educational dysfunction, we need to, whenever possible, establish this very important communication contact with the family physician. By working hand in hand and by each one monitoring the effects of the other's interventions, a great deal can be done to help the youngster—much more than if each one works independently.

## PERSONNEL—PARAPROFESSIONAL OR INSTRUCTIONAL AIDES

In recent years, more and more schools have recognized the need and value of a teacher's aide to assist in the classroom for the handicapped. There is virtually universal agreement that an extra pair of trained paraprofessional hands in the classroom is of value to the educational program within that room. Some might say that the task of teaching is made more difficult with another person in the room for whom the teacher has to be responsible. However, these isolated opinions may be the result of a personal, negative experience with an aide. The problem

**Figure 8-6.**   *A room where the pupils move from center to center according to their individual programming.*

is not whether to have an aide when the teacher wants one and when financially feasible; rather the problem lies in determining exactly where the priorities should be placed regarding the duties that are performed by the aide. There is a great deal of disagreement on the part of school personnel as to what the aide's role should be. Special-education administrators, principals, teachers, and even the aides themselves would have varying perceptions of an appropriate job description.

This confusion stems from the lack of training on the part of the people involved in establishing and implementing an instructional aide's role. From one special-education room to another the aides will be doing entirely different kinds of things—some appropriate and some inappropriate. Therefore, each district or school must determine where it wants to place the major emphasis among the many activities of the instructional aides. A job description should be developed, and the district must then proceed to train the classroom teachers or supervisors as to how to make maximum use of these very valuable paraprofessional personnel. To turn an aide loose in a room of students without any training, with a teacher who has only a vague notion as to what the aide's function is, can be a real problem and may lead to chaos. More time will be wasted in trying to determine the role than if the time had been taken originally to establish the role.

*Figure 8-7.   A highly motivating bulletin board used to reinforce color discrimination.*

Preservice time is another important factor in assuring an aide's effectiveness. There should be some planning time before school starts in the fall, or at least before the aide comes into the classroom situation. This will allow the aide to discuss with the teacher how each of them perceives the other's role in the classroom. Many frustrating situations could be eliminated if this were done.

In summarizing the role of the teacher's aide, it can be said that an aide is an extension of the teacher, within the instructional program in the classroom. To provide and maintain an effective relationship between the teacher's aide, the teacher, the pupils, the parents, and other professionals, planning time must be allowed for within the schedule, on a daily basis whenever possible. School districts must set up training programs for all persons concerned with the aide program—the aides, teachers, principals, etc. A brochure should be sent to the home so that parents can understand the role of this other adult in the child's academic life. The aide should never be found doing things that can be done by volunteer help. This is an inexcusable waste of already scarce educational dollars. The paraprofessional's time has arrived in education, but we must prepare all interested individuals to maximize the effectiveness of this type of help. The role of the aide will be discussed more fully in Chapter 9 when discussing the student in the classroom.

**Figure 8-8.**   *Whimsical figures help the child who has visual discrimination problems discern and retain abstract symbols.*

## THE PARENT

We often forget that the most influential persons in the life of every child are his parents. Only by working together with the parents can we ultimately achieve the most for each youngster. We can never accomplish very much by working at cross-purposes. The teacher should always contact the home early in the year and see the parents on a positive basis. The teacher needs to let the parents know what is happening at school and why. The parents should be told how they can be team members and what they can do to follow through in the home. The teacher and other school personnel are also sometimes the best resource to let the parents know what they can do through the use of other agencies to help the youngster. All school personnel ought to let the parents know that the school's goal is the same as theirs, and that only by walking hand in hand down the road of success for the child can we really achieve what we are all aiming for.

When parental goals and school goals differ, a concerted effort must be made to understand the parents' point of view. Rarely can we change an attitude by confrontation. We must deliberately and methodically attempt to come to an agreement on goals through conferences, exchanging information, and compromise.

# OTHER CONSIDERATIONS

## Communication

Many times in this book the importance of communication has been stressed. When we are talking about programs, it is certainly very important to again bring the subject of communication to the attention of the reader in the context of these programs. We must communicate with the parents, physicians, other professionals on the staff, and other ancillary personnel who are a part of the program in order to function optimally and get the job done properly. Improvement in this whole area of communication is probably the single greatest need in special education today. We need to develop the concept of the team approach rather than having each discipline operating independently with very little attention to what has preceded or what will follow.

Remember, the parents know the youngster better than anyone else. Rely on them for basic information about the youngster. Be aware, certainly, of their biases and prejudices. Be aware of their tendency to sometimes blame someone or something for the youngster's problem. But *do* communicate with them. Only through this, the simplest of media, can the youngster ultimately benefit to his full potential.

When appropriate and proper, and when permission is given, the physician is a very important member of this team. One of the very good reasons why he should be involved is his rather special relationship with the child and his family. Very often he can be a great ally to school personnel in helping the parents recognize, internalize, and deal with the true problems and what can be done to bring a child to his full potential. The physician is also a great ally when it comes to recommendations that might be made for assistance from outside agencies. He has a lot of prestige in the community and may be listened to where school personnel may not be.

Special educators do themselves a real disservice when they don't communicate properly with other professionals on the staff—the regular teacher, principal, counselors, etc. If the regular staff members don't know what the specialists are doing or why they're doing it, or if the regular staff doesn't understand the youngsters, it might be because the specialists haven't taken the time to communicate properly. Special educators should help themselves, their pupils, and certainly the regular staff members by communicating with them (the regular staff) as to the nature of the special program and explain exactly what they're doing with the pupils. The regular staff will probably be much more receptive to the concepts of integration and mainstreaming and will cooperate in moving the youngsters to regular classes if this kind of communication is done in an innocuous and positive way.

## *Grouping*

Grouping is a subject that has led to quite a bit of misunderstanding. Historically, the youngsters were, and in some instances still are, grouped on the basis of their disabilities, on the similarity of the things that are wrong with them, i.e., on the negatives. With the introduction of federal legislation for all handicapped school children (PL 94-142), we now can and should begin to look at our students from the standpoint of their *educational* needs. We should begin to group youngsters not by negative categories, but rather by positive criteria, based on what the teacher can honestly be expected to accomplish in the remedial or developmental program. For example, in some cases, there should probably not be more than 3 or 4 youngsters per class. In other cases, 20 or even more might be appropriate. There is no magic number that is right for any particular category of youngsters. There is only a number that is *right* for a *particular teacher* and a *particular group of youngsters* at a *particular time.*

The size of the room, the equipment and material available, whether or not there is an aide (and for how long each day), how much cooperation there is from parents, how much cooperation there is from the ancillary personnel, and how much understanding there is on the part of the regular staff are all components in determining what the group size and group makeup should be.

We can say, generally, that there should not be more than a two-year age range in a class, although this is not an inviolable law. The reason for this is that youngsters of the same age with similar needs are generally of the same maturity, size, social level, and interest level. Where these factors vary, we might have to move a youngster in with an older or younger group, depending on his individual characteristics.

We find approximately ten boys for every girl among our learning handicapped population, and certainly we would not want to have this ten to one ratio in our classes. It would be better in almost all cases to have the girls grouped in one or several classrooms to avoid any possible problems associated with creating a sex minority.

Another general concept that is true most of the time is that the student should be on a school site with his age mates. If a particular district is a 6-3-3 district, then the first six grades in special education should also be housed on an elementary campus, the middle three grades on a junior-high campus, and the tenth through twelfth grades on the high-school campus. Age is a viable criterion for grouping only in a very general way. There is nothing inherently wrong with a very mature 11- or 12-year-old who needs the junior high-type experience being moved to seventh grade, with the understanding that he may have to repeat seventh grade. By the same token, there is nothing wrong with a very immature

13-year-old being in the sixth grade. These illustrations assume that everyone who has involvement with the child—especially the parents— understands and concurs that the action is proper in this particular case.

There is no single criterion that can be set down as a universal rule for grouping. IQ, mental age, physical size, chronological age, etc. are all very poor individual harbingers of school success. Grouping should be decided by a team comprised of those who know the child best. The grouping should also take into consideration the individual teacher's competencies and her training and personal desires and likes and dislikes. The team approach, using the total gestalt of the youngster, his abilities and his disabilities, is certainly the best way for any kind of grouping to be accomplished properly.

## *SUMMARY*

Philosophically, special-education programs should offer zero-reject, no-fault learning. We should meet every child where he is, accept him for what he is, teach him at his level, and provide a positive climate where success is imminent. Failure is always possible, but should not be allowed to happen without the assurance that the failure can be turned into a corrected learning experience. Children *must be allowed to face the consequences* of their *conscious acts,* but there should be *no negative consequences for an honest attempt* at *proper performance.*

Programs, whether remedial or developmental, must be geared to the educational needs of the child. Programs must be flexible, eclectic, and different from the "normal" classroom offering.

The most important components of good programs are intangible— attitudes, philosophies, and communications. The tangibles—personnel, equipment, supplies, physical layout of the teaching station, human resources, and financial resources—are important only to the extent that the intangibles are positively or negatively affected.

There is no magic formula for success in the special-education classroom. Only diligent, dedicated, and informed effort will have the desired effect—success for *each pupil.*

# Provisions of Public Law 94-142

The provisions of PL 94-142 are numerous and some are quite complex. We will list only those tenets that are important to the delivery of service to children.

## STATE'S RESPONSIBILITIES

1. Each state is responsible for developing and adopting an annual state Master Plan for special education which is in compliance with PL 94-142.

2. Each state must monitor the comprehensive plans of Local Educational Agencies (LEAs) to insure compliance with the state plan and PL 94-142.

3. Each state is responsible for receiving and disbursing the federal funds included in PL 94-142.

4. States must assure the legal possibility of interagency agreements including those with private schools and services when appropriate.

5. State facilities for the handicapped must be in compliance with PL 94-142 and must be part of the statewide Master Plan.

6. States must assure that other federally funded programs are in harmony with the state's Master Plan.

7. There must be a statewide advisory commission composed of a cross-section of persons interested in handicapped pupils.

## LOCAL RESPONSIBILITIES

Each LEA (Local Educational Agency) must be capable of delivering full services to all handicapped pupils. School districts may join other districts in a consortium, districts may form a county-wide cooperative LEA, a district may elect to go it alone, counties may join other counties, and so forth.

1.    Each LEA must submit an annual Master Plan which assures compliance with PL 94-142 and the state plan.

2.    A search effort must be made to find unknown handicapped children who are in need of service.

3.    Except where illegal, all handicapped pupils aged 3 to 21 must have available to them a free and appropriate educational program by September 1, 1980.

4.    Each pupil must have an annual IEP (Individual Educational Program—see Chapter 9). The plan must detail present levels of functioning, long- and short-term objectives, and all services and interventions deemed necessary to educate that child to his highest potential without regard for the availability of services. The plan must also include a timeline, the personnel to be involved, a plan for evaluating effectiveness, and a justification for the plan. The parent must also be involved in the development of this plan.

5.    The IEP must include provisions for educating the child in the least restrictive environment.

6.    Each child must be educated with nonhandicapped pupils to the maximum extent appropriate.

7.    Funds must be spent first on the unserved population and then on the inadequately served students.

8.    Programs for personnel development are required, including in-service training.

9.    Work experience and career education are required areas of an IEP as appropriate.

10.    Sincere and documented attempts must be made to insure parent/guardian involvement.

11.    Local and state plans must provide for the participation of other private and public agencies when appropriate.

## *Procedural Safeguards and Due Process*

1. Regular parent or guardian consultation is required in all cases.

2. Disagreements between parents/guardians and public school officials may be resolved by due process hearings.

3. An independent appraisal of the pupil may be made at no cost to the parent under certain conditions.

4. Parents/guardians must be given prior notice of all matters relating to identification, evaluation, and placement of their child.

5. All contacts with parents/guardians must be made in their native language.

6. The terminology used in all notices must be understandable by the general public.

7. The implications throughout PL 94-142 are that parental consent must be obtained on the basis of informed understanding.

8. Appeals may be made by parents/guardians anywhere along the process of identification, evaluation, placement, or release of a pupil. Appeals are made to an impartial hearing officer or panel according to the approved state and local plan.

9. All parents/guardians must be apprised of their rights under PL 94-142.

10. The confidentiality of all information must be assured.

11. Parental/guardian consent for all activities must be in writing.

12. Parents/guardians may examine all relevant records.

## *Funding*

PL 94-142 establishes a formula of progressively implemented funding wherein the federal government pays a gradually escalated percentage of the average national expenditure for public school pupils. This formula is:

| | |
|---|---|
| Fiscal 1978— 5% | ($387 million) |
| Fiscal 1979—10% | ($775 million) |
| Fiscal 1980—20% | ($1.2 billion) |
| Fiscal 1981—30% | ($2.32 billion) |
| Fiscal 1982—40% | ($3.16 billion) |

(The dollar amounts are maximum allocations based upon estimated numbers of children to be served.)

1.   Funds are allocated to LEAs on the basis of a specified dollar amount for each identified handicapped pupil, but not to exceed 12 percent of the total school population.

2.   State Departments of Education may use 50 percent of the money in 1978 and 25 percent thereafter.

3.   An inflation factor is part of the formula.

4.   Incentive grants are available for providing service to the pre-school age handicapped.

# CHAPTER 9

# *What Happens to the Student in the Special-Education Classroom?*

## THE INDIVIDUAL EDUCATIONAL PLAN

Before a youngster is admitted to any special-education program, there must be an assessment of that youngster's educational needs. Notice the emphasis is on *educational* needs. So often the laws and the ancillary personnel involved with education are only concerned with the decibels of hearing loss or the actual IQ scores. These are really less important than some other factors with which we must be concerned. As stated earlier, we must know the statistics to give us a starting point, but beyond that we must be concerned only with their effect on the educational needs of the particular student.

### Assessment Roles and Phases

There are many people involved in the assessment of a pupil, starting with the initial referral, and ending when the pupil is "assessed out." The initial evaluators may include audiologists, physicians, psychiatrists, psychologists, previous teachers, counselors, speech and language specialists, nurses, and others. Also included are all of the people who are in any way involved in determining the progress of the child once he has entered the program.

We essentially have three types or phases of assessment. Phase one is the preliminary assessment prior to entering the program. Phase two is the ongoing assessment, which will lead to a successful, well-adjusted and self-motivated learner. Phase three is the pulling together of all data, educational plans, and modifications for a final "pregraduation" assessment.

## PHASE ONE

The assessment roles of the individuals who are involved in the initial screening, or phase one, are pretty much laid down by laws, customs, and procedures established within the particular public or private school system.

We need to have enough information, both historical and current, to support the fact that the youngster does, in fact, need some kind of modification of his school experience. The need may be for a special class, for part-time assistance, or for the regular teacher to modify something within the regular classroom. These initial assessors generally bring together their findings at a staffing or admissions meeting, at which time it is determined whether or not the youngster "fits the mold" or qualifies for the kind of service being suggested.

At this point, we must look not so much at the "evidence" submitted, but rather at the verbal pictures being painted by those presenting the evidence. What kind of a child is this *really,* not statistically? What kind of a program does he need? We can give the child everything from a total developmental program to a part-time remedial program; from a very highly structured program to a very permissive program; from a grandmotherly teacher to a younger, "hep" teacher, or a teacher of a specified gender if that's what is required. These are just some of the things that can and should be considered for every placement.

Let us think of a clockwork composed of many cogged wheels meshing with one another (see Figure 9-1). The main wheel represents the youngster, and the teeth represent his needs. The other wheels represent the curriculum, the educational environment, the home, the parents' attitudes and aspirations, the child's self-concept, the child's medical condition, any deficits he may have, his facility for language, his physical size and shape, and sibling attitudes, among other factors.

Obviously, there are some wheels that educators and other professionals cannot modify or change. The ones that we can control, even in part, should be very carefully changed, bent, and modified in order to make them mesh as closely as possible. Too often we try to distort the wheel that represents the child too quickly, or we try to make him fit a pre-existing notion as to what the curriculum should be for another youngster who has *almost* the same kind of problem. Instead, we should file the teeth of the curriculum wheel to fit the teeth (needs) of this one-of-a-kind youngster who is being considered because of his *own special and unique problems.*

## PHASE TWO

Phase two of the assessment is primarily the responsibility of the special-education teacher. She may call on any one or more of the experts

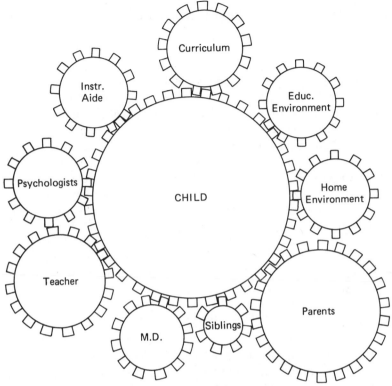

**Figure 9-1.** *A clockwork kit.*

*1. Assemble as shown. Main gear labeled "Child" is made of a special material called "flesh and blood," (F & B), and is capable of human emotions. DO NOT FOLD, BEND, SPINDLE, OR MUTILATE. Any necessary modifications to this gear should be made in accordance with the note below.*

*2. Other gears may be modified as necessary to create a fine meshing with the main gear.*

> *Note:* Since F & B material is somewhat pliable and is responsive to careful "tender loving care" (TLC) molding, the other gears might need to be slightly out of mesh so as to carefully perform this TLC molding and modifying function. This is especially true in cases where the main gear is bent or "out of sync."

available for their input and assistance. The process of phase two consists of keeping work samples, doing achievement testing, keeping anecdotal records, and generally accumulating pertinent information regarding the pupil's adjustment and progress in the special class. There may also be updates on the formal standardized testing and information from other agencies.

## PHASE THREE

Phase three consists of pulling together all of the information from phase two and the original information from phase one. This third phase is also primarily the responsibility of the special-education teacher. This is a more formal evaluation than phase two. The objective is to bring together all data and personnel with the thought that the child may be ready to leave a certain special-education program. Usually, a meeting is held to give all persons, including the parent, a chance to present information. A decision and recommendation should be made regarding the child's readiness to "graduate" back to a full-time regular class or perhaps to a less restrictive alternate program. This is when we would determine whether the pupil is remediated to grade level, remediated to expectancy, in need of a more comprehensive program, not benefiting from the program, in need of additional interventions, or whether we need to continue service with or without modification.

### Accentuate the Positive

The educational assessment cannot be expressed in numbers; we must use words. One of the problems we have had in education is the lack of standardized words to describe the handicapped pupil. If we are really to do what federal and state legislation says we should do, we must drop all labels. We must begin to call students not by a categorical word or phrase, which is in reality a catchall phrase for all of the students who happen to have the same types of deficits or problems (negatives). Instead, we must use descriptive terms that will talk about the educational needs (positives) of the child. We must then put this information together for instructional purposes. In the past, there has been too much definition and redefinition of relatively undefinable and ambiguous terms. We must now resort to good old-fashioned adjectives and adverbs (see Chapter 2, "Labelology"). We have for too long dwelled on the negatives—the things the child could not do—his handicaps. The time is right for a switchover to a recognition that the positives—i.e., a student's intact modalities, his interests, and his ambitions—are a much more viable tack for special educators to take.

Thus, we must talk about a youngster who is ten years old and is having difficulty with short vowel sounds at the third grade level or about the youngster who has mastered addition and subtraction facts to 20. Any teacher can then very quickly ascertain *exactly* where that particular youngster is in those subjects, and can design an individualized program at his level of skill and experience. We should not try to condense these bits of information into test scores, or into single profile numbers, in order to convey what we wish to pass along to a new teacher. The sum and substance of this suggestion is that we must *communicate.* Remember, communication is complete only when there is a *sender and a receiver,* and then only when the thought or information is transmitted *accurately* and with *understanding.*

## Communication

Communication should be simple and in a language clearly understood by sender and receiver, which is usually basic English in the United States, not "psychologicalese" or "medicalese." If we talk about *visual acuity* or *auditory distortion* or *visual perception,* each of us has a slightly different notion as to exactly what these terms mean. Therefore, instead of employing such terms, we should describe the material or test used, and the success or failure the child is having with *that particular material or test*—which should leave little doubt in the mind of the reader as to exactly where *that* child is and where he needs to go to progress further.

All of the school personnel who come into contact with the youngster, once he is found to be eligible for special help, can be considered to be practitioners or treaters of this youngster with the educational dysfunction. Once his uniqueness is defined in good, descriptive terms *that we can understand,* the teacher, the nurse, the psychologist, the teacher's aide, the administrator, and certainly very importantly, the parent, all should be brought along into the scheme of action that will get the job done. This team approach (including the parent) is a must if we are to maximally affect the child's learning. The most important process involved is communication. Don't try to write a thesis or dissertation. Stick to simple, descriptive words that will have essentially the same meaning to all who read the document.

Be aware of the value of verbal communication. If a phrase is not quite clear in a student's records, or if a bit of information is hazy or a meaning is unclear, if the semantics are shady, or perhaps when a youngster is in your class you just don't see him quite the same way, ask the other teacher about it. "What did you mean by this?" "Help me figure out why this is happening when you said this other is true." Very often there is a very simple solution to what appears to be a very complex problem, and the pathway to the solution is communication. (Also see Chapters 6 and 7).

## Teaching as an Art

Too often, we are still "flying our curriculum by the seat of our pants." We're still barnstorming and "playing it by ear" in the days of the 747s and trips to the moon. Special education will never be a true science, that is, a systematized field of knowledge utilizing methods based on scientific principles. As long as a teacher has even one choice to make regarding whether to use resource A or resource B, or material 1 or material 2, teaching is an art. Choices must be made daily, by the hour, by the minute, choices that affect the youngster and what is offered to him in the classroom. Therefore, we need to talk about education as an art, as a series of choices. These choices should be knowledgeable and should be based on sound information and systems, but they nevertheless are choices. Ultimately, the decisions must be left up to the individual practitioner as he or she interacts with the individual youngster in the classroom, with its own particular set of constraints, resources, and personalities.

Most important in the area of ongoing assessment is the idea, the notion, the knowledge that every time something is attempted and the youngster either succeeds, succeeds partially, or fails, this becomes a bit of information that must be added to the assessment and information already in the books.

Of course this means adequate record keeping. Many commercial publishing houses now produce some sort of tabulation profile for keeping track of the progress of youngsters in various programs. This system is fine as a starting point. However, where possible and practical, the teachers in a given district, program, or level should get together and develop their own profile to track a youngster's progress. The value in such a "homemade" document is not only in the finished profile itself, but also in the values accruing to those who develop the device, in the meeting of the minds, in the semantics of the words used, in the discussions, and finally in the conclusions reached.

## The Complete Blueprint or IEP

The initial assessment that is done by people who see the child for only short periods of time, prior to the youngster's coming into the program, should serve only as a rough sketch. We now have the beginning of an individual educational plan or IEP. We have some ideas and directions that should be different and unique. The information should represent the needs of *this* child so that he may become what we all want him to be (and usually also what he wants to be). The plan at this point is not something that can be used optimally for more than just the first few days. Once the teacher has a youngster in her class for a day or two, she may be able to judge the proper direction for the curriculum better than all of the special personnel who have spent only a short time in the assessment process prior to the actual enrollment. The initial assessment made prior to enrollment should obtain general information to establish general goals and general objectives. It should contain statistical data that are important for some of the preliminary decisions we need to make about the youngster. The teacher should be cautious, though, and be aware of the limitations of these statistics. Once the child is in class, the teacher will know if he is very bright, average, or dull; whether he has a hearing loss; or whether he has visual problems. Therefore, the teacher should consider these initial bits of information to be like working sketches. The final and complete blueprint or educational plan will be developed out of the profiles and the other kinds of data that the teacher and others will collect as they take care of the youngster in the program.

What we really want to do is to take a youngster who exhibits an educational dysfunction and transform him into a successful, well-adjusted student, using all the materials, techniques, assistance, tricks, and other positive modalities we can muster. We need to develop some working sketches using the expertise of all the educators, physicians, psychologists, specialists, and parents. From these working sketches will evolve the blueprint, known as the *individual educational plan* (IEP).

Everything that happens from the time the first notion is presented that a youngster is having difficulty, until he becomes a well-adjusted student, functioning at grade level, is part of the individual educational plan. Included are all of the experiences that have happened, are happening, or will happen to the youngster in the course of his educational program, experiences both planned and unplanned.

In summary, we must take the working sketches prepared by individual experts in pupil assessment, and treat them as general goals and objectives. Based on that fund of knowledge, we must then work with the youngster and build the blueprint that becomes the program or IEP for all the practitioners who work with that youngster. The sum total of everything from the time of the first referral to graduation becomes the educational plan for that child. It is never finalized, always viable, never static, always flexible; and at the same time that it is the educational plan, it becomes the educational history for that youngster.

## Emotional Climate

Creating and maintaining a positive emotional climate within the classroom can be an important contributor to success for the handicapped pupil. This emotional climate is largely the result of the teacher's attitudes as well as the attitudes of the other professionals and paraprofessionals who work within the classroom. As has been said many times, these youngsters are frustrated youngsters. They are failure-oriented and are easily discouraged. They don't need someone else to "bug" them about their lack of skills. If a child takes a spelling test of 20 words and misses 15, he still has 5 right, and that is the thing that should be pointed out to him. He also deserves and needs a chance to go back and correctly spell the other 15 words. After all, the educator's job is not to reinforce failure or to continually remind a dysfunctioning child of his disabilities. How much better to allow the youngster to "get them all right." Maybe 20 words was too many in the first place—then the error is the teacher's, not the child's.

Included among the worst things that can happen in special education are the nonsmiling face, the red check marks denoting *"Wrong!!"* on the papers a youngster completes. A youngster—particularly a handicapped one—doesn't need the straight-lined or down-curved mouth showing disappointment and displeasure in something that he has tried. Also, we should eliminate negative check marks on papers indicating that something is wrong. The child has had failure thrown up to him all of his school life, and no one continues to try very long in the face of sure defeat. It would be wiser to use a brightly colored pencil to mark those things that are *correct,* return the paper, and give the youngster a chance to correct those that *aren't* marked correct. Then everything he does will ultimately be a successful and positive experience and will bear a symbol attesting to the student's *effort* and *achievement.*

Too often, when a paper is handed back with a number of check marks indicating errors, the youngster just shrugs his shoulders and thinks, "Oh well, another failure." Nothing happens to correct any misconceptions or negative learning that has taken place. It would be much better to give him the chance to go back over those items that have not been properly done and give the correct response. This way, he goes back through the thinking, and comes up with the correct response so that there is no negative learning. Thus, there is no reinforcement of a negative concept. Also, the student eventually has a paper with all correct responses, something he can be proud of. Only you, the teacher, and the parent whom you have informed as to your strategy, need know that all were not correct after the first attempt.

## USING CASE-STUDY INFORMATION

### Danger—Scores Ahead

Throughout this book we have indicated that it is wise for teachers and others who are working with handicapped youngsters to utilize all of the information that is available. There is no need to go back to ground zero each time a new person undertakes the education of a youngster. There are several cautions, however, about how to use the information that may be available. The most important misuse of information is in interpreting a score on any test as a *point* rather than a *range.* All that the score on any test or other evaluation device tells us is a particular respondent's reaction to those test items at a given time, feeling as he did at that time, with whatever attitudes he brought with him to the testing situation (see Chapter 10).

Chances are that if a number of test scores over several years all indicate that a child is functioning at a high level, the trend is proper, and the youngster is probably capable of high-level performance. By the same token, if a number of scores given over a period of time by different examiners are all in the subnormal range, we can assume that the youngster is at least functionally operating at a below-normal level. The caution is to recognize the variables that may be a part of any test situation. Some of these variables are:

1. Is the child confused about this particular test?

2. Is he apprehensive?

3. Is he malingering?

4. How does he feel physically?

5. What are his attitudes at this point in time?

6. What are the capabilities of the tester?

7. What rapport has been established between the tester and the person being tested?

8. Is this test actually going to give us the information we are seeking?

9. Is it the proper test for this youngster?

10. Is it the proper test for this subject area or area of inquiry?

11. Is it at the proper level for this youngster?

12. What is the child to gain or lose by passing or failing the test?

When we consider factors such as these, we begin to recognize that many variables can come into play and may be hidden within the confines of the one- or two-digit test score.

It is just as important to know what tests do *not* tell as it is to know what information we might get from a given test. Find out what tests are commonly used in your district to determine a child's achievement level or his intellectual level. Sit down with a psychologist and become familiar with the concepts involved. Become familiar with the content of a test, so that you may better interpret the scores that are shown on a profile. The apprehensive child responding to a test situation may not be the same youngster in the relatively tension-free atmosphere of a classroom.

Conversely, when another youngster is surrounded by people, movement, and visual and auditory distractions of various types in the classroom, he is likely to respond more negatively than he did in the test situation. The better you know the child, the better will be your interpretations of the test results.

## The Self-Fulfilling Prophesy

Too often, in the course, of following a child's progress in school, we see the self-fulfilling prophesy come into play. A teacher is told that a youngster is "subnormal" or "above average," so materials are chosen and the pace is set. The child is thrust into a pattern of expectancy to fulfill the "known" quantities, even though these "known" quantities may actually be false. We know that too often, under these circumstances, the child does fulfill the expectancies of the teacher, be they low or be they high, as long as they are within the child's capabilities. Therefore, things that we should look for beyond the variables in the test situation, when reviewing a student's records, are:

1.   Was the test an individual test whereby the tester had a much better control at one to one than might be found in a group situation in the classroom?

2.   Was it a group test where a child found it very difficult to settle down to the test because of distractions around him?

3.   If the instructions were standardized, and this youngster has problems with encoding or decoding information, we might expect the youngster to have difficulty with the test.

Always read the psychologist's or other tester's narrative report. The numbers themselves are of little value unless we know the frame of reference of the tester. The tester will often explain a score that deviates from a pattern and often will give clues as to the probable validity of the scores.

## A Better Way

The test scores should generally be used only in setting up your class initially. Once you have a youngster in your class for even a short time, you will have a better knowledge of his day-to-day functioning and his levels of competencies than all of the test scores can tell you. A better way would be to keep anecdotal records, narrative reports, and a progress profile on a child's progress or lack of progress.

In your anecdotal reports and other notes, tell the next teacher in writing what the youngster's interests are, what his levels of accomplishment are, what turns him on, what turns him off, what riles him, what things spook him, does he like to be touched, or is he "goosey"? (We know that many of the children diagnosed as emotionally disturbed actually respond negatively to physical contact with another human being.) The narrative report takes more time to write, and obviously takes more time to read, but is infinitely more valuable than test scores. As you are reading another teacher's comments, try to read between the lines. By looking for patterns of statements or what is meant by a particular phrasing, very often valuable insights can be gained as to the child's problems of behavior control and learning.

Test scores should never be regarded as infallible and constant. Only by comparing the child's current performance with his stated, tested potential, can we really know whether the potential indicated is in fact true. It is not uncommon to have a pupil in class for only one week (and sometimes less) when an astute and alert special-education teacher properly and correctly refutes the reported scores with some new and much more valid information regarding the child's functioning. Perhaps for the first time the child "finds a home" in the educational jungle that has been so unkind and unfeeling toward him, and his true level of functioning is finally uncovered.

## THE ALL-IMPORTANT FIRST DAY

We never get a second chance to make a good first impression. Whatever happens in the classroom on the first day is difficult to counter. The first day is perhaps the most important day of the year for all concerned. The teachers have perused the case study folders and have contacted each parent and know all about the youngsters (or so we hope). The pupils have talked to last year's students and know all about the teacher (they think). Everyone will be playing games to establish the pecking order and to test all limits and most new teachers are surprised to find that the students are probably better players than they are.

The youngster with a learning disability is not proficient or expert in many areas; if he were, he wouldn't be in a special class! However, one area in which this type of child does seem to excel—with exceptions, of course—is in the game of human manipulation. Many of these children seem to be able to steer peers, parents, teachers, and virtually all others in whatever way they want to. A remark, a look, a well-placed foot or elbow, a question, an angelic excuse, any seemingly innocuous minor event can be setting the stage for their ultimate victory in the game of human interaction. You and I may take courses in assertion training, or in leadership roles and styles; but we don't necessarily become experts. Perhaps the child with the learning disorder should teach the classes in these subject areas!

## Preparation for Individualized Learning

Teachers should always read the case-study folder, read the cumulative reports and talk to last year's teacher; but most importantly they should *get some positive handle* on each student in preparation for the first day. Time will never be better spent. Many successful teachers of pupils with learning disabilities visit each home before school starts every year. After the ice is broken, it's a very positive meeting for future liaison. Very often the only contacts the parents have had with the school have been negative—such as, "Johnny goofed again." It's a treat and a relief for the parent to have a nonapprehensive, nonthreatening visit with the teacher.

Another *must* for the first day is to have many appropriate activities planned for each pupil. These activities should be highly individualized and highly motivating. Many times the pupils will come into class daring the teacher to teach them. Unless she's teaching kindergarten, she is not their first teacher, and unless she's teaching twelfth grade, she will not be the last. Other expert teachers have tried, and many have failed. Therefore an effective teacher should put the odds for success in her favor as much as possible by being like a boy scout—"Be prepared."

By utilizing individualized materials, the teacher can set the stage for the year. In this way the children will not be looking at one another's work for hints. By never giving two students the same work in remedial academic areas at the same time, the teacher can insure that each youngster will be doing his own work. Teachers will find that once the scope and sequence of activities and materials in any subject are set up, keeping the material current and properly paced for *each student* requires no more effort than planning group activities or trying to modify or justify the same materials for all. This certainly is much easier than trying to find an activity or material for the whole class that is at the proper level of difficulty, paced properly, within the experiential limits of each child, and is challenging everyone but frustrating no one.

Teachers need to establish an accumulation system and a retrieval system for materials. Once set up, these systems are beautiful. There are several systems commercially available to assist in the codification and retrieval of materials. The best, always current source of information regarding available systems is the Council for Exceptional Children's publication service.* Also check with local and state consultants for availability of these and other systems.

## Activities

Another first day *must* is the posting and discussion of the rules of the room—setting the limits. Everyone must understand what is expected, what will not be tolerated, and, perhaps just as importantly, what are

---

*Council for Exceptional Children, 1920 Association Drive, Reston, Virginia 22091.

the consequences for noncompliance. Some things should be negotiable, and others are inviolable "laws." The youngsters need not agree or approve of the rules, but they must understand them and the consequences. Students everywhere will always "test" the limits imposed, but the students with a learning disability will often test the teacher, her semantics, the logic behind the rules, the "Who says?" the efficacy, and at the same time look for loopholes. The teacher must be careful not to make unenforceable or unreasonable rules or suggest untenable consequences. She should keep the rules at a minimum and involve the students as much as is appropriate for their grade level and sophistication. She should deal with the "why" of the rules; i.e., "Why don't we wander around the room, or why don't we talk out in class?" The students should be used whenever possible to help develop the "whys" as well as the "no's."

Another activity that will be beneficial to all and will give the teacher some insights into the intricacies and dynamics of the individuals and the group is the interview. The teacher can interview the youngsters, or they can interview each other—with careful guidance. The age and severity of the learning problems will have to be considered when planning this activity. All humans are ego-involved and love to talk about themselves. In order to take advantage of this, the teacher should:

1. Find out about the children factually.

2. Find out about the children emotionally. How do they handle verbal encounters?

3. Find out how the children feel about one another.

4. Find out how each student feels about himself.

5. Find out how each student feels about school and learning.

6. Pull out positive aspects of each youngster's background. (Some of this will have been learned from the home visit and/or the case study.)

7. *Provide an ego boost for each child.*

These activities will not only give the teacher good information regarding individuals and group dynamics, but will give the students a chance to feel important and be an integral part of the class immediately. The teacher is in effect saying, "I care about you, so do others, and we'll listen." For some youngsters, someone listening to them is a rare and treasured experience.

### Bribery—A Frame of Reference

Success must be built into the first day. The child must *want* to come back, not come back because he has to. Making him want to come back might be handled in a number of ways, one of which could be referred to as "bribery."

There's nothing inherently wrong with bribery—at least not educational bribery in a classroom setting. We can call it a "token reward system," "contractual teaching," "contingency management," or a "token economy." Whatever name it has, it all means the same thing, the presentation of a learning system. This sort of system helps by:

1.  Setting a realistic goal.

2.  Providing the means to achieve it.

3.  Telling the students what will happen when they accomplish the task, and what "tragedy" will befall them should they not succeed.

We all work for a remuneration of some kind. We are rewarded by all those around us when we do well. We are rewarded by our employer, our spouse, our children, our friends, our neighbors, and our colleagues. The student with a learning disability is largely failure-oriented, at least in educational pursuits, and has probably had little success except in nonconformity. He needs some of the bribery we all live on and thrive on.

Our personal goals can be, and most often are, long-term: a paycheck once a month, a vacation trip once a year, a new house or car. The normal child gets his grade rewards quarterly and other rewards vicariously because he is "in tune" with his environment. Some of these vicarious rewards are frequent and some are long-term. But the youngster with a learning disability *constantly* needs the reassuring word, the pat on the shoulder, the star on his paper, the positive note home, the paper displayed on the bulletin board, even tidbits of food—if this works. Very often this youngster is a failure at age seven or eight or even earlier. Very often Mom and Dad are "on his back," and he's being unfavorably compared to siblings or other age mates. Pretty soon this child will stop trying. It's easier to say, "I can't," than to try. At least if he says, "I can't," he's right and no one can prove him wrong. It is the teacher's job to change the "I can't," or "I won't" to "I'll try," and educational bribery is one effective way that often works.

## THE INSTRUCTIONAL AIDE

As mentioned in Chapter 8, the instructional aide is a fairly recent and fantastically valuable asset to a special-education classroom. The major problems seem to arise when we try to define the role.

### What the Role Should Not Be

It may be easier to start by trying to determine what aides should *not* be doing in the classroom. More agreement might be found among the professionals if we start from this point of view.

**Rule #1:** The aide should *not* be the teacher. That is, decisions that reflect the curriculum in the classroom—what shall be taught, how it shall be taught, when it shall be taught, and under what conditions it should be taught—should only be made by the teacher. The aide is there strictly to assist, not to make these original or supplementary professional determinations.

**Rule #2:** The aide should *not* be used for purely clerical or nonprofessional activities. It would be very difficult to justify an aide being paid for instructional time with children if his or her chores included mainly such activities as running the ditto machine, taking milk money to the office, and doing countless other unimportant tasks that are required in the course of the school day. Volunteers can be found to perform many of these mechanical tasks, although the aide can, of course, assist when necessary.

**Rule #3:** An aide should not be *the* disciplinarian for the classroom. The teacher must be the one in charge. The aide can assist within the parameters and procedures set up by the teacher.

**Rule #4:** The aide should *not* be the main liaison with the home. The teacher must be in charge, must be the one who knows what's going on, and therefore must be the one who is the main communicator with the home. There may be individual circumstances such as bilingualism, or a particular rapport that has been established in a certain situation, where it might be appropriate for the aide to be the communicator with the home. However, even in these circumstances, the teacher must always be the one in charge of the communication, the one who's calling the shots and determining what is to be communicated.

**Rule #5:** The aide is *not* paid to do the things that the teacher doesn't care to do, or would rather have someone else do to free the teacher for social or other nonclassroom activities.

### Some Appropriate Roles for the Instructional Aide

Since this book deals with handicapped pupils, we can assume that every pupil being discussed needs some measure of remediation or some type of specialized developmental program. Obviously, the remediation or developmental, sequential presentation can be performed much more effectively and efficiently if more adult presenters are performing the tasks of remediation or teaching the developmental skills. The role of the aide, then, becomes one of being an *extension* of the teacher. The aide is able to almost double the teacher's potential to work with the students on an individual or small-group basis.

Most educators would agree that the only justification for spending educational dollars for a teacher's aide is to utilize the person mainly in the role of instruction—that is, working with the children. A properly oriented aide who knows what he or she is doing can be an invaluable asset in extending the teacher's range of influence within the classroom. Tasks and activities should be planned to include the aide's role in the fulfillment of those tasks. The teacher may wish to do some individual work with the students while the aide is doing group work. Conversely, the aide may be the one who is better equipped, or for some special reason better able to perform, some individual work, while the teacher is doing group work.

As mentioned above, the aide should not be the disciplinarian, but nevertheless the aide must follow through as an adjunct and arm of the teacher in disciplinary matters. The aide doesn't tell Johnny, "Wait until the teacher comes and you'll be punished," but rather the aide must be consistent within the disciplinary framework of the class. The aide must be sure that the teacher knows of the problems encountered, and the solutions the aide is using to maintain order within the classroom. An aide should be part of the lesson plans every day, just like the teacher is. Those lesson plans should include all of the activities for the day for each youngster. Only with this kind of intensive planning can maximum use be made of the efforts of all the individuals involved—the teacher, the students, and the aide.

Time for the teacher and the aide to summarize and reflect is another basic need. Some daily periods should be allocated when possible for the aide and teacher to summarize the day's activities and do some mutual planning for the next step of the instructional program. The aide needs to understand his or her role in the total program. There needs to be a preview of materials and other media that will be in use in the classroom.

When problems arise with a student, the aide should ask the teacher for the proper course of action if it has not already been established. These discussions need to be held as often as is appropriate and in great detail. There should be no miscontruing the intention of the teacher in handling situations that arise within the classroom.

The effective teacher's aide learns very quickly to say, "I don't know," when queried by another adult, and to defer questions to the teacher, unless there is some very definite understanding as to the proper way to handle a particular subject. The aide who gets into difficulty is the one who guesses when asked questions by a parent or other professionals. This aide may then be at odds with the teacher as to what someone believes about a particular child or class or situation.

## SUMMARY

This chapter has attempted to give a brief and concise look into what makes a special-education program good from the student's point of view. There is only one reason for special-education programs, classes, and teachers to exist—they must provide an *effective educational service* to handicapped pupils. Unless we recognize this service aspect and make our every action work toward effective remediation or developmental programs, *we* have failed the child—the child has not failed us. Be *positive,* be *supportive,* be a *friend.* Also, be *consistent, fair,* and *flexible.* Always be willing to modify or change yourself so as to effect a change in the pupil.

We've looked at the individual educational plan and the roles of the people involved in its preparation and implementation in the classroom. The IEP must be a viable and flexible instrument aimed at the child's level of skills and experience. Constant evaluation keeps the IEP current and keeps interested parties informed as to the pupil's progress or lack of progress.

The importance of communication, attitudes, and a positive atmosphere cannot be overstated. We should always be aware of the intangibles and their importance in educating a youngster.

We also must recognize the *dangers* and *values* of case-study information. It's a good place to start, but an unproductive place to linger. The teacher's experience with a pupil when properly assessed and interpreted is a much better indicator of potential and progress.

Being informed and being prepared are two well-established criteria to insure success as a teacher.

# CHAPTER 10

# The Psychological Approach

In Chapters 7, 8, and 9, we briefly discussed the role of psychological personnel in the assessment and care of the child with a learning handicap. We identified the two general areas of psychological intervention—evaluation and treatment. We also discussed the various professionals who operate in this general area, including the school psychologist, educational psychologist, clinical psychologist, and other professionals who may be involved in the testing. Finally, we touched on the wide field of psychological help and remediation, and the different types of workers who operate in this field. In this chapter we will take a closer look at this entire picture.

## THE IDENTIFICATION AND
## EVALUATION PROCESS

Any child who exhibits educational problems should have a total evaluation by a competent educational psychologist. The majority of school districts have a staff of psychologists who function in this area, although in many situations the need far outstrips the availability. In this case, or when the child attends a private school or one with no staff psychologist, a private psychologist should be consulted. No child can be scholastically remediated to his optimum without a quality evaluation by a competent educational psychologist. Teachers and other therapists need base-line data and knowledge of impaired and intact modalities for learning, in order to proceed efficiently and effectively.

Each school district usually establishes role responsibilities and job descriptions for its psychological personnel, designed to meet that district's own needs. Therefore the role of the individual psychologist will often vary quite a bit from district to district. It will also vary somewhat within a district because of the different backgrounds, training, interests, and experiences of the various professionals. However, for the most part, each district is able to formulate a program suitable to its own needs, utilizing the resources that become available to the teachers, students, and others working with the children. In the following sections we shall attempt to point out some of the important facts concerning this very important segment of the team serving the child with a learning handicap.

## The Role of the School Psychologist

The school professional is often characterized as the person who is constantly scurrying about, pulling individual children out of their classrooms and testing them, conducting conferences, writing reports, and generally making himself quite visible on the school scene. The student who needs help beyond what can be offered in the regular classroom is usually the one the psychologist has focused on quite early in the child's school career. The services that the psychologist offers are extremely important to students, teachers, administrators, parents, and the physician (who sometimes may use the information to assist in his medical intervention).

There are many areas in which the psychologist operates, including diagnosis, assessment, and treatment. The typical school psychologist can be a specialist in special or regular education, counseling, administration, or other pupil personnel services. The ideal school psychologist has credentials in teaching and psychology, perhaps an advanced degree, and often has had teaching experience. The services he can provide may include any or all of the following.

1. Assessment.

2. Diagnosis.

3. Treatment.

4. Consultancy.

5. Instruction for teachers, students, and other personnel.

6. Supervision for the same individuals as listed in #5.

7. Parent-teacher-student conferences.

8. Parent-education classes.

9. Counseling (individual and group).

10.  Child-study team member.

11.  Curriculum advisement.

12.  Program development and maintenance.

In recent years, there has been a trend to train school psychologists to be more than just "testers." A relatively new treatment model has supplemented the old "test—write report—recommend program—conference—go to next case" model. The psychologist is now becoming more actively involved and provides services beyond the "old" model. This is a "total interest" role, including ongoing evaluation, communication, sharing of information, and responsibility-taking. This type of model will supplant the older one on a fairly universal scale.

## The Psychological Report

The psychological report should give as much information about the student as possible and should assist the teacher in developing greater knowledge about the student as well as suggesting ways in which to improve instruction of the child. There are certain very important basic *prerequisites* for a well written and usable report. The prerequisites are:

1.  It should be written in clearly understandable language.

2.  It should help the teacher to better understand the student she is working with.

3.  It should give adequate information in a relatively short format.

4.  It should present practical suggestions and recommendations that can be easily implemented.

5.  It must relate things that are in the student's best interests and can be of help to him in the future.

The actual content of the psychological report will vary somewhat from district to district, but there is usually a well-defined format that is fairly universal. A typical test report will contain most of the following information.

1.  Background information:
    a.  Why the testing was conducted.
    b.  Family history.
    c.  Educational summary.
    d.  Important health and developmental history.

2.  Description of the student.

3.  Description of the testing situation.

4. Tests administered along with scores and percentiles.

5. Overall impressions.

6. Recommendations, including whether the student qualifies for special educational help, and if so, what type and how much.

7. Suggestion of treatment strategies, including an educational plan.

### Testing Instruments*

The school psychologist alone decides which tests to administer to the student. There are literally hundreds of tests to choose from,* and the psychologist should choose the ones that will give the most accurate and valid information about the student. It is not the intent of this section to describe or even name all of the instruments available to the educational psychologist. We will attempt to define some basic terms, give a short description of the more basic and well-known tests, and discuss in greater detail probably the most widely used test—the Wechsler Intelligence Scale for Children, Revised (WISC-R).

### TYPES OF TESTS

#### Global Intelligence Tests

The global intelligence tests attempt to measure the full range of a child's intellectual abilities. A particular test may assess both verbal and performance skills, or it may concentrate on one or the other. Some of the most widely used tests in this group include the Stanford-Binet, Wechsler Intelligence Scale for Children—Revised (WISC-R), Merrill Palmer Scale of Mental Tests, Wechsler Pre-School and Primary Scale of Intelligence (WPPSI), and Quick Screening Scale of Mental Development.

#### Verbal and/or Vocabulary Tests

These verbal and/or vocabulary tests measure a child's intellectual abilities in the verbal areas. There is no performance or written component to this type of instrument. Some examples are the Full-Range Picture Vocabulary Test, Peabody Picture Vocabulary Tests, and Lorge-Thorndike Intelligence Tests.

#### Performance (Visual-Motor) Tests

The performance instruments measure a child's intellectual abilities by nonverbal methods. They include such tests as the Draw-A-Man Test, Leiter International Performance Scale, and Raven Progressive Matrices.

*Refer also to Chapter 2 for general description of tests.

## Achievement Tests

Achievement tests generally measure academic abilities in specific subject areas. The scores provide a grade-level equivalent and a percentile ranking. Achievement tests can be administered both individually and in groups. One of the most commonly used is the Wide-Range Achievement Test (W.R.A.T.), which measures reading, spelling, and arithmetic achievement levels. Other achievement tests include the Gates Reading Tests, Gray Oral Reading Test, Spache Diagnostic Reading Scales, and the Lincoln Primary Spelling Test.

## Criterion Reference Tests

The purpose of the criterion reference tests is to reveal to the teacher exactly which skills the student has mastered. There are no grade equivalents or chronological age comparisons. The teacher keeps a profile chart or card on each student listing the skills in some type of sequential order. When a student somehow demonstrates proficiency in a skill, the teacher records this on the student's individual card and then develops strategies for instruction in unmastered skills. This type of record keeping allows the teacher to instruct the student in those areas that need special help. These tests are usually designed and established by each individual school district.

## Gross and Fine Motor Tests
## (Including Perceptual Tests)

Gross and fine motor tests attempt to measure gross or fine motor coordination development and perceptual abilities. Some examples are the Benton Revised Visual Retention Test, Beery-Briktenica Visual-Motor Integration Test, Frostig Developmental Tests of Visual Perception, Bender Visual Motor Gestalt Test for Children, and the Purdue Perceptual-Motor Survey.

## Projective Tests

Projective tests attempt to discover an individual's attitudes, motivations, and defense mechanisms. They are used to define and describe personality traits. Since the examiner must make some subjective evaluations in these tests, the results are sometimes suspect as to validity and reliability. The Rorschach is an example of this type of test. The Bender Gestalt and House-Tree-Person Tests are also helpful in this area.

## Language Tests

Language tests are instruments that attempt to measure a child's language functions to see whether either receptive associative or expressive language problems exist. The Illinois Test of Psycholinguistic Abilities (ITPA), the Porch Index of Communicative Abilities in Children

(PICAC), and the Auditory Discrimination Test (Wepman) are in this group.

## Vocational Assessments

Vocational assessments attempt to measure abilities, strengths, and attitudes regarding career choices and aptitudes. There are many specialized tests in this group, including the Kuder "General Interest Survey."

## Adaptive Behavior Rating Scales

Adaptive behavior rating scales are designed to indicate whether a child is operating at lower than normal levels in areas other than intellectual. Persons other than the child are interviewed (parents, teachers, etc.), and the results are compared with age scales for other children in the same functions. The social competence tests such as the Vineland Social Maturity Scale would fit into this group.

## GLOSSARY OF SOME COMMON TESTS

### Bender Visual Motor Gestalt Test for Children

The Bender Visual Motor Gestalt Test is used to measure fine motor skills, visual perceptual abilities, and often shows up personality problems such as anxiety. The test is also often used to suggest the presence of organic brain dysfunction. The test involves the copying of ten specific geometric figures, and utilizes a specific grading scale by age equivalents.

### Draw-A-Person

By having the child draw a picture of a member of the same sex, we can get an idea of his mental age, fine motor development, and developmental maturity. There is also some projective and personality information to be gained from this instrument.

### Gesell Index of Maturation

The student is asked to duplicate full geometric shapes in the Gesell Index of Maturation test. This is a good measure of fine motor skill and visual motor development in children under eight years of age.

### House-Tree-Person

In the House-Tree-Person test the child is asked to draw the above three objects. By analyzing these drawings we can get some good ideas of his personality development.

### Leiter International Performance Test

The Leiter International Performance test is an intelligence test that is designed to be culture-free and is completely nonverbal. It is quite valuable for testing children with hearing or language disabilities and is useful for ages two to adulthood.

### Peabody Picture Vocabulary Test

The Peabody Picture Vocabulary Test is a verbal intelligence test that is untimed and can be used for children from 2 to 18 years of age. It is an individually administered test of intelligence estimated by measuring receptive vocabulary.

### Stanford-Binet Intelligence Test

The Stanford-Binet is used to measure intelligence and is primarily a verbal test. It is highly regarded for assessing high and low levels of intellectual functioning and is a standard instrument for the identification of the mentally gifted child.

### Wechsler Adult Intelligence Scale (WAIS)

The WAIS is an intelligence test that is used for persons 16 or older.

### Wechsler Pre-school and Primary Scale of Intelligence (WPPSI)

The WPPSI is an intelligence scale for children 4 to 6½ years of age.

### Wepman Auditory Discrimination Test

The Wepman Auditory Discrimination instrument measures a child's ability to differentiate between similar and dissimilar phonemes. It is useful for the diagnosis of language disabilities.

### Wechsler Intelligence Scale for Children— Revised (WISC-R)

The WISC-R is probably the most widely used instrument utilized by school psychologists when assessing children for special educational placement. The average IQ (intelligence quotient) is 100 with a standard deviation of 15 points. The WISC-R measures two areas of intellectual potential:

1. Verbal intelligence

2. Performance intelligence

A full-scale intelligence quotient is then interpolated from the results of the verbal and performance scales. There are 12 subtests of the WISC-R, 6 on the verbal scale, and 6 on the performance scale. The various subtests are listed below, along with a very brief description of what they measure.

1. Verbal Scale

a. *Information:* The examinee responds to questions calling for general facts and information. This subtest is an index to how observant, interested, and experienced the child is in the world around him.

b. *Similarities:* This subtest measures the ability to tell how two things are alike and is a measure of concept formation. These concepts are measured at abstract, perceptual, and functional levels.

c. *Arithmetic:* This subtest shows how the child computes mathematical problems. It measures numerical reasoning, concentrating, and attention to task, and is not an achievement test.

d. *Vocabulary:* The examinee defines words with their major uses. This subtest is highly correlated with the information subtest. It measures general overall verbal knowledge and is one of the best single measurements of intelligence.

e. *Comprehension:* This subtest measures the response to commonsense questions and is a measure of social knowledge and practical judgment. It shows how socially experienced and sensible the child may be.

f. *Digit Span:* The examinee repeats a series of digits forward and backward. This subtest measures auditory recall and the ability to concentrate. It also measures memory span and the ability to make mental manipulations. A low score on this test is often correlated with learning disabilities. This is an optional subtest and is not used in scoring the full scale IQ.

2. Performance Scale

a. *Picture Completion:* The child shows what parts are missing in a picture. This is a measure of visual acuity, alertness, logical reasoning, and perceptual vigilance.

b. *Picture Arrangement:* The examinee arranges a series of pictures into a sequence so that they tell a sensible story. This subtest measures social understanding, sequencing ability, cause-and-effect relationships, and integration of thinking. Reading success depends on mastery of this skill.

c. *Block Design:* This subtest calls for the child to arrange blocks to duplicate a three-dimensional design. It measures abstract thinking, spatial relationships, and the ability to solve problems. This subtest is considered by many workers to be one of the best indicators of natural intellectual potential.

d. *Object Assembly:* The child is asked to put together puzzles. This activity measures visual motor skills and the ability to distinguish the whole from its parts. It shows the ability to organize one's approach around an idea or plan.

e. *Coding:* The examinee duplicates a specific code pattern, which provides a measure of the speed of learning and of the ability to solve problems involving spatial relationships. This subtest measures the ability to work well under pressure and dexterity in eye-hand coordination. This subtest is a good predictor of which students will have problems with paper and pencil activities.

f. *Mazes:* This subtest shows how the student is able to use a pencil to draw his way out of a printed maze. It measures fine motor skills, coordination, planning abilities, and techniques in measuring difficult problems. This is also an optional or supplementary subtest.

The verbal scale section of the WISC-R requires the examinee to respond in some verbal fashion, and these subtests are not timed. In the performance scale, time is a factor in scoring the test.

There are some very important things to look for when reviewing the results of the WISC-R. Each subtest has an average scale score of 10, with a range of 1 to 19. We should be aware of the following facts concerning the WISC-R.

1. Look to see if there is a discrepancy between the verbal and performance areas. A range of 15 or more points in the total scores may be significant in diagnosing a child's problem.

2. We must also be aware of wide differences in the subtest scale scores, which may be a clue to the presence of some neurological dysfunction.

3. Areas of strength shown in some of the subtests can indicate where our educational strategies should be aimed. Children respond best to instruction that is geared to their intellectual strengths rather than to their weaknesses. *Specific subtest performance may be an excellent clue to unlocking a child's educational box.*

## SUMMARY

There are a great many testing instruments available, and most psychologists become proficient in a small number of these in order to be able to work more efficiently. It is not necessary for the teacher, parent, or physician to know how to administer or interpret the results of a specific test. It is quite helpful, however, for the psychologist to review the test results with concerned individuals in order that all may know what the child's entire psychological profile is like and how strategies may be devised to help the child. Test results should be freely accessible to all concerned with the child, especially the parents, and uncertainties should be thoroughly explained to all. This type of total communication and cooperation will advance the educational team to the next step in help for the child—remediation.

## THE THERAPEUTIC AND REMEDIATION PROCESS

As we have so often mentioned in this book, the final educational plan for each child is the responsibility of the teacher. However, we have seen that many children with educational dysfunction are desperately in need of both medical and emotional or psychological help (see Chapter 7). This section will expand on the types of help (emotional or psychological) which may be needed. And the next chapter, Chapter 11, will again cover the medical approach.

A child may be identified as having a specific emotional problem by psychological testing, or the teacher may suggest this possibility by virtue of her observations of the child in the classroom and school. It is fairly well accepted and agreed upon that almost all children with learning handicaps of one type or another will need *some* type of psychological help—if only to learn how to deal with the fact that they *are* having some problems.

The remediation process often begins when the regular teacher works together with the school psychologist and/or the counselor or school nurse to determine the existence and nature of a perceived problem. This might happen when the teacher feels that the child is in need of some special help either within the school setting or in the community. Upon evaluation and verification of the need, the school psychologist will usually know where to direct the search for help and which professionals may be called upon. Some of the sources may include the following:

1.  The school principal.
2.  Other school psychologists.
3.  Counselors.
4.  School nurse.
5.  Career-guidance experts.
6.  Physicians.
7.  Clinical psychologists.
8.  Welfare workers.

9.  Social workers.

10.  Occupational therapists.

11.  Speech and language specialists.

12.  Curriculum specialists.

13.  Adaptive physical education specialists.

14.  Librarians.

15.  Administrators.

16.  Law-enforcement officials.

17.  Child-protection agencies.

18.  Any or all private and public agencies.

19.  Other teachers, both regular and special. (This last source is most important of all.)

There are many types of programs that can be considered as being appropriate to meet the psychological needs of a child. Within the school itself, the child can often receive the aid he needs simply through an understanding teacher, or perhaps through some time spent each day in a classroom or special area with a teacher specially trained in such care. Many children with learning handicaps need only to be understood more thoroughly, or perhaps to be allowed to spend more time with a teacher with whom they have developed a "special chemistry."

If this simple approach does not meet the child's needs, perhaps the school psychologist can spend some time with the child, either in the classroom or individually. Occasionally the psychologist is trained to bring a group of these children together—to let them share some of their difficulties with other students with similar disorders. The psychologist can often help the teacher formulate some educational as well as emotional strategies while observing the child in this manner. Whatever type of classroom approach *is* undertaken, it is usually a good idea for the teacher-psychologist team to formulate a plan for each child and to work together in the direction of understanding, accepting, helping, and perhaps changing the behavior of the child when necessary. There are many different types of approaches to accomplish this end. These include behavior modification and many others. Most often, the particular vehicle of assistance is not nearly as important as the people who are running it.

Many children will not respond to the classroom type of help and will need a more intensive approach. This will usually mean that the school team will work with the parents and child *outside* of the classroom and the approach will often include referral to outside sources.

There are many professionals in the community who are actively engaged in varied programs available to children with educational disorders. In fact, the plethora of such assistance is often a source of more confusion than aid to teachers, parents, and others. As we mentioned in Chapter 7, the range of training, expertise, and experience of the professionals active in this field is panoramic. With all of the programs that are available, and considering the huge diversity of workers offering their services, a parent literally needs a guide to sift through the super-market of psychological options and services. This type of guidance might be provided by the school psychologist, counselor, and often the physician. The type of psychological assistance the child and his family will need varies greatly from case to case. The training and degrees-manship of the therapist are quite often not as important to the end result of therapy as is the relationship of the child and his family to the therapist.

It is impossible to present any list of comprehensive review of psychological therapy in this type of book because of the vast quantity of approaches and theories. This is especially true if we go back to our basic premise of each child needing his own individual approach to remediation. What we will attempt to do is to present a short summary of the most popular, most often utilized, and seemingly most successful programs that are currently in action.

## Categories of Psychological Remediation

### PARENT-EDUCATION PROGRAMS

Children with educational dysfunction may be afflicted with many different types of problems, but they all have two things in common:

1. Because of some known or unknown cause, they are not learning to full potential; and

2. Because they are not learning properly, they are different from the "normal" children, and may behave in a quite different manner in other areas besides educational pursuits. If we also add to this the group of children whose behavior problems *precede* the learning disorder, we are truly dealing with a very large group.

Parents and teachers who deal with children with learning handicaps usually find out quite early that these children need a very different type of behavioral and disciplinary approach than is necessary for children without such problems.

Because of the need to fully explore different types of approaches for different children, we believe it to be of the utmost necessity to expose all parents of children with behavioral and educational disorders to one or more programs that explore the basic problems and possible solutions. Many schools have set up programs offering assistance for parents either on a regional or district level. There has also been a proliferation of parent-education programs on a community level, either privately run or perhaps as part of one of the local governmental mental health agencies. There have also been many books published on this subject, most of which we do not believe are very effective in most cases because of the need for an individual, personal approach in this field.

The majority of programs that seem to be of value are headed by an individual or team consisting of psychologists, marriage-family-child counselors, educators, social workers, and occasionally psychiatrists. Here again, the credentials are often not as important as the actual communication and learning that take place in such a program.

Some parent-education programs are vibrant, meaningful, and deal with issues and problems, whereas others consist of merely empty words and catch phrases. It is important for those of us involved with children with learning handicaps to find out about these programs before we refer our parents to them. It is often very helpful to include the child's teacher, baby-sitter, and others in his life as participants in these sessions so that all of the people who have an influence on the child are working together to help him.

It is almost a necessity that a child's parents become involved in some type of program that helps them learn about their child and how to understand his problems and deal with them more effectively. This cannot be done overnight, and most programs consist of somewhere between 15 and 30 hours as a starter. Often after a course like this is finished, the parents may have to keep right on working with some professional in order to further help them deal with their own problems as well as the child's. However, even if no other form of psychological help ever takes place for one reason or another, we strongly urge everyone who comes in contact with the parents of a child with behavior or learning disorders to become involved with a parent-education program— and the sooner the better!!

## FAMILY THERAPY

Since children do not exist in a vacuum, there is a great need to help each child fit into his own home environment as comfortably as possible. Because many children with learning disorders have associated emotional and/or behavior problems, there is usually a price to pay as far as the "happy home" is concerned. We have found it to be increasingly necessary to refer children and their families—including brothers and sisters—to therapists who have the experience, ability, and training to conduct some type of family-oriented therapy with the entire group. This may be some form of behavior modification, reality therapy or, perhaps other type of model—according to the needs of the family and the expertise of the therapist. There are many professionals involved in this type of work, including psychiatrists, clinical psychologists, marriage and family counselors, psychiatric nurses, social workers, and psychiatric technicians and aides. The important thing is the ability to work effectively with the family and to produce desirable results.

## GROUP THERAPY

Some children with learning and behavior problems have a need to learn to accept more responsibility for themselves. They also often need to learn how other children and adults perceive them—and how to accept responsibility for their own actions. We have had a most satisfactory experience with a group-counseling type of approach with this type of child over the past several years.

The group-therapy approach to emotional problems received its biggest boost from the large-scale involvement of adolescents in this type of therapy in the 1960s. This approach was especially effective in the case of "substance abusers,"* and has now mushroomed into an effective approach for persons of all ages with problems.

We have seen children as young as 6 or 7 respond quite well to this type of approach, although the attention span of the younger children is often a limiting factor. The most receptive age group for this type of intervention seems to be in the prepuberty group of 10- to 12-year-olds, and often in children who have had multiple problems and are just ready to enter junior high school. Often children who are currently being taken off psychotropic medications are found in these groups.

There are not many therapists trained for this type of treatment, and therefore there is not a large reservoir of experience in this area. It is imperative that the person who engages in this type of approach be able to roll up his sleeves, get on the floor with the kids, talk their language and love and respect them, and be ready for any eventuality! It takes a very special kind of person to be able to do this kind of work, but it is a very necessary adjunct to the other types of therapy available. There are currently some school psychologists and counselors who are conducting therapy groups in schools, which can be a helpful approach for some children.

---

*"Substance abusers" refers to people who are users of alcohol and drugs to a degree that causes physical and emotional abuse of their person.

It is very important for the parents and teachers of children involved in group therapy to be kept fully informed on the progress of the children. It is frustrating to see a child improve his behavior, but regress because his parent or teacher did not know what was going on in his life. The field of group therapy for young children is a sometimes confusing but quite necessary addition to the therapies available. Group therapy must not exist in a vacuum—and also must not be continued with a child who does not seem to fit into or benefit from this approach. We would welcome additional professionals becoming involved in this very challenging endeavor.

## INDIVIDUAL THERAPY

There have been countless studies to determine the results of psychiatric and psychological therapy on children with learning problems, hyperactivity, and other behavioral disorders. The results have often been less than satisfactory for many reasons. To begin with, we are dealing with many different types of children with diverse etiologies— thus, there would be no one general form of psychotherapy suitable for every child. Even in the group of children who are classified as neurologically hyperactive, there are diverse opinions as to the results of psychiatric or psychological therapy.

A second reason for the difficulty in assessing the results of this type of therapy is the very type of approach we are dealing with— individual. We have seen throughout this book that any type of isolated individual intervention in the care of a child with a learning handicap is likely to be much less successful than one that encompasses a comprehensive approach. Thus a child who is given psychiatric or psychological therapy without the total involvement of the entire team (especially without his family) will very often fail to show substantial improvement in the behavior that prompted such therapy.

Another important reason for the apparent inefficiency of individual psychotherapy in many of these children is the problem of assessment of the results of the therapy. Since so many of these children have multiple problems, there may be other things going on in their lives at the same time as the psychotherapy. Thus, it is difficult to assess just how much the psychotherapy itself has really helped.

For these and other reasons, the child with educational dysfunction is perhaps more suited to some other form of psychological remediation than individual therapy for his emotional problems—with some notable exceptions. For example, there are a small number of children who fall into the severely psychologically or behaviorally disturbed category. These children may be identified by the results of psychological

testing, and/or by a history of behavioral deviation in school and home—
or both. The severely emotionally disturbed child should be under the
care of a competent psychiatrist or a well-trained and experienced clinical
psychologist. Much of the therapy may be of the individual variety.
However, even the severely emotionally disturbed are becoming involved
in other types of therapy including group and family therapy.

### Summary of Common Psychological Approaches

The psychological help that is provided for most children with
learning and school problems is usually geared to remediation of the
particular problem, amelioration of the disturbing symptoms or behaviors, and in general helping these children to live with their handicaps.
Most children with learning handicaps are not severely emotionally
handicapped to start with, and it is most important to make sure that
the child and his family do not become emotionally sicker because of
his educational problems. Thus, a combined approach utilizing parent-
education programs, perhaps some group counseling, often a period of
family therapy, and occasionally some directed individual psychotherapy
might all be utilized in the long-term care of these children.

### OTHER TYPES OF PSYCHOLOGICAL APPROACHES

There have been many other methodologies developed in the
general area of psychological therapy to provide aid for children with
learning handicaps and there is no one school of psychological therapy
that is more successful with these children than any other. Again, we
must state that the child usually does best with the person he can best
relate to and who has had the most successful experiences with children
with similar problems. It is important that parents, teachers, and other
individuals working with these children do not become devoted to one
special school of therapy. These children are very much individuals, each
with his own unique problems, and whatever is necessary to help him
must be attempted, whether it fits into a certain current fad or not.

Other techniques of therapy have also been developed, which,
although not quite accurately classified as psychological, might
loosely fit into this category. One of the most recent developments in
the field of behavioral therapy is known as "bio-feedback." This type
of therapy involves the use of body functions such as hearing and vision
to monitor the occurrence of various symptoms or behaviors such as
headache, blood pressure elevation, or hyperactivity. The subject is
taught to recognize certain undesirable symptoms or behaviors by the use
of an electronic or mechanical monitoring apparatus that usually gives
a visual or auditory signal. He then learns how to control the particular
trait through his awareness of the actual behavior or symptom on his

sensory system. Bio-feedback has become a very useful experimental tool in the control of headache, tension, and some other symptoms, and recently has undergone some surveillance in hyperactive children of various etiologies. There may be some promising results from this type of approach in the future.

## SUMMARY

To summarize the psychological approach to the child with a learning handicap, we would like to reiterate the following points.

1.  All children who are having educational problems should have complete psychological testing done, including at least intellectual and achievement testing.

2.  Other testing such as language evaluation and personality inventory should be done when indicated.

3.  The school psychologist is a very important member of the evaluation and remediation team and should be used as a valuable source of help by the teacher.

4.  Teaching strategies may often be formulated by utilization of psychological test results.

5.  Children with learning handicaps may have psychological or emotional problems either as a cause for or as a result of their educational problems.

6.  The parents of children with educational and/or behavior problems should be strongly urged to attend at least one good parent-education program.

7.  Many children with educational dysfunction will need some type of counseling to help them deal with their problems.

8.  The most effective forms of psychological therapy at the present time seem to be family and group counseling, with individual psychotherapy being reserved for the more seriously disturbed children.

9.  The credentials of the therapist in many cases are not as important in the results of intervention as the relationship of the therapist to the child and his family and his experience in the field.

A final word might be added here concerning the effects of the pressures of the classroom on the teacher of children with learning handicaps. There are terribly stressful situations inherent in routine classroom activities of even normal children; but when the teacher becomes involved with children who are having learning or behavioral problems, these stresses are multiplied and are sometimes unbearable. Therefore, it is often wise and necessary for the school psychologist, counselor, and other professionals involved with the care of the child to turn some of their attention to the needs of the teacher. An occasional counseling session, rap group, or just an understanding word from time to time can go a long way toward making the classroom situation less burdensome for the teacher. This in turn is sure to pay handsome dividends in the educational remediation of the child with a learning disability.

# CHAPTER 11

# The Medical Approach

In Chapter 7 we discussed the role of the physician in the management of children with educational dysfunction. The importance of interdisciplinary communication and the ways this can be accomplished have also been mentioned. In this chapter we shall discuss the various specific noneducational, nonpsychological forms of treatment used for these children, and we will try to summarize the current status of medical therapy. Treatments dealing with nutritional categories such as vitamins, blood sugar metabolism, and food additives will also be included here. There are also a number of nonmedical but commonly used types of therapies that will be mentioned in this chapter. These include perceptual training and similar categories, which will be discussed along with the "paramedical" therapies.

## CONSTRAINTS

The entire field of medical and paramedical therapeutics for the child with a learning handicap is fraught with controversy. There have been numerous reviews of all aspects of this field that often present very conflicting and confusing points of view. Thus, it is extremely difficult to present this type of material without the probability of one or another group of interested parties disagreeing in one area or another. Another problem we must face is the fact that the information we are using as a base for our therapeutic recommendations is usually collected from many different and varied sources. As we previously stated, the diagnosis of one condition or another is often not based on solid data, and information we do have is often conflicting. Thus, the accepted medical model of a specific diagnosis-treatment form is often not available in this field.

Another problem lies in the diversity of the experience and interest of the physicians and other professionals who initiate and suggest the treatment programs. As we discussed previously (see Chapter 7), it is imperative that the care of these children be undertaken by doctors who are fully acquainted with all of the manifestations of the problem and who have the time and resources to carefully follow their patients. One of the important points we stress here is the extreme lability and total state of flux in the treatment of children with learning disorders. Not only does the treatment itself need constant reevaluation as new and changing concepts are uncovered in research, but we must also remember that we are dealing with constantly changing and developing children. Thus, the total remediation picture must be in a continuous state of reevaluation.

## HAWTHORNE EFFECT

A final but extremely important concept must be stressed before any specific therapies are presented. This is the so-called Hawthorne effect, whereby the degree of success of any form of treatment is often directly proportional to the enthusiasm of the professional who prescribes the particular therapy. For example, if a certain medication is given with a positive assuredness of its ability to modify certain symptoms, the doctor's positive feelings and words will often have a lot to do with the success of the drug. Conversely, if the physician prescribes a medication with a very negative approach, the treatment is not as likely to be a success.

This type of approach also applies to other forms of treatment besides medicine and to professionals other than doctors. If a teacher or parent feels strongly enough that a child will be helped by a special diet, that child *will* be helped; if a psychologist thinks that a certain form of psychotherapy is the *only* way to go, it will work for him; if someone else feels that perceptual training is going to help a child read better, and is enthusiastic enough about the approach, progress will be seen. Nowhere in the field of medicine or science do we see this type of phenomenon as clearly as in the treatment of the child with a learning handicap. Thus, with any of the treatments we propose for these children, we may be dealing with a "Hawthorne effect." The enthusiasm of the prescriber often has a major significant effect upon the success of a particular therapy. Whether this is a real improvement or exists only in the eyes of the people involved with the child is often hard to say.

Because of the overwhelming presence of this phenomenon, we must be very careful in judging the results of any type of treatment.

Anyone who attempts to help these children must be as relatively free of biases toward one form of treatment or another as is reasonably possible. We must learn to accept the results of well-constructed scientific research evaluations concerning various modes of therapy, even if it is not favorable to our own "special" approach. A person who stubbornly clings to a particular type of treatment, after it has been proven to be of less benefit than another approach, is not really helping the child. We all have various feelings about a certain therapy or approach, and it is all right to explore these avenues if we do not do it to the exclusion of another well-proven method. We must remember that we are dealing with children with multiple problems, often caused by diverse etiologies. We should try to use any kind of treatment that seems to work for a particular child as long as it is not harmful and doesn't take time, effort, and resources away from a more proven type of treatment. It is important to stress again that we are usually dealing with children with mixed types of problems. Therefore, we should not try to treat a *diagnosis,* but rather a *child* with *various specific, different,* and unique problems. Finally, it is urgent to restate the fact that the treatment of the child with educational dysfunction must be under constant surveillance so that the child can benefit from the changes that are constantly occurring in this field. *If the therapist becomes unchanging or complacent, it is the child who suffers from the lack of progress.*

## MEDICAL TREATMENT OF LEARNING HANDICAPS

This section will deal with diets, nutritional theories, and medications. In the following section the authors will try to present the material as briefly and objectively as possible. For each type of treatment, the majority opinion will be presented whenever possible. Well-tested and documented therapies will be stressed. However, we will try to mention *all* of the more popular modes of therapy. We will try to submerge the biases of the authors as much as possible in dealing with this material (and this is sometimes the most difficult part of presenting such information). Whenever possible we will present the material in outline or brief short-statement format, since this is the most informative and easy to understand method of handling this type of information.

### Nutritional Approach*

#### FOOD ADDITIVES, ARTIFICIAL

Over the past several years, many children have been placed on diets that eliminate foods containing food additives, preservatives, artificial coloring, and salicylates. The author of the popular book

*See Chapter 4 for background material on the nutritional approach.

describing the "KP" diet (*Why Your Child Is Hyperactive* by Benjamin Feingold) has made a case for many children with behavior and learning disorders fitting into this group.* There are isolated reports of workers throughout the country who report similar glowing results. However, the majority of the reports of children being placed on these stringent diets are quite equivocal.

There is no doubt that a diet free of artificial coloring or food additives might be healthier for a child. However, to attain such dietary purity, a child must often be placed in the position of being very different from his peers. This could negate any beneficial systemic or chemical effects of such an approach. In addition, the entire food-shopping and preparation habits of a family must be drastically altered to follow the diet, which might in itself be quite disruptive and explosive. This diet prohibits such commonly used foods as breakfast cereals, luncheon meats, soft drinks, and most fruits, as well as most medications and tooth paste, so that its acceptance is often not too easily managed.

There have been several recent well-controlled and unbiased studies sanctioned by the National Institute of Mental Health concerning the efficacy of this approach. One study by Conners showed a slight statistical improvement in some of the children, but it was far from conclusive and included only 18 children.** The results of other trials at this writing show no major benefits from the diet.*** Other studies using larger groups of children are now in progress. It is probable that occasional children will be found to benefit from this approach, but it is far from being a panacea.

However, it is certainly a worthwhile effort to acquaint parents with the "KP" diet. If the family wishes to embark on this type of approach, we *must* be supportive. We have seen some children in the younger age group (three to six) with multiple neurological defects seem to show benefits from the diet. It is very difficult to get older children to accept it—or to stick to it. Many parents who feel that the diet is working would be shocked to find out how much their child is actually cheating! We must always be careful with this diet to assure that we do not make the child feel he is *more* different than he was before. If this happens, the resultant rebellious behavior is often a good deal more disturbing than the behavior that suggested the diet in the first place!

We feel that if the emotional climate of the home is such that there would be no hardship involved in placing the family on such a regimen, it may be worth a trial. We might expect to see the best results in younger

---

* The "KP" diet was so named because Dr. Feingold was working at the Kaiser-Permanente Clinic in Oakland, California, when his book and the diet were popularized.

**Conners, C. Keith *et al.* "Food Additives and Hyperkinesis: A Controlled Double-Blind Experiment," *Pediatrics,* 58, No. 2 (Aug. 1976), pp. 154–166.

***Wender, E. "Food Additives and Hyperkinesis," *American Journal of Diseases of Children,* 131, No. 5 (Nov. 1977), pp. 1204-1206.

children with serious global neurological dysfunction. It must be stressed, however, that the changes seen with this particular diet must be as carefully documented as if dealing with a medication. Finally, this approach should not be undertaken without medical guidance since there can be some nutritional and vitamin deficiencies associated with a rigid diet of any type. This is especially true for the intake of vitamin C and the general nutrient value of breakfast for the "KP" diet.

## FOOD ALLERGY

As we have previously discussed (Chapter 4), many workers in the field of food allergies feel that some, or many, of the children who manifest learning and behavioral problems do so because of some type of allergy. This may take the form of any type of environmental stimulus, including foods.

The actual treatment of a child with allergic disease is often quite difficult. This is especially true in the case of the child with suspected food allergies. There can be all kinds of problems associated with a diet that eliminates various special groups of foods—problems such as hidden cheating, making the child different, and the improper documentation of results because of bias of the patient, physician, or both.

If a child has major allergic manifestations of the respiratory or gastrointestinal tracts, such as wheezing, nasal stuffiness, or severe diarrhea, he may show many signs and symptoms very similar to those exhibited by a "hyperactive" child. Therefore, it is often prudent to suggest a trial of a special diet for a short period of time. This might make the child feel better as far as his respiratory or gastrointestinal tract is concerned, and thus he may learn better. In some cases the diet could conceivably produce a positive effect on the central nervous system itself. However, it is often very difficult to know which children to treat in this manner and what foods to eliminate. Most people feel that milk and milk products, sugar, white flour, and chocolate are the greatest offenders. Since a period of three to four weeks of the elimination diet will usually be sufficient to note the difference, this approach is viable in a cooperative family.

It is very interesting to note along these lines, that there seems to be a very high correlation between children who show learning, behavior, and hyperactivity problems and those who had signs of respiratory or gastrointestinal "allergy" when younger, especially in infancy. The allergists tell us that this is proof of the high correlation between these conditions. Many workers in the field, however, feel that there is a strong predisposition in these children to develop *many* different kinds of problems, and that *chronic individual and family stress situations* are the *common denominator* for the behaviors and symptoms, *not foods or pollens.*

Whatever the real truth, we do see many children who show "allergic" signs such as nasal stuffiness, dark circles under the eyes, aches and pains, sneezing and coughing, and abdominal symptoms who *also* show educational dysfunction. Whether the milk, chocolate, or other food is the real culprit or not, it may sometimes be worthwhile placing the children on the proper elimination diet along with other methods of allergy control to document any benefits from such therapy. We must remember here as in other types of similar treatment—this should be considered a plan of treatment, not a religion.

## SUGAR

The entire matter of dietary sugar in the approach to behavioral and educational problems is discussed in Chapter 4. As we mentioned, there are some workers in the field who feel that either low blood sugar or direct exposure to sugar-containing foods can be a determining factor in the symptomatology of children with learning problems. We have also seen that the actual documentation of hypoglycemia or behavioral quirks secondary to sugar ingestion is extremely difficult and most of the time impossible. Actual measurement of the blood sugar in children who are having behavioral problems has been quite unrewarding in most cases. Also, the glucose tolerance test is often normal in children who seem to respond to dietary changes in sugar. Thus, it is very difficult to know exactly what to do as far as this controversial field is concerned.

We know that a diet rich in sweets and "junk foods" is certainly not a healthy one. We also know that the theoretical after-meal drop of a person's blood sugar is not as likely to occur if many small meals are eaten rather than a few large ones. It is also true that protein foods are less likely to be associated with a rapid drop of blood sugar than are pure carbohydrates. Finally, we know that the child most likely to show a detrimental sugar reaction has certain characteristics such as extreme sensitivity, touchiness, often blonde or red hair, fair skin, and he may show extreme fluctuations in behavior and sleep disturbances (see Chapter 4). If this child is also a greedy "sweets" eater, especially at breakfast (including sugared cereals and doughnuts), it might be worthwhile trying to change his dietary patterns. A positive response to this type of dietary manipulation will often be seen in several days to a week. (As a matter of fact, it is probably a good idea to get *all* children—not only those with problems—on a more sensible and nutritious diet.) It is therefore a good plan to ask the parents of those children who have learning problems to make sure that their children eat a good breakfast with no sugared cereal or doughnuts. These children should eat foods such as eggs, meat, milk, and perhaps some whole wheat toast and peanut butter. We should ask that these children use cheese or peanuts as a snack rather than cookies or candy. And we should also try to make sure that there is no more than a two-hour spacing between some type of intake, preferably proteins. The teacher can sometimes notice the difference in behavior in these children by seeing an improvement when they are allowed to nibble on cheese and nuts instead of sweets, as well as having them eat more meals with less carbohydrates.

The children who respond to this dietary change may really belong to the neurologically hyperactive group who are already under stress due to their inability to handle all of the incoming stimuli presented to them by the classroom situation. The fall in blood sugar after the pure sugar ingestion may be just enough to prevent the child from functioning optimally. Perhaps when these theoretical blood-sugar fluctuations are controlled, the neurological components become easier to control also. This dietary therapy is quite speculative according to most workers, however, and also because of the similarity of symptoms in this group of children to those symptoms and signs caused by stress alone, the total picture of sugar metabolism versus emotional stress must be carefully understood before ascribing positive results to this one type of therapy.

We have certainly seen some children who seem to respond positively to this dietary approach, although it is far from the total answer. Furthermore, because of the highly speculative nature of this theory, we must remember to use it in a nonthreatening, sensible manner. We must not make a child a total outcast from his friends so that he cannot attend birthday parties and other such events without feeling too different. If this type of moderation is followed in the sugar controversy, the child may derive the full benefit from this approach.

## THE DIETARY TOWER OF BABEL

In their zest to latch on to all of the latest trends and fads in the field of behavior and educational problems, many well-meaning but ill-informed people have started giving nutritional advice to parents. This may be all right in some cases, but can occasionally be quite confusing, or at times even dangerous.

We have heard of a case where parents were told that their child looked like he was allergic and also probably had hypoglycemia; they were also told that the "KP" diet should be started to cure his school problems. Thus, the parents were told to feed the child increased milk for breakfast, fruit for snacks, and lots of eggs and fish. What the "expert" didn't realize was that milk is the first food we would want to eliminate in an allergic child, and eggs and fish might follow closely. Also, most fruits are prohibited in the "KP" diet since they contain the prohibited salicylates. Thus, the parent was doing nothing to really prove or disprove any kind of food sensitivity by the change in diet as suggested by the "friend."

There is a great deal of confusion and difficulty deciding how to formulate diets that will be nutritious and will also eliminate possible offenders at the same time. A person who is driven by zeal instead of some type of scientific approach based on sound nutritious and medical facts is of no help in this field, especially if the parents are made to feel guilty about what they can or cannot accomplish.

The logical conclusion to this type of dilemma involves a sound approach with a nonthreatening type of format—and lots of understanding. And finally, we must all remember that if we think our children follow our dietary directions completely and without diversion, we are totally ignorant of the facts of life about children and their eating habits!

## VITAMINS

We have previously discussed the roles of some of the vitamins in the metabolic chain of events in our bodies. There are some chemomedical problems over which there is no controversy regarding the necessity for an increased daily intake of vitamins. For example, children with malabsorption problems do need an increase in Vitamins A, D, E, and K. An occasional child will need increases in Vitamin B6 because of a metabolic disorder which produces seizures. Sometimes children being treated with dilantin need increased amounts of folic acid and Vitamin D. And in some instances of certain genetic disorders, increased vitamin intakes are indicated.

In Chapter 4, we referred to the school of orthomolecular therapy, where large doses of vitamins, especially the water-soluble B and C groups, are utilized to treat behavior and emotional problems (megavitamin therapy).

Over the past decade large numbers of adults with various mental and emotional disorders have been treated with megavitamins. Treatment usually included large doses of nicotinic acid (niacin or B3) riboflavin (vitamin B2), ascorbic acid (vitamin C), pyridoxine (vitamin B6), calcium pantothenate, vitamin B12, folic acid, thiamin (vitamin B1), and others. The results have been reported as very encouraging by a small group of workers, but as valueless by the vast majority of observers. This has obviously become a very controversial subject.

Where the megavitamin therapy was carried over into the treatment of children with behavior disorders, the same type of controversies rage. There is still a small group of workers who feel that it may work in certain children with severe learning problems, neurological dysfunction, or psychoses. However, most people who have tried or evaluated this type of therapy feel that it is of no value, or at times may even be dangerous because of possible overdoses. There may sometimes be a fair amount of nausea and vomiting associated with the ingestion of such large amounts of vitamins. There is also some evidence that long-term administration of nicotinic acid (vitamin B3) may lead to skin redness, itching, rapid heartbeat, liver damage, and high blood sugar.

Thus, it is fairly well agreed upon, except for a small number of dissenters, that behavioral, neurological, and learning problems in children have very little to do with the disordering of brain cells that are dependent on large doses of vitamins to restructure them. It might be added, however, that there is some current research going on in areas of brain function and memory that could ostensibly include some limited role for vitamin therapy. The results of this approach will be worth waiting for.

The chief difficulty in evaluating vitamin therapy is that there is no simple laboratory test to determine an individual's specific needs for some of the vitamins. It is postulated that some people need more than the minimum recommended dose. Also some people may have an intestinal absorption problem that requires more vitamins than are usually obtainable in the average diet. And some people may want the vitamins to work—and so they do! This is considered a placebo effect and is seen with other types of medications also.

Advocates of vitamin therapy feel that vitamin B6 and others in the B group are essential for memory skills, and that they may play a role in the total care of some educationally dysfunctioning children. It is thought that those who respond best are children with so-called psychosomatic symptoms such as asthma, hay fever, eczema, migraine, fatigue, ulcers, abdominal pain, and bed-wetting. However, the obvious trap of emotional versus physical causes must be very carefully considered both in therapy and in symptomatology in this group of children.

In general, the field remains quite controversial, and the bulk of evidence does not support a proven cause-effect relationship between vitamin therapy and behavior. However, if the adherents to and recipients of this approach work within a sensible, open-minded framework, we can continue to judge the results of such therapy at the same time as we use all of the other available treatments to provide optimum care for the child.

## MINERALS

Calcium and magnesium therapy are sometimes used to treat hyperactive children because of a theoretical low level of these minerals in the blood of such children. Restless children with insomnia would theoretically tend to benefit the most from this type of therapy. Zinc is essential to the proper functioning of many enzyme systems, and a deficiency of this mineral may be present in a child who shows white spots in the nails, or short stature with sparse hair. A few weeks of a zinc supplement would give us the answer as to whether any deficiency exists. The recent emergence of hair analysis has been considered a valid scientific method of assaying the level of minerals in the body. Future positive findings along these lines may be helpful in the treatment of children with an educational dysfunction. At the present time, however, there is no widespread use of mineral therapy in this field except in limited cases. Controlled studies up to the present time have shown no major benefits. However, an open mind must be kept in this area as research goes on.

## COFFEE THERAPY

There has been a recent attempt to substitute one or more cups of coffee for stimulant medication in the treatment of neurologically hyperactive children. Thus, the children who seem to respond favorably to a stimulant drug are given a "socially acceptable" substitute—coffee— and they often react in the same manner as they did to medication.

This approach is perhaps helpful to the parent who feels guilty about the use of medications in his child, but it is actually likely to be detrimental. The effect of the coffee is the result of the caffeine, which is a stimulant similar to amphetamines such as dexedrine and methyl-phenidate (Ritalin). Caffeine also comes in a little white pill as well as in a dark brown liquid in a cup. The rest of the contents of the coffee are certainly not healthy for the child, and the amount of caffeine is totally unregulated from "dose" to "dose." This type of therapy is looked upon with total disfavor by most professionals in the field, although it has achieved a certain amount of notoriety. It has become less popular over the past several years.

## Medications

## GENERAL INFORMATION

We must reiterate at the start of this discussion: *A pill does not cure the problems inherent in a child with learning disabilities!* What we are trying to do when we prescribe medication for these children is to correct any medical or chemical disabilities. We attempt to get the child into the best possible physical condition so that the educational process can proceed as normally as possible.

If we consider all of the medical conditions that can interfere with a child's proper learning (see Chapter 5), we are aware that many differ-ent types of medications may be useful at various times in a child's life. Infections, hormone imbalances, and allergic disorders—all may be treated and often cured with one type of medication or another. However, there are certain groups of drugs that have been associated with the treatment of learning disabilities as a separate entity. These drugs are usually classified as *psychotropic* (having an effect on the mind or brain). Many different types of psychotropic medications have been tried for children with learning disabilities over the years, including stimulants, tranquilizers, depressants, antidepressants, antihistamines, and anticonvulsants. The information concerning some of the results of these treatments is controversial and often unsubstantiated. Although extensive studies have been carried out on drug therapy, workers in the field are still not in complete agreement on many aspects of this type of medication. In spite of this lack of accord, we will attempt to make some statements of a general nature, and then proceed to a description of the more common medications.

1.   The most widely used psychotropic drugs are the mild antidepressants or stimulants, such as methylphenidate (Ritalin) and the amphetamines (Dexedrine).

2.   By far the most beneficial results in the total chemotherapeutic approach to these children have been achieved with the use of stimulants.

3.   In the authors' opinion there is very limited application for the use of tranquilizer drugs in most children with learning disorders, although some workers would disagree with this.

4.   Each child may respond to a medication in his own special way. Thus, dosage and follow-up must be carefully monitored.

5.   It is important to judge the results of drug therapy in the broad context of all persons concerned with the child—including the teacher, the family, the physician, and the child himself.

6.   There are basically four groups of children who may respond to medications given expressly for a learning problem.

      a.   Neurologically hyperactive children with a short attention span.

      b.   Children with convulsive disorders.

      c.   Children with emotional disorders such as severe anxiety, depression, deep neurosis, or psychosis.

      d.   Children who seem to manifest a pure reading or other type of learning disorder and who seem to be more motivated or show a positive attitude change if given very small amounts of medications, especially the stimulants.

Medications should be given with the full approval and understanding of all parties involved, including the child. Effect and duration of therapy must be meticulously monitored through close communication between all persons responsible for the child.

## TYPES OF MEDICATION

In each category below we will list the chemical and brand names, theory of action when known or surmised with high probability, important side effects, and dosage when applicable. In the case of the stimulants, since this is the largest group used, we will also try to present a glossary of important and often-questioned points of interest.

### Stimulants (Mild Antidepressants): Theory of Action

Stimulants are the most widely utilized medications in the field of learning and behavioral disorders. They have been used to treat children with behavior problems since 1937, and they are felt to be the most useful of all of the drugs used for this purpose.

We are not absolutely certain of the specific actions of these drugs, but it is widely thought that they exert their effects by the stimulation of certain arousal mechanisms in children who are lacking this stimulation due to a genetic or other cause. The children who lack this arousal system fit into the neurologically hyperactive group. The specific stimulatory action of the medications promotes a better control over attention, as well as more organized motor activity, and also helps the child screen out unimportant or disruptive environmental stimuli. If we use the model for short attention span and hyperactivity that we first presented in Chapter 4, we can graphically show how these medications most probably exert their effects.

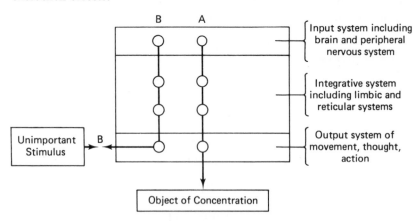

A    Stimulation of train of events to concentrate properly

B    Stimulation of train of events to block out unimportant stimulus at Point B

It is postulated (see Figure 11-1) that the blockage at positions C and D (which when operating interfered with A, attention span, and B, the desired blocking out of environmental distractions) is overcome by the stimulants, which neutralize these blockages at C and D. Thus, these medications help to normalize the areas of chemical and/or electrical blockage in the brain and facilitate the smooth passage of the impulses necessary for arousal, attention span, and screening out. These drugs do not act as depressants in these children as some people think. Rather, by promoting control over attention and environmental annoyances, the side effect of less impulsive, undirected behavior is attained—thus a hyperactive child becomes more controlled and less active. The stimulants seem to exert most of their action on the following areas of the brain: the reticular activating systems, hypothalamus, and limbic systems. These areas are in the mid-brain and not in the cerebral cortex. If stimulant medication is used on people with a normal arousal system, the result is overstimulation.

## Types of Stimulant Drugs

**Amphetamines:**   There are several different chemical forms of amphetamines. These include:

Amphetamine (Benzedrine)

Dextroamphetamine (Dexedrine)

Methamphetamine (Desoxyn, Methedrine)

The most commonly used drug of this group is Dexedrine, which is usually given in dosages of between 5 and 40 milligrams (mg) daily. These drugs have been used for hyperactivity since 1937, but are not currently used nearly as much as other medications such as Ritalin. The

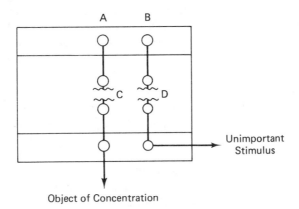

*Figure 11-1.   Mode of action of stimulant medications.*

side effects of the amphetamines include overactivity, stomach upset, loss of appetite, growth delay, sleep problems, and heart palpitations. They are not addictive nor habit forming when used to treat hyperactivity and short attention span.

**Methylphenidate (Ritalin):**   Ritalin is the most popular medication used for learning disorders and hyperactivity today and has been in use since 1956. Ritalin seems to have less side effects than the amphetamines and may work in a higher percentage of cases. Some workers believe that if Ritalin does not give a desired effect, the amphetamines should be tried, and vice versa. Others feel that there is no evidence to support this view. The daily dose of Ritalin is usually from 5 to 60 mg, although some doctors will use doses up to 80 or 100 mg daily. A dose of 1½ to 2 mg per kilogram of body weight (or lower) will usually produce no serious side effects. Most children will respond nicely to 10 mg once or twice daily, and some to as little as 5 mg. Occasionally children will need up to 15 or 20 mg several times a day for a desired effect, but we rarely go above this dosage. Although adverse effects such as loss of appetite, sleep problems, skin rashes, and growth depression are seen, these are usually rare except for the appetite suppression. This may be quite a problem in some children and occasionally may necessitate either stopping the medication or administering it *with or after meals,* which cuts down its effectiveness. Another way to deal with this problem is by giving the child drug "holidays" on weekends or during the summer where possible. An occasional child will show signs of headache, crying, abdominal pain, or depression when first started on Ritalin, but these symptoms usually quickly disappear in several days.

There have been several recent reports of skin rashes secondary to Ritalin therapy which should necessitate stopping the medication for a time until the rash disappears. Another rare but disturbing adverse reaction has been the development of facial tics and grimaces, sometimes associated with the use of foul language. The authors have seen this in only one patient who was on a very large dose of medication, but nevertheless, this can be a disturbing consequence of treatment when it occurs.

If a child has trouble sleeping at night when he is being treated with Ritalin, it is usually necessary to cut down or stop the evening or afternoon dosage. Some physicians administer a mild sedative at bedtime to counteract this side effect, which the authors would disagree with for the most part.

Ritalin is usually given 30 to 45 minutes before mealtime, since it can be destroyed by stomach acid produced by the ingestion of food. The duration of effectiveness is usually 4 hours, but this may vary from child to child. A more complete discussion of the philosophy of the use of stimulant medications will follow the listing of the other drugs in this category.

**Pemoline (Cylert):**   Cylert is a newer medication that has been in use for a shorter period of time than the other stimulants. The way it works is similar to the other drugs, but the duration of its effect is longer—perhaps up to 10 hours. This drug is therefore effective in children who might have to take several daily doses of medication to keep on an "even keel." Cylert has been used for older children (over nine or ten) for the most part, and seems to be particularly effective in the younger teen-ager. The side effects are similar to those of the amphetamines and Ritalin. One of the drawbacks to the use of Cylert is the fact that it often takes several weeks to see a beneficial effect, while side effects may occur earlier. The dose of Cylert varies from 37.5 to 112.5 mg daily, and the medication can be given with meals without losing any potency.

**Deanol Acetamidobenzoate (Deaner):**   Deaner was one of the first drugs used, but it is very rarely prescribed today. It is a mild stimulant that does not seem to have as beneficial an effect as some of the other drugs. There are really very few children actually being treated with Deaner today, and experts are in disagreement as to whether it is very effective. The dose is from 25 to 300 mg daily.

There are other stimulant medications on the market, but they are only rarely used for learning and behavior problems, so we will not list them here. Before moving on to the other psychotropic medications used in children with learning or behavior disorders, we will present a list of facts about the stimulants that might be useful to know since they are the most commonly used medications. The following statements apply to the use of the stimulants only, and most specifically to Ritalin, Dexedrine, and Cylert, which are the three most commonly used drugs in this group.

*Facts about Stimulant Medications*

1.   Stimulant medications are most effective in the child between 5 and 9 years of age. They are often either ineffective or poorly tolerated below age 5, and their action is sometimes difficult to document over ten years of age.

2.   Many workers discontinue the use of stimulants entirely by 12 years of age, although some children do continue to show positive effects through the teen years. This is a highly individualized situation.

3.   There are really no specific physical, psychological, or laboratory tests available to pinpoint which children will benefit from the

stimulants. The best we can do is to make an educated appraisal on the basis of the child's history, the school report, and a thorough examination. *However, a short trial of medication, carefully monitored, is usually the only real way we have of telling which children will actually benefit from such therapy.* The beauty of using these drugs (except for Cylert) is that they act so quickly, and the effect stops within several hours. Therefore, we can find out if the medication will be beneficial or detrimental quickly and easily.

4.   A trial of stimulant medication is often the only method of differentiating the true neurologically hyperactive child from other types of "hyperactives."

5.   Stimulation medication is usually given only to help the child pay attention better. Behavioral control is often a desirable secondary effect.

6.   Children do not become addicted to stimulants when they are given for the proper indications.

7.   These medications must not be prescribed without a *total* evaluation of the *child* and his *home* and *school* situation.

8.   There must be a careful monitoring of the effects of any medications, but especially when used in children with learning disorders. It is imperative for the physician to seek the help of parents and school personnel to decide whether a drug is helpful to begin with, and most importantly if it *continues* to aid the child's performance.

9.   Stimulant medications at the proper dosage level do not make neurologically hyperactive children sleepy or subdued. These medications *do* cause the children to be calmer and more able to focus their energies in an effective manner.

10.   The learning that takes place while a child is taking stimulants may be "state-related" (related to the effect of the drug at that time); in spite of this fact, the educational process in the majority of these children seems to be enhanced.

11.   The question of when to give the medications—once or several times daily, including weekends and during the summer—is highly debatable. Some physicians feel that a child should be in the same neurological "condition" at all times and thus should have medication as frequently as three or four times daily every day of the year until it is stopped; others feel that once each day before school is sufficient. The answer probably lies somewhere in between, and according to our experience we would recommend highly individualized treatment for each child.

There are some children who have an attentional problem only in school and can do well with one or occasionally two doses daily. Other children have such enormous swings of behavior that it becomes necessary to use the medication more frequently, including weekends and summer vacations. In any case, each child must be followed carefully and evaluated frequently to see what *his* particular needs are.

12.    In children who show very wide swings of activity when taking a medication like Ritalin, a longer acting drug such as Cylert or Desoxyn might be useful.

13.    The action of the stimulants is very individualized. Some children might become quite drowsy or even stuporous if given too high a dose; others may just show increased activity. Dosages may also vary a great deal from child to child. Occasionally the effect may be U-shaped, whereby a small overdose may cause overactivity and a larger one withdrawal or stupor. The overtreated hyperactive may become irritable, withdrawn, tense, or appear to be paranoid. Massive overdosage causes gaze avoidance, abnormal movements, and perhaps intense withdrawal. If the point of overdose and effective doses is similar, the drug should be withdrawn.

14.    Children with learning problems who show no obvious overactivity and have a seemingly normal attention span may still occasionally show a very positive effect with stimulants. This may be due to the child's arousal centers not being stimulated to the fullest capacity without the medication.

15.    The best results with the use of the stimulants for this condition are seen in the seven- or eight-year-old with a supportive family.

16.    The changes that the stimulants may produce in a child can be seen in his behavior, school work, handwriting, and motor performance. The changes may also be manifested in better performance of certain psychological tests including block design, coding, mazes, continuous attention test, Bender, and draw-a-man. The documentation of the effects of medication should be in the form of objective information including retesting, rather than totally by purely descriptive or anecdotal methods. In this way, biases are less likely to be perpetuated.

17.    As stated above, the enthusiasm with which any type of treatment is prescribed, including these medications, will have an effect on its evaluation—often a very great one. This may lead to various inconsistencies in the reporting of effects and should be taken into consideration.

18.    A child who is started on stimulant medication occasionally may actually seem worse and have some negative side effects for as long as the first week. Often he will then start to respond beautifully.

19.   Physicians and teachers may vary in their feelings as to whether a teacher should be notified when a child is placed on medication. The most accurate method of evaluation of the effect of medications is where the observer does *not* know what has been given. This eliminates the possibility of bias. However, in many instances because the teacher is such a valuable and objective member of the team, this is really not a big problem.

20.   The appraisal of the effect of a particular medication must be received from parent, teacher, *and* child.

21.   Occasionally the positive effects of a medication cannot be appreciated until it is stopped, and the child's activities are monitored without the drug.

22.   Drug therapy is important and sometimes essential, but *never sufficient* by itself for the total approach to the care of the child.

23.   Psychological testing and other types of evaluation should be done under the best possible conditions for the child. If a short attention span interferes with testing, it should be repeated with the child on the medication. Some very useful information can be gathered by this before- and after-type of evaluation.

24.   All children with learning or behavior problems do not need and should not be given medication. However, stimulants are effective in approximately 70% of the children with neurological hyperactivity. When the drug is effective, it will produce a very positive effect in the child's entire approach to education and life in general. This far outweighs any minor side effects that have been attributed to the stimulants.

25.   All children who are being treated with stimulant medications should have periodic assessment of growth and weight gain as well as complete blood counts (at least every six months).

In summary the stimulant medications such as amphetamines, Ritalin, and Cylert stimulate the child's nervous system's arousal mechanisms, which increase the tone of the attention centers, enhance the capacity for selective inhibition, and organize the motor performance. Thus, the child is able to attend better and more selectively, control impulsive behavior, improve various performances, and engage in the educational processes more skillfully. Other effects of these medications may be a decrease in aimless, uncontrolled activity, improved visual and auditory perception, enhanced language function and speech synthesis, and an improved self-image. Not all effects may be seen in all children because of the great variability of the action of medications on each individual child.

*Major Antidepressants*

The major antidepressant drugs have a different chemical action on the brain than the milder stimulants. Most of their action is not exerted by primary stimulation. They are much more potent medications for the most part, and have not been used as widely or for as long as the mild stimulants. There is some difference of opinion as to the efficacy of these drugs for learning disorders or attentional problems, and the reports are not as conclusive as for the amphetamine-Ritalin group. The side effects and actions of this group are in general much stronger than with the previous medications and must be regarded very carefully when used. The principal uses of these drugs are in the treatment of depression.

**Imipramine Hydrochloride (Tofranil, Imavate, Janimine):** Imipramine has only very recently been used for hyperactive children. The earliest use of imipramine in children was for bed-wetting (enuresis), where it still is widely used, although with mixed reviews. Although there are reports of some success in the modification of undesired behaviors and in the enhancement of attention, there is still some controversy as to the use of this drug in the neurologically hyperactive child. The most likely indication would be in the depressed, mildly neurotic, or disturbed child who also exhibits a short attention span. Another use for imipramine would be in the child who is neurologically hyperactive and has a major bed-wetting problem also. The medication seems to allow the child a lighter sleep pattern and thus enables him to recognize more easily the stimulus of a full bladder.

The side effects of imipramine as well as the other drugs in this group include:

| | |
|---|---|
| Blood pressure fluctuation | Dry mouth |
| Nervousness | Visual problems |
| Confusional states | Rashes |
| Anxiety | Vomiting |
| Restlessness | Blood changes |
| Sleep disorders | Jaundice |
| Hallucinations | Hormone changes |
| Nightmares | Constipation |
| Numbness and tingling | Seizures |

The dosage of Tofranil in children varies from 10 to 75 mg daily.

The other major antidepressant drugs are very rarely used in children, and only in very special circumstances. Their potency and side effects must be carefully evaluated before prescribing. These other medications include:

1.  Nortriptyline (Aventyl)

2.  Amitriptyline (Elavil)

3.  Phenelzine (Nardil)

4.  Desipramine (Norpramin; Pertofrane)

5.  Doxepin (Sinequan)

6.  Combination of Amitriptyline and Perphenazine (Etrafon; Triavil)—a tranquilizer-antidepressant combination.

7.  Combination of meprobamate and benactyzine (Deprol)—also a tranquilizer-antidepressant combination.

8.  Isocarboxazid (Marplan)

9.  Tranylcypromine Sulfate (Parnate)

The above group of drugs has found its most common usage in enuretic children and also occasionally in children with extreme school phobia. The side effects are similar to those of imipramine (Tofranil), and because of their potency most of them are not suggested for use in children.*

### Tranquilizers: General Characteristics

Tranquilizers include many different drugs, most of which are not of proven value in the care of the neurologically hyperactive child, except as an adjunct when the child exhibits other manifestations of emotional illness, such as severely uncontrollable behaviors, loss of reality (psychosis), extreme agitation, and other such major emotional disorders. The prescribing of such drugs is usually done most effectively by a well-trained child psychiatrist or neurologist.

The tranquilizers are supposedly given to produce mental calmness without extreme dulling, such as might be seen with sedative drugs such as phenobarbital. Some of the tranquilizers are used in conjunction with the stimulants, but there is no solid proof that these combinations of drugs are any more effective than the stimulants alone in most of these children.

The tranquilizers are divided into two groups—major and minor. The major tranquilizers are suggested for use only in severely emotionally disturbed children, because of the side effects, as well as the questionable efficacy in less affected children. Side effects may include:

*The use of some of these drugs on children diagnosed as being psychiatrically depressed is advocated by some workers (see Chapter 3).

1. Skin rashes

2. Bowel problems

3. Weight problems

4. Blood disorders

5. Breathing difficulty

6. Motor and sensory disturbances

7. Severe spasms of the face and body

8. Convulsions

It is also thought that some of these drugs create a reduced attention span in most children, and thus *learning may be adversely affected.*

We will list the more commonly used major and minor tranquilizers with a statement as to their general usage, when applicable.

## Major Tranquilizers

**Chlorpromazine (Thorazine):** Thorazine is used mostly for psychotic children and has very little use for the usual "hyperactive" child.

**Thioridazine (Mellaril):** Mellaril is probably the most widely used of the major tranquilizers in these children. Mellaril seems to promote appetite and sleep and thus counteracts some of the bad side effects of the stimulants. It is also reported to be useful in very anxious, emotionally labile, and disturbed children who also show hyperactive behavior. Mellaril is popularly used in conjunction with Ritalin or the amphetamines, but its beneficial effects are far from proven. The toxicity and side effects are perhaps less than with the other major tranquilizers.

**Trifluoperazine (Stelazine):** Stelazine is also used in conjunction with a stimulant by some medical personnel, although proof of efficacy again is lacking. Stelazine is an extremely potent drug and is quite toxic. Its main value is for severely disturbed and psychotic children. There is some stimulatory effect of stelazine that has made the drug popular for the child with a short attention span. The drug is still not widely approved for use in children under 12 years of age.

The following drugs are rarely indicated except in severely emotionally disturbed or psychotic children.

**Fluphenazine (Prolixin, Permitil):** Fluphenazine is quite stimulatory like stelazine and is used by some physicians for this effect.

**Perphenazine (Trilafon)**

**Promazine (Sparine)**

**Prochloperazine (Compazine):**   Prochloperazine has been widely used to treat nausea and vomiting, but because of its extreme toxicity is not used in children.

**Triflupromazin (Vesprin)**

**Chlorprothixene (Taractan)**

**Thiothixene (Navane)**

**Haloperidol (Haldol):**   Haloperidol is a highly potent and toxic drug used for psychotic children. However, it has crept into limited usage for children with educational problems. This use is unproven at the present time and perhaps dangerous. The drug is currently not recommended for use in the pediatric age group, except perhaps to treat tics and other movement disorders.

## Minor Tranquilizers

The minor tranquilizers are not as potent and produce less side effects than the major tranquilizers. Their main use is for anxiety, mild neuroses, and tension. There are also muscle-relaxant effects attributed to some of these medications. Most of these drugs will aggravate the short attention span and impulsivity of the true hyperkinetic child and therefore should be used with the greatest of care and selectivity. The more common drugs in this category include:

**Diazepam (Valium):**   Diazepam is a good muscle relaxant and is effective against some forms of convulsions. There is very little use for it in children for reasons other than to reduce anxiety states.

**Chlordiazepoxide (Librium)**

**Meprobamate (Equanil, Miltown)**

**Hydroxyzine (Atarax, Vistaril):**   Hydroxyzine is a mild tranquilizer with some sedative and antihistamine effects. It used to be quite popular for the treatment of young children with anxiety or sleep disturbances. However, it is capable of produciong extreme hyperactivity when used for a neurologically hyperkinetic child.

**Oxazepam (Serax)**

**Trihexyphenidyl (Artane):**   This drug is useful for severe neurological problems such as Parkinsonism. It is occasionally tried in children with muscle spasms or similar problems.

## Antihistamines

Antihistamines are primarily used to alleviate common symptoms produced by allergic diseases such as nasal stuffiness, sneezing, hives, and itching. Occasionally a few of these drugs may be tried in hyperactive children for a primarily sedative effect. This may especially be seen in the case of insomnia produced by stimulant drugs. Two of the more common medications used for these types of children include.

1.  Diphenhydramine (Benadryl)

2.  Promethazine (Phenergan)

There are many other antihistamines in use, but the above two are the ones most commonly used in children with behavior and learning problems.

## Anticonvulsants

**Phenobarbital:**  Phenobarbital is primarily used in seizure disorders of a major type, such as grand mal. Phenobarbital and other barbituates have a tendency to magnify hyperactive behavior and should not be used if at all possible in hyperkinetic children.

**Diphenylhydantoin (Dilantin):**  Dilantin is a very useful drug for many types of seizures, especially major motor and grand mal. It seems to work better in neurologically hyperactive children then phenobarbital does. It is often used to treat behavioral disturbances in children where the electroencephalogram is abnormal but shows no specific identifiable seizure disorder. The use of Dilantin for this type of condition is very controversial, but it seems to have a beneficial effect on the aggressive behavior of certain children with wildly abnormal EEGs. Side effects may include skin rash, gait disturbances, drowsiness, gum problems (overgrowth), and blood disorders.

**Primidone (Mysoline):**  Primidone is useful in the treatment of various types of major motor disorders. It is quite potent and can be very toxic.

**Ethosuximide (Zarontin):**  Ethosuximide is the most effective and nontoxic drug for the treatment of minor motor and petit mal seizures.

**Phensuximide (Milontin):**  Same as above but more toxic.

**Trimethadione (Tridione):**  Trimethadione is effective for the treatment of petit mal epilepsy, but is more toxic than Zarontin.

**Mephobarbital (Mebaral):**  Mephobarbital is very much like phenobarbital.

**Carbamazepine (Tegretol):**  Carbamazepine is an extremely potent drug used in patients who have not responded to safer anticonvulsants. It is useful for temporal lobe, grand mal, partial, and mixed forms of seizures. The drug may be extremely toxic.

There are other anticonvulsant medications on the market, but the above are the most widely used, least toxic, and most effective for the majority of children with seizure disorders.

### Final Statements on Drug Therapy for
### Educational and Behavior Problems

1.    Of all the medications that have been used to treat children with learning handicaps, the stimulants (minor antidepressants) are still the only ones with proven reproducible, beneficial effects in most instances. This type of effect is mostly in the area of increasingly effective attention span, improved coordination of motor function, and improved screening out of bothersome stimuli. Thus, the overall effect of the use of stimulant medication is often a more attentive child who is able to learn more effectively. Another effect is the proper direction of impulsive behavior with a secondary "calming" effect on undirected hyperactivity. The most useful and commonly used medication in this group at present seems to be methylphenidate (Ritalin).

2.    Stimulant medication may be an early and effective step in the differential diagnosis of the neurologically hyperactive child.

3.    Sedatives and tranquilizers have a limited place in the treatment of these children. Their use should be reserved for severely agitated, disturbed, depressed, anxious, or psychotic children. These drugs can have negative effects, such as a reduced attention span, more overactivity, and poorer learning capabilities.

4.    A drug should not be employed before a careful study of the child has been undertaken. Any child who is being treated with a medication must be carefully followed, and meticulous documentation of the effects of the drug must be available to all parties concerned with the child. Changes in doses and medications must be related to the actual performance of the child, rather than the opinion of the physician, parent, or teacher.

5.    Dosage and length of treatment must be totally individualized, and a drug should not be used longer than necessary.

6.    Medications are used only to treat symptoms. They cannot substitute for a poor cultural, nutritional, familial, or educational environment. The taking of a pill by the child does not make him learn better—but it *may* help the *teacher* to be more effective in *helping* the child to learn.

## PARAMEDICAL TREATMENTS

Because of the existence of a diversity of causes for learning handicaps, as suggested by workers from many and varied fields, it is only natural that many different types of therapies have sprung up over the years that embrace these diverse etiologies. Among these, some of the most popular include:

1.   Motor training programs (including laterality training, balance board exercises, and crawling).

2.   Visual perceptual programs.

3.   Orthopic programs (eye-muscle training).

The above programs vary from place to place, and from worker to worker. However, the main thrust to this type of approach is that the child with a learning handicap owes that particular problem to the presence of certain defects in motor or sensory abilities. Thus, it has been postulated that reading difficulty may occur because a child sees words or letters backwards (perceptual problems), or perhaps because of a problem in moving his eyes in a left-to-right scanning procedure (orthoptics). Others theorize that a child's reading abilities are related to his coordination and developmental abilities (motor training, creeping-crawling programs). Throughout the years many children, both within and outside of the classroom, have been subjected to a whole host of exercises based on these theories. At present, many classrooms are still "hotbeds" of perceptual training of one sort or another. The big question we must ask ourselves is whether a child's reading, spelling, or other educational endeavors are directly helped by this type of approach? The vast majority of well-documented recent information we are seeing now tells us that the answer is probably no!

As we discussed in some of the earlier chapters, the actual cause of a child's learning problem is usually quite difficult to pinpoint. In fact, we have seen that most children have more than one etiology for their own special problem. A large number of children with learning problems also have immaturities of the nervous system. Thus, these children may exhibit coordination and perceptual problems as part of their general immaturities. However, it is not likely that the learning disability is directly related to the immaturity, since many children with severe neurological, perceptual, and coordination difficulties learn to read and write perfectly well, and others with severe learning handicaps are beautifully coordinated.

We also know that children who have never walked, due to some congenital problems, or those with complete paralysis, can learn to read perfectly well. As far as eye-motion problems are concerned, we see just as many reading problems in other countries where the child must read from right to left or top to bottom as in our own left-to-right system. Also, children with learning disabilities seem to have the same incidence of refractive errors and muscle imbalance as normal achievers, and eye defects do not cause reversals or perceptual problems.

It has been shown that children exposed to perceptual training programs in kindergarten do no better with their reading in later grades than those taught conventionally. Various research projects have shown no relationship between any type of motor-coordination exercises and reading ability. There is also no evidence that the failure to develop at one motor level or another actually influences capabilities at higher levels of development.

Although perceptual problems are often associated with reading difficulties, it is not clear which factors relate to which events. We certainly *do* see reading difficulties in the same child who has coordination deficiencies. It is most probable that the two coexist rather than act as cause and effect. The normal child in today's world has developed far greater abilities to discriminate forms, sounds, and figure relationships in order to survive in his environment than he needs to read. Therefore, the minor perceptual problems that we see blamed for reading problems are in reality probably not a factor at all.

There has been recent evidence that children with reading and other learning problems do not have any problem at all in perceiving the letters and forms, but rather in the memory areas. Thus, the areas of auditory memory, perhaps visual memory, sound discrimination, and our old friend—attention span, may be intimately involved here. No type of motor exercises, eye training, or finger-hand-body coordination programs can correct these deficiencies except as they increase memory. Recent research in the field of memory, including various chemical and nutritional approaches, may yield some beneficial results in the near future.

With this knowledge as a background, it is fairly clear that the types of programs dealing with perception, motor coordination, and eye movements do not actually improve anything except those functions that are being worked with. Physical training programs will certainly improve fitness and self-image if they are not forced upon a child who is opposed to so exposing himself (which is often the case with immature children who have poor coordination). It is unlikely, though, that the programs will help these children learn to *read* any better. The people who advocate such programs very genuinely feel that the child's specific learning is enhanced. However, it is quite likely that the major beneficial results of such endeavors will be produced by the increased attention and stimulation given to the child, rather than by the program itself.

Educational goals are quite specific, and the more closely related to the ultimate learning task the experience is, the more directly beneficial will be the results. The teaching of children with learning disabilities is a problem for educational experts. There is only a limited amount of time, money, and human resources available to each child and his family.

Thus, one should direct these resources to the most important goals and concentrate on these particular areas. If a child is having difficulty learning subject "X," then the precious time allotted to this child should be concentrated on helping him to learn subject "X," and perceptual, motor, and eye exercises that do not relate directly to subject "X," are largely a waste of precious time.

There is no doubt that a child's self-image could be helped by increasing his skills in an area of his growth that might be poorly developed. However, this type of approach should normally be used only as an adjunct when extra time and resources are available. In most cases, it is best to try to find out the most successful strategy to help a child learn a particular subject in which he is deficient, and stick to that task rather than try some parallel type of approach.

It is certainly helpful to have on hand a large number of people interested enough in a child to want to help him overcome his handicaps. However, it would be beneficial to the child if the people trying to help him would put aside personal biases in their efforts. We still have a lot to learn ourselves about the child with educational dysfunction, and the first step in this direction is to unclutter our own minds so that the child's mind can expand with clarity. We know that many people who have been trained in the schools of perceptual and similar therapies might disagree with the approach we suggest. Nonetheless, we feel the time has come to more closely inspect this entire area, and we feel confident that a direct approach to the specific problem will turn out to be the most rewarding and viable answer to this particular question. The actual remedial educational procedures must always remain the responsibility of the educators!

## SUMMARY OF MEDICAL APPROACH

Nowhere in the entire field of remediation of educational dysfunction does individualization mean so much as in medical, dietary, and paramedical therapies. As we have previously stressed, each child we see usually has a variety of problems at the root of his special disability. Thus, there are often many different things that have to be considered in helping the child. We have seen that the educational team must use many types of strategies for each individual child at various times. There might also be several types of psychological approaches necessary to help a child. Obviously then, we must approach the medical model in the same manner.

Each child we see must be fully evaluated. Parents must be apprised of all of the possible therapies that are potential options in this field.

The physician must keep abreast of the documented results in all areas and utilize all available information in his approach to each child.

There is usually no one special way to treat all of these children. We must try to achieve the best possible nutritional status for each child, and perhaps suggest various types of specialized nutritional approaches or elimination diets where appropriate. We must remember that a well and properly nourished child will be more likely to benefit from any type of treatment. At the same time we must be careful that our efforts in the culinary areas do not disrupt the social ecology of the family or make the child even *more* different than his peers, which would totally override any benefit that the particular diet might achieve.

If medication is thought to exert a possible beneficial effect on various symptoms a child might show, this therapy should also be approached with an open mind. However, the careful documentation of the results of drug therapy is again stressed. We also emphasize that the treatment of each new symptom with a new drug is not usually an acceptable approach either.

We must do our best for these children, whatever seems most appropriate. We have to keep our minds open so that all of us can work together to honestly evaluate the results of our medical and para-medical approaches. Finally, we have to be sure that all parties interested in the child totally understand that this area of the remediation of educational dysfunction is only a key that might open the door to the educational house where all of the *real* work takes place!

In order for the reader to develop a feeling for some of the objective changes we look for in children who are placed on special diets or medications, we have included several photographs of self-drawings and Bender-Gestalt diagrams done by children before and after treatment was instituted.

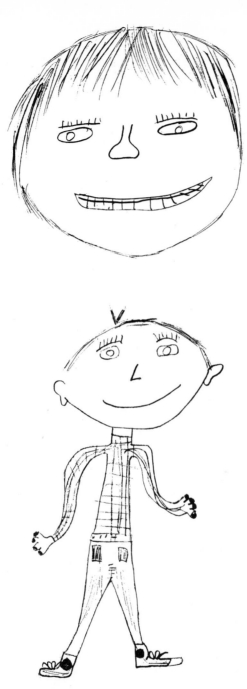

**Figure 11-2.** *Kerry's self drawing on October 5, 1976, without medication (*top*) is much less complete and shows less detail than the one completed two years previously (*bottom*) while on treatment with Ritalin. This is probably due to an increased attention span.*

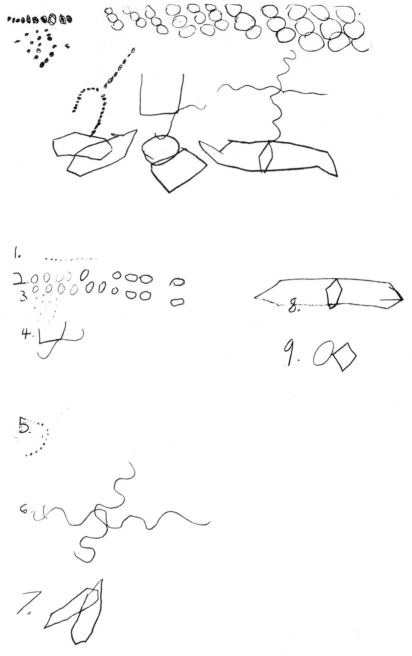

**Figure 11-3.** *The Bender drawings Rachel completed on April 9, 1975, (*top*) show much less detail and organization than the ones accomplished just eight months later while Rachel was taking medication (*bottom*).*

AGE 11¾ yrs.
9/12/75

AGE: 12¹¹⁄₁₂ yrs.
10/13/76

*Figure 11-4.*   *Billy's self-drawing on September 12, 1975, shows a much smaller self-image with less detail than the one done one year later with the help of Ritalin. The improvement is much greater than would be seen with just one year of chronological growth.*

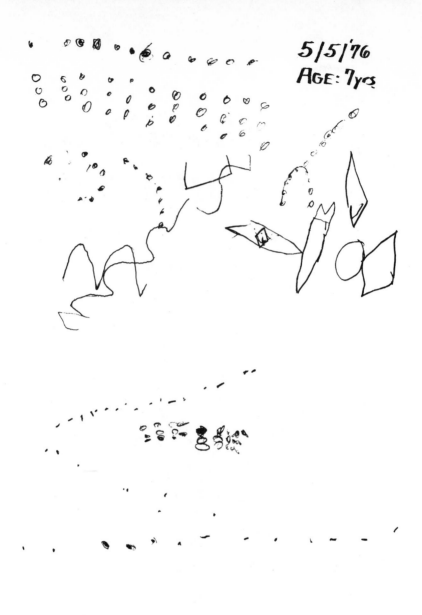

**Figure 11-5.** *John's Bender test on May 5, 1976, shows striking change in reference to detail, finishing the task, and pencil manipulation over the same test given one year previously without medication.*

5/18/77

11/1/75
2½ Hour Post
Medication
(Ritalin)

*Figure 11-6.* *Even though he was eighteen months older at the time, David's self-drawing on May 18, 1977, was more immature with less detail than the one completed on November 1, 1975, which was done while on Ritalin.*

Troy

1|16|76

SELF DRAWING
RITALIN 3 hrs. AGO
5|3|76

1
2.
3.
4. 4
5.
6.
7.
8.

9.

Troy

AGE 8yrs.
1/16/76

*Figure 11-7.* *Troy's self-drawings with and without medications are shown. The May 3, 1976, drawing shows much greater detail and a better self-image. Bender drawings are shown without treatment, on a diet free of food coloring ("KP" Diet) and with Ritalin. Although the changes are not as striking,*

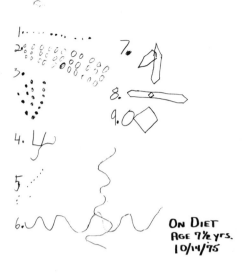

On Diet
Age 7½ yrs.
10/14/75

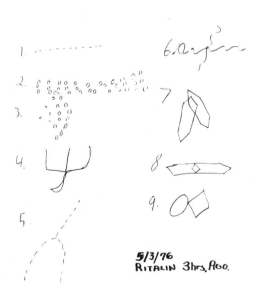

5/3/76
Ritalin 3 hrs. Ago.

it can be seen that there is much greater attention to detail, a much more even distribution of the figures, and much less sloppiness on those done while on the diet and medications.

# CHAPTER 12

# *Recapitulation*

We have covered a rather large amount of information in this book, and we felt it might be helpful to recapitulate some of the material presented. There is a twofold reason for this.

1.  The learning process is always aided by a careful, specific, well-organized review of information.

2.  The writers are able to more clearly focus their own ideas if the material is restated and perhaps more finely honed.

The purpose of this chapter, therefore, will be to repeat some of the more important ideas covered in the book, perhaps to restate some areas that might lend themselves to redefinition, and in some cases to include new material that will aid in understanding the main concepts of the book. We will attempt to follow loosely the chapter content as presented, but in some cases this will not be possible nor serve the best purposes. We will keep the material as concise as possible, with a short statement sufficing where feasible. We hope both writer and reader will benefit from this exercise.

The first part of this chapter will be devoted to a presentation of ten case histories. We have attempted to select a representative cross-section of educational dysfunctions to show how teamwork can be effective in the treatment of these children. This representation is, of course, only a minute part of the entire problem, but will provide the reader with some idea of our approach.

## CASE HISTORIES OF SOME CHILDREN
## WITH EDUCATIONAL DYSFUNCTION—
## HOW THE TEAM WORKS

1.  Mary G. is a ten-year-old girl who was noted to be having difficulty with reading in first grade. There had been no previous problems in Mary's history, and she had been a healthy girl. The teacher referred her to the school psychologist after a consultation with her parents. Testing revealed that Mary's intelligence was normal, but there was a wide scatter on a few of the subtests of the WISC-R. Some of her lower areas identified problems with auditory and visual perception, and it was felt that she needed a somewhat different approach to the learning process than she was already receiving. She also seemed to do much better dealing with people on a one-to-one basis.

Mary was referred to her physician for a complete evaluation and it was felt that she showed some signs of developmental delay, especially in the neuromuscular areas; but no other problems were noted. Consultation among the teacher, psychologist, physician, and Mary's parents was held. A decision was made to place her in a part-time group for learning disabled children, with a special education teacher several hours each day to work on reading and any other difficult subjects. Mary was also followed carefully by the psychologist to see that her feelings about school stayed on the positive side.

At the present time, Mary is in the fifth grade in her regular classroom all day. She occasionally stops in to work with the special education teacher, but she is essentially performing grade-level work. She is a happy, well-adjusted girl who generally likes school, and her reading disability seems to be behind her. The teacher's early identification and referral in this case saved Mary from a possibly difficult, or even disastrous, school career.

2.  Carl W. is an eight-year-old boy who was first seen by the physician at two months of age because his parents were not sure he was seeing properly. Carl received very careful medical study over the next eight months, and at the end of that time it was felt he had brain damage and also showed very definite signs of infantile autism. Carl and his parents were referred to a special center where they worked with people who had had experience with children like Carl. These people included language specialists, physical therapists, child psychiatrists, and pre-school teachers.

At three years of age, Carl was referred to the special education administrator of the school district where his family resided. He was evaluated by the school psychologist, nurse, and language specialists and was found to be eligible for a special pre-school program. The severe-oral-language handicapped program in this particular district seemed best suited for him because of the teacher's experience in working with children like Carl.

After several months in the program, Carl was noted to exhibit some bizarre behavior and body movements, and the school nurse was asked to evaluate him. She felt that he might be showing signs of a convulsive disorder, so she spoke to the family physician. Carl was referred to a pediatric neurologist who did indeed diagnose a seizure problem and prescribed anti-convulsant medication.

Carl did well for the next few years, but at the age of five it was felt that he would benefit more from a program for multihandicapped pupils, since his language was coming along very nicely. Carl's behavior has also been a problem almost from the start, and his parents had been enrolled in a parent education program very early. Because of the ongoing difficulty with his behavior, family therapy with a counselor experienced with this type of child was undertaken from time to time as the need arose.

When Carl turned six, his behavior suddenly became more of a problem, and after consultation between the school nurse, teacher, physician, and his parents, several special diets were tried—none of which seemed to work. A trial of stimulant medication was then attempted, and with careful monitoring and the aid of the teacher, a definite improvement was noted. After one year, the teachers reported that Carl's behavior was no different with or without medication, so the stimulant drug was stopped. He is currently still in the multihandicap program, where he is doing as well as can be expected. He still has many problems, but seems to be happy and his education is coming along nicely. Carl will continue to need careful follow-up in future years from all concerned parties.

3.   Tracy F. is a nine-year-old girl whose birthday is on November 2. She is very bright and up to now has always done well in her studies. Tracy has, however, missed quite a bit of school right from the start. In first grade she seemed to have a cold every two weeks, and second grade marked the start of a bed-wetting problem. In the past year she has started to complain of constant abdominal pains, and her physician has not been able to find any physical problem. Because of the common association of abdominal pains with emotional problems, the school psychologist was asked to see Tracy. A superficial examination revealed no major problems at that time.

At the start of fourth grade, however, Tracy began to rebel at finishing some of her work, and by the end of the year she had become somewhat of a disruptive force in the classroom. Tracy's parents and the physician then spoke about the possibility of a chronic stress situation which might be secondary to the fact that Tracy was the youngest in her class. This had been considered previously, but was dismissed because of her outstanding school achievement. Her parents were very much against the thought of retention, but after consultation with the teacher and doctor, it was decided that this was the most logical way to proceed. When Tracy was asked whether she wanted to repeat fourth grade, much to her parents' surprise she immediately developed a huge smile and seemed almost relieved at the suggestion. She is now repeating the year, has stopped her bed-wetting, and has had no belly pains for four months.

4.   Steve S. is an eleven-year-old boy who was diagnosed as "hyperactive" at the age of four and who had been on stimulant medication since he turned five. He was attending a private school and there were no learning problems until he entered fourth grade. At that time both his parents and teachers noted that Steve became more stubborn and defiant and that his work became very sloppy and incomplete. An attempt to control Steve's behavior and problems by more and different medications failed, and his parents and teachers became quite distraught.

After speaking with some friends whose child had similar problems, the family was directed to a parent seminar sponsored by their local school district. There they met a school counselor who directed them to the school psychologist and finally to the special education administrator. There was also a referral to another physician who evaluated Steve and then met with the school counselor and psychologist and came up with another plan for him.

It was felt that Steve's problems were being caused by diverse factors, and the following suggestions were made:

a.   Steve was found to be under quite a bit of pressure in the private school. With 40 children in the classroom, the teacher had no time to really communicate with him. It was decided that Steve would be withdrawn and placed in public school with one period a day to be spent working with the school counselor.

b.   Steve was also found to be quite unhappy at his lack of physical coordination; the boys in his class were all playing organized sports, at which he was a failure. He was therefore placed in an adaptive physical education class where his coordination was worked on and where he learned to appreciate things he *could* do well. This took the pressure of competition off him, and when it was found he could kick quite well, he was on his way to becoming a relatively competent soccer player.

    c. Finally, Steve's parents were asked to change his dietary habits in an attempt to see if his increased activity might be due to any type of food sensitivity. A trial on a diet free of salicylates, artificial coloring, and food additives showed that there *were* some items, like candy bars, cola, and certain fruits, that always seemed to make him more irritable. Exclusion of these foods has enabled Steve to enjoy a more even-keeled behavior and his medication is now at a minimum.

The future still holds some perils for Steve and his family, but at least he now seems to be happy and well adjusted to his particular situation. Without the total cooperation and communication of everyone involved, this would not have been possible.

    5. Harvey A. is currently twelve years of age and is a student in the program for educable mentally retarded pupils. He had been a problem since birth, when it was noted that he had some paralysis of his right arm and leg, thought to be due to a difficult labor and delivery. When Harvey entered school he had physical and educational difficulties which were immediately recognized by the teacher. (Harvey's parents had never enrolled him in pre-school because they were afraid of the reaction of the other children to his problems.)

    During the course of his first year in school, Harvey was evaluated by the teachers, psychologists, school nurses, and physical therapists, and was referred for a complete medical examination. Before the year was over he was receiving special therapy for his physical handicap and was registered in the special education program for the following year. During the next few years, several different classes were tried until the best program for Harvey was found. The first recommendation for the program for retarded children came when Harvey entered junior high school. Harvey is not retarded in the true sense of the word, but it was noted that he needed a developmental program for low-functioning children. He also found that he got along better with the children in this program than in any other, so he asked to be placed there. Harvey attends "regular" classes for some subjects where he does well, including music and shop, since he has become quite adept at working with his good arm and hand after years of work with physical and occupational therapists. From time to time he has needed some counseling, and the family has benefited from referral to a marriage, family, and child counselor. Harvey's future outlook situation has turned out bright because of the good work and cooperation between all concerned.

    6. David L. is a ten-year-old who was enrolled in the gifted program because of his very high intelligence. He had been in the pro-

gram for four years, but had been finding it increasingly difficult. Finally, in fifth grade he just seemed to come to a halt—he wouldn't do any work, became disruptive in class, and started to show signs of behavior problems at home.

David's teachers had been told over the years that David was very bright, and they had difficulty trying to decide just why he was not doing as well as his 145 IQ said he should. A series of psychologists, counselors, doctors, and others were consulted to see if they could find out what was wrong. When David finally started to really "blow it" in the fifth grade, everyone seemed to be at a loss and felt that David had some emotional and motivational problems.

Because of the difficulties David had gotten into, a meeting of everyone concerned with his progress was held. After a prolonged discussion it was decided that perhaps everyone was looking at David in the wrong light. Maybe he *was* extremely bright, but maybe he *also* had a specific learning disability. It was then quickly ascertained that David indeed was a gifted boy with a learning problem, especially in reading. It was only because of his superior intelligence that he was able to maintain his educational level before this time; but the pressure had finally gotten to him and he "cracked." When David's unique educational needs were re-evaluated and a special program was drawn up for him, he immediately started to bloom and the behavior problems disappeared.

There are many children like David—gifted intellectually, but manifesting specific learning disabilities. Only a concerted, cooperative, and open approach by the school team can avert educational disaster in these children.

7.    Kim S. is a shy, pretty eight-year-old who was found to exhibit educational dysfunction in first grade. She was of average intelligence, but could not seem to learn to read. She was also very much a loner who did not play well with the other children. She had been examined by both the school nurse and her doctor and no physical defects were found. The school psychologist was able to test her with difficulty in spite of her apparent inability to relate to him, but he could find no clear reason for her problem.

Because of her obvious communication deficits, it was decided that the speech and language specialists would test and work with her, even though there seemed to be no specific recognizable language disabilities. After prolonged and intensive investigations, it was found that Kim *did* have some rather obscure but very relevant language problems, both in her receptive and expressive areas. This was interfering with both learning (since she was unable to learn by using the phonic system) and her relationships with others (because of expressive problems).

After two years of intensive work with the language specialists,

Kim has come a long way. She is now reading quite well since her teacher has employed methods that suit her own particular way of learning. She is also now able to express herself quite a bit more comfortably, which makes her happier both in school and at home. And in the language specialist she has a very special friend whom she can seek out from time to time when the going gets rough. Many children in school would benefit similarly from this special kind of friend—whether a language specialist, physiotherapist, counselor, or in most cases a certain teacher the child has grown to love and trust.

8.   Derek P. is a seven-year-old who has been diagnosed as having asphasia, cerebral dysfunction, a learning disability, hyperactivity, autism, and mental retardation. He has been a problem for his parents almost since birth because of his unmanageable behavior, lack of communication, bed-wetting and soiling, and poor learning ability. Derek had been seen by many physicians, each of whom had affixed one or more of the above labels to him. By the time he was four, Derek's family was in a state of turmoil.

When Derek's parents were first introduced to the idea that a label was not necessary in order to work with Derek and that *each individual* problem should be attacked, they became more cooperative and seemed somewhat relieved, although they knew that Derek was a very unique child. Over the next year Derek was enrolled in the pre-school language handicapped program in the family's home district, he was given medication for his severe lack of attention, and the parents were enrolled in a behavior education program.

Derek improved greatly during that year, and at the end of the term a meeting was held among the physician, teachers, psychologist, language specialists, and school nurse. It was decided that Derek had benefited about as much as he could from his present class, and another one was suggested where more classroom personnel were available to work with him individually. It was also decided that the medication was not working as well, and a different dosage format was instituted, which was much more effective.

Derek is now in the second program and is doing quite well. The aide who is spending the most time with him is officially listed as a physical therapist, but the work going on between the aide and Derek includes very little physiotherapy—it is the contact and the time spent that are so important. Derek's parents know that the future is uncertain, but there is at least some hope now. Derek probably fits into the category we called the "Global Atypical Child," but as you can see the attempt to label him really does no good—and in this case probably slowed down the process of remediation.

9.   Becky J. is a fifteen-year-old who was first brought to the

physician because of a chronic problem of constipation. She had been seen by many other physicians for this problem and many different kinds of medications, diets, and other approaches were tried—but the problem remained. It was only when another physician looked at the whole Becky, not just her bowel movements, that things started to happen.

During the course of the total evaluation other problems, such as Becky's increased weight, poor speech, skin problems, and school difficulties, were brought out. A phone call to the school psychologist and another to the nurse set the wheels in motion for a complete about-face in Becky's approach to life.

Psychological and language testing revealed that Becky was having learning and emotional problems secondary to a speech difficulty. Language therapy and a change in her classroom status were then instituted. She was then put into a group counseling situation with a female counselor who worked on her personal habits, dress, and awareness. Some minor medical manipulations helped her to some degree with her health in general, and by the end of the year Becky was a much happier, more well-adjusted teenager.

Becky's constipation has also disappeared. Her increased ability to express herself intellectually and emotionally also solved her inability to express herself organically.

10. Eric E. is a twelve-year-old boy who was diagnosed as hyperactive at six years of age and placed on medications. At seven he was found to have a reading disability and was put into a special education classroom. At the age of eight he was an extremely unhappy child and just about a school dropout.

There were various people around the school, however, who noticed a few important things about Eric that changed his life. The principal saw Eric in a ball game, the nurse noticed him constantly rubbing his nose, and one of the other teachers saw him at a model-building contest. These three seemingly unrelated events were to make the difference between a school dropout and an excellent, honor-roll student.

Eric had always been an excellent athlete and was one of the best players in little league baseball, soccer, and football. Eric's parents did not like the idea of his consuming interest in sports and were so adamant about it that he was not even allowed to read about sports, let alone play. This made him quite unhappy and made him more resolved not to try hard at school.

Eric was also very good with his hands and loved to build models of all kinds. Because of his poor grades, however, his parents discouraged this element of his activities until his grades improved. Finally, it became apparent after some fact finding by the nurse that Eric had been bothered by a constant runny nose, sneezing, headaches, and weeping eyes for many years—he was a very allergic child who really was uncomfortable much of the time.

When all the people interested in Eric's progress finally sat down together, a plan of action was outlined to try to eliminate the problem areas and utilize his strong points. Thus, in a short period of time, the following took place: Eric's physician instituted a strict anti-allergic program and when some of his symptoms started to clear up, he began to feel much better, was able to sit still in the classroom, concentrated on his work better, and did quite well without any medication at all.

Eric's parents were persuaded to let him play ball, and within a short period of time he had established himself as one of the outstanding athletes in the school, as well as the community. His self-image rose by leaps and bounds and he became a happy and easy to handle boy once again. He was also picked by the principal to play on the little league team he coached, another very positive experience. In addition, Eric began to read his favorite sport books and this helped his overall reading to a great extent.

Finally, the teacher who recognized Eric's model-building ability formed a hobby club in the school which elected Eric as its president. This also gave him some very positive feelings about himself and added to his newly enhanced self-image.

Because of the interest of some of the people around him and the cooperation of his parents, Eric had become a very popular, happy, and well-adjusted student by the time he entered the sixth grade. His classwork, including reading, is now on grade level or above. Eric is on his way to a very good school experience with the help of a lot of his friends.

We would like to see every child with educational dysfunction receive this type of individual interest and help. If the child's parents, teachers, doctors and the other people in his life were to become his friends as well, this could very well be the case.

Many children do not realize their full educational potential for many reasons. Each child must be fully investigated to see what his own problem might be.

## SUMMARY STATEMENTS

The child who does not learn as well as expected may have physical, emotional, neurological, psychological, or other causes for his problem. We have chosen to call any learning handicap—for whatever reason— *educational dysfunction.*

Each child with a learning problem may have one or many causes for this difficulty. This means that each child has his *own particular* learning disability that must be treated in a very individual manner.

As stated above, there is no single cause for learning disorders. They can be secondary to many diverse factors—often a combination of many. There is also no single way of diagnosing these children and no one way of teaching them.

A child with educational dysfunction should be totally evaluated by educational, psychological, medical, and other necessary personnel. All of his problems should then be listed and handled by whatever and/or whoever is necessary to correct these individual problems.

There are many causes for educational dysfunction. These can be grouped into those pertaining to the child himself and those in the child's environment. The majority of children with this type of problem fit into several different categories so that the causes are almost always varied and comprehensive. This means that the identification and remediation of such problems must be just as comprehensive.

Labels such as "minimal brain damage, "minimal brain dysfunction," and "minimal cerebral dysfunction" are not helpful in the treatment of children with learning handicaps and are best forgotten. Labels such as "aphasia," "dysgraphia," and "dyslexia" are also not helpful in the care of these children and should be abandoned when possible. Each child with a learning problem has his *own distinct* problem with its own unique treatment. Labels do not help this process.

Several other labels and terms are commonly used in conjunction with children with learning disabilities; we will define these terms now. These are only descriptive terms and should not be used as diagnoses.

**Dysarthria:** This term refers to a speech problem secondary to some type of disability of the actual mechanism of the production of speech. Dysarthria usually refers either to an actual articulation defect caused by poor motor control, or to an anatomical abnormality in the speech-producing areas (mouth, tongue, throat).

**Dyspraxia:** This term refers to impaired or painful functioning of any organ of the body.

**Apraxia:** This term refers to the inability of a person to perform a voluntary movement even when there is no known problem of motor, sensory, or other specific neurological function.

A child who is considered a likely candidate for the possible development of learning problems may show any of the following: a history of perinatal problems, delay in developmental milestones, repeated or chronic illnesses, and cultural or family disturbances. He may also manifest a short attention span, poor impulse control, poor frustration tolerance, poor fine-motor coordination, and most important, some language delay or disturbance. Oral language development may be the most important factor here!

It is important to identify a child as having a learning handicap not later than kindergarten or at least first grade, before frustration and a sense of failure set in.

Children with possible educational dysfunction should be diagnosed before school entrance if possible, and this process should be assisted by extensive and careful screening by all persons involved including parents, physicians, preschool teachers, and other interested parties.

Every child should have a thorough evaluation and screening of developmental, social, and intellectual skills before entering kindergarten. A child who shows any areas of delay should be thoroughly investigated before he starts school. If a child's fifth birthday occurs *just before* or certainly *after* the start of kindergarten, it is wise to question his entrance into the program, especially if the child is a boy!

It is quite important to identify a child who shows developmental deviation or behavioral disturbances as early as possible. It is sometimes not possible to do much with the child himself at a young age (under five), but the parents should be counseled on methods of dealing with the child's behavior; and most important—provisions for the child's education should be made as early as possible, *especially for children with language delay!* These children may be placed in educational programs dealing with their language problems as early as three years of age.

A child must be ready for school in three areas of development—intellectual, social, and neurological. If any of these is below average the child may well fail to reach his full potential.

Many boys are 6 to 12 months behind girls in social and neurological development at 5 years of age. Thus, a boy who starts school who is not yet 5—or better yet, 5 years and 4 months—may be under a great handicap!

A child who is misplaced in school will often suffer a needless learning handicap.

The term *hyperactivity* is so confusing, poorly described, and difficult to pin down that it would be better if it were not used at all.

Children who are labeled "hyperactive" can fit into many different categories. These include behavior disturbances, emotional disorders, normally overactive children with impatient observers, normally active children with abnormally impatient observers, and neurological abnormalities.

The only type of hyperactivity we are really concerned with is that group of children who are suffering from some type of neurological handicap that causes them to exhibit a short attention span and impulsivity. Other behaviors attributed to this group of children are probably secondary to the impulsivity and short attention span.

This particular group of neurologically hyperactive children may have this condition because of some previous central nervous system damage or infection, but in most cases may have no specific history of any identifiable etiology.

The majority of children who have neurological hyperactivity with short attention spans have no specific known reason for their problem. These children fall into two categories.

1. True, genetic, neurological hyperactivity,

2. Medical or chemical hyperactivity.

Group 1 children have some type of neurological dysfunction whereby they are lacking a central stimulation of their arousal system for concentration and for blocking out environmental stimuli. Group 2 children have adverse effects from environmental substances such as food colorings, sugar, certain allergies, or other factors that cause the same problem (or perhaps *set off* the problem) as children in Group 1 have.

Children with neurological hyperactivity often show other behaviors such as impulsivity, distractibility, poorly directed control of emotions, awkwardness, lability of emotions, easy frustration, perceptual defects, and perseveration. All of these traits are probably secondary to a short attention span and poor impulse control.

It is extremely difficult in many cases to specifically diagnose the neurologically hyperactive child. Physical examination, neurological examination (including "soft signs"), psychological profile, and electro-encephalogram all may give clues, but *are not diagnostic.* The one true diagnostic test at present may be a trial of stimulant medication.

Most children with true neurological hyperactivity have a history of symptoms dating back to infancy. They were often colicky, fussy babies with sleep and feeding disturbances. They often were described as running as soon as they walked and as "always into everything." Other traits frequently ascribed to them are discipline problems, immaturity, and occasional speech delays. However, not all hyperactive children have this kind of background, and many children *with* this type of history may easily fit into the category of emotionally disturbed. Thus, specific diagnosis is difficult.

The physician who diagnoses a child as neurologically hyperactive must rely on observations by the teacher and/or parent much more than on anything he can do himself to make this diagnosis.

Often the only true method of a final diagnosis of medical or neurological hyperactivity is by changes seen in the child after dietary manipulation or a trial of stimulant medication.

A child with developmental or maturational lag will often look and act very much like one with a true neurological handicap. There is no way to tell one from the other (if in reality there *is* a difference) except by the passage of time!

A child with a developmental or neurological cause for his learning handicap is not always recognized in the first few years of school. Sometimes the problem does not surface until the stresses of later grades (fifth or sixth) are encountered.

Children with neurological or medical hyperactivity may have learning disabilities. Children who have specific learning problems may be hyperactive. However, not all hyperactive children have learning disabilities, and vice versa.

A specific learning disability is one where the child has no other major physical defects (such as vision or hearing), has normal intelligence and motivation, and for some reason fails to be educated to his full potential in one or more areas—after receiving adequate conventional instruction, and thus reveals an unexpected learning problem.

Specific learning disability is only one of many reasons a child may show educational dysfunction.

Many children with specific learning disabilities (in the absence of other recognizable physical or emotional disorders) may represent a product of genetic factors, neurodevelopmental lags, and environmental problems and stresses. The result is usually a child with a mixture of several disabilities for which there is no one diagnosis, and certainly no one specific therapy.

Specific learning disabilities can be due to inefficiencies in the brain in many different systems. There may be disturbances in auditory memory, auditory perception, the synthesis and integration of perceived sounds, or the transfer of auditory signals into motor-equivalents for speech, among others. Thus, each child has his own, unique, neurological prerequisites for learning disabilities.

In the majority of cases, reading disability is due to a physiological, developmental, or maturational lag that may in itself be accompanied by other signs of immaturity such as "soft" neurological signs.

It is often quite difficult to tell whether a child in the 4-to-6-year range is suffering from a neurological dysfunction or from a maturational delay, when he exhibits many signs of neurological immaturity and behavioral problems. Thus, the *individual components* of his problem must be treated rather than some possible spurious all-encompassing diagnosis such as minimal cerebral dysfunction.

Many children diagnosed as neurologically handicapped at 6 years of age are perfectly normal at 9. These children had only a delay and not a dysfunction of neurological maturation. If we support them during the delay period, they will usually be all right.

Neurologically hyperactive children do not "outgrow" their problem at age 12. They will still often continue to need various types of help throughout adolescence, including medications in some instances.

The problems of perceptual problems, reversals, and fine-motor coordination difficulties are parallels to learning problems, not the cause of them.

Poor readers are more likely to suffer from an auditory perceptual problem than from a visual perception difficulty.

Perceptual development may be a *necessary* condition for reading, but not a *sufficient* one. Some children with poor perception are excellent readers, and others with fine perception may be poor readers.

Visual-motor perceptual abnormalities and neurological "soft" signs" are in most cases those types of responses that would be normal in a younger child. They may coexist with reading and learning problems but are not diagnostic or etiologic. Reversals in writing and reading are in the same category and are not a predictor of any kind of brain damage or reading disabilities. Perceptual problems and reversals are more likely to be seen when a child is under stress.

Neurological "soft signs" are only a reflection of immaturities of the nervous system and are not diagnostic of neurological disease or dysfunction.

There are almost no children whose reading disability essentially consists of reversals and right-left problems, or whose reading and writing would have improved had they not had these problems.

There is no evidence that failure to develop at one level influences capabilities at higher levels of development. Thus, children who never learn to crawl may be perfectly fine readers, and vice versa.

There are many children under the age of 5 who exhibit the following characteristics: hyperactivity and driven behavior, slow or absent speech, severe discipline problems, and coordination immaturities. These children are often diagnosed as brain-damaged, autistic, aphasic, hyperkinetic, or retarded. In reality they should be considered as manifesting severe, diffuse neurological delay and/or dysfunction, affecting many areas of the brain. We have called them "globally atypical children."

The global atypical child must be treated by many different professionals including language specialists, special-education teachers, psychologists, and physicians. A variety of educational programs may be necessary for them as they grow, including language programs, classes for the educationally handicapped, occasionally programs for the severely emotionally disturbed, classes for the multihandicapped, and rarely, classes for retarded children. Often more than one of these programs are necessary for each individual child with this problem.

If a child has difficulty in school, it is important that his teachers, parents, physicians, and all of the other people concerned with his educational progress work together in an understanding and openly communicative manner. We have called this our "educational triangle," and each side is an important one for the support of the child.

Professionals who are dealing with children with learning handicaps should not waste valuable resources and time hypothesizing about the specific neurological status of the children, but should instead concentrate on appropriate psychosocial and educational assessment and remediation.

Any personnel dealing with children with learning handicaps should remain open to new information and suggestions that could possibly contradict any previous training and understanding.

A child with a learning disability and normal intelligence must obtain educational evaluation to find out just what his strengths and weaknesses are and what can be done to help him become educated to his full potential.

The physician can perform many tasks for a child who has a learning handicap. These include early developmental screening of possible problem cases, providing medical care for illness and physical defects, and diagnosing the presence of neurological handicaps that may be at the root of learning problems. The physician may also prescribe nutritional or medical therapy for specific problems such as medical or neurological hyperactivity. Finally, he may provide guidance and counseling for the family, and help to unite the whole team that is helping the child. The physician is not expected to, nor should he attempt to, prescribe educational therapies for the child.

Medical evaluation can be helpful in diagnosing and treating physical disabilities and illnesses where present. Medical management may also play a part in the care of a child who cannot pay attention to his work due to chemical or neurological dysfunctions. However, the physician has a minimal role in the assessment of reading disabilities, which should be dealt with within the school system.

There are many illnesses, both acute and chronic, that can interfere with a child's school progress. The physician can greatly benefit from input from the teacher to help him in his medical treatment of the child.

A neurological examination does not identify which of the areas of the central nervous system is contributing to a learning disturbance except in the case of a child with a major neurological disturbance. Since most children with learning handicaps do not fit into this category, the usual neurological exam will not help in the educational remediation of these children.

Every child who attends school should be in as good health as possible in order to best benefit from the educational process. This means especially that the child's state of nutrition must be optimum— including a good breakfast. Some children who exhibit abnormal behavior or learning problems may need even more attention to dietary measures such as in the case of the problems that may be caused by food allergy, hypoglycemia, or artificial coloring and additives.

Chemical factors affecting learning and behavioral problems not only may occur because of congenital or genetic biochemical defects, but they may also result from the effects of a stressful environment. Thus, emotional and environmental stress may *cause* chemical abnormalities, abnormalities that may interfere with brain function and ultimately learning.

Every professional who is involved with a child with educational problems must *be free* and *feel able* to communicate with the other professionals in the field. This can be done by phone calls, written messages, or meetings. The information communicated should be concise, easy to understand, and to the point. Interdisciplinary communication must also use terminology that can be understood by everyone involved, including the parents.

The particular type of therapy used to correct learning disorders usually does not relate to whether the problem was structural, genetic, or environmental. We must find out what works best for each child and utilize it, no matter what the cause was.

Each individual child has his own unique learning profile and level of attainment. His education must be geared to that specific profile and level of ability.

In order to effectively remediate a child's learning problems, observations must be made to determine how he solves tasks and what his strengths and weaknesses are as far as learning channels. This must be done by way of extensive psychological and educational testing.

We must develop processes to measure exactly what is involved in the task of reading itself, so that we would not have to care about perceptual problems, "soft signs," and neurological examinations.

Each child with a reading problem has his own unique pattern of difficulty. There are so many mental processes involved, each of which can be impaired to varying degrees, that you cannot treat any two children alike.

When a child exhibits a selective difficulty in reading, it must be determined what it is about the traditional instructional methods that this child fails to benefit from, as well as what methods might best be used to help him succeed.

Most children with learning handicaps should be retained in regular classrooms as much as possible. In order to accomplish this, teaching methods that have been developed in the field of special education will have to be taught as part of the general education curriculum.

Remedial educational programs can promise effort but not results. Developmental programs can promise results if all parties are tuned to the proper goals. This of course depends on proper identification of pupils and on competent personnel.

The tangible features of a special program (room size, furniture, equipment, and materials) should be an eclectic collection for that particular teacher and group of students.

The intangibles of a special program (attitudes, communication, personality) are by far the most important features of the program.

If the authors could positively influence just one component of any remediation program, we would stress communication between the home and school.

Assessment of a child with learning handicaps must be aimed at what kind of program is needed for the child, not whether the child "fits" into an existing program or class.

Students should be described in a simple, narrative style, not with labels. We should attempt to accentuate the child's positive traits, not his deficits.

Test scores and other technical data are very important, but the limitations of the information must be recognized. A competent teacher's observations are often of more value than test scores.

Any medical, nutritional, or psychological therapy a child receives must be closely monitored by a person concerned with the child. The most meaningful feedback on the effect of such therapy will usually come from the teacher.

Drug therapy is an important, and sometimes essential, but never sufficient, form of management. The most important indication for medications in children with learning problems is in the neurologically hyperactive child for the control of the attention span.

Stimulant medications exert their effect on these children by reinforcing the normal stimulation of the arousal systems, which in turn causes better attention, less distractibility, and better organization, and eventually cuts down on hyperactive behavior where present.

Although the nutritional approach to learning problems is still controversial, it does no harm, and certainly it is more beneficial, to be certain that these children eat good, well-balanced diets as free as possible of pure sugar, "junk" foods, and any foods that may specifically bother them (such as milk in some cases).

Children who are being treated with psychotropic medications, as well as their families, need counseling help. Reliance on a pill or medication alone is inadequate treatment as regards the entire remediation program.

Children with serious emotional and psychosocial problems cannot be remediated by the school alone. Educational help by itself will not change these childrens' lives.

The more closely a learning experience is related to a specific task, the more directly beneficial will be the results. Thus, even though physical training and eye-muscle programs may improve fitness, motor, and visual skills, it is not clearly shown that they will enhance learning or reading capabilities.

Professionals who deal with children with educational dysfunction should inspect the resources available to the child's family and help the family direct the resources to the most needy areas. Thus, if poor reading is the problem, this should be the target area, not other controversial methods of training.

In any type of program dealing with children with educational or behavioral problems—no matter whether these problems are psychological, perceptual, nutritional, or otherwise—the greatest amount of success has usually been achieved by the proponent of the particular method.

The question of what finally happens to the child who exhibits learning, behavioral, or hyperactivetype behavior is difficult to assess. Many of these children will develop into adolescents with serious emotional and educational difficulties no matter what is done to or for them. However, the more help these children receive in their younger years, the more likely they are to develop normally as they grow into adolescence and adulthood.

## SUMMARY OF LABELOLOGY

### Minimal Brain Damage, Minimal Cerebral Dysfunction, Minimal Brain Dysfunction

All of these terms—*minimal brain damage, minimal cerebral dysfunction,* and *minimal brain dysfunction* have been used to try to lump a whole host of behaviors into a certain diagnostic category. Children with hyperactive behavior traits, learning disabilities, neurological and coordination immaturities, perceptual disabilities, and other signs and symptoms have been grouped into these "catchall" categories. Because of the very diverse types of problems that can cause these behaviors, and the confusion of the various professionals dealing with such children, and most important—the total lack of correlation of diagnostic, therapeutic, or remedial endeavors with such labeling—it is best to completely *avoid the use of these terms* altogether.

### Hyperactive, Hyperkinetic

*Hyperactive* or *Hyperkinetic* is a term used to describe children who exhibit impulsive behavior, a short attention span, perceptual problems, distractibility, and immaturities of various types. Hyperactivity is a poor term to use because of the absence of true diagnostic criteria and the diversity of people describing these children. Of all children labeled in such a manner, there *are* a select few who have some type of neurological dysfunction manifesting itself by a short attention span, or perhaps have a medical problem related to previous brain damage or nutritional dysfunctions such as hypoglycemia. These few individuals are the true neurological or medical hyperactive and are only a small portion of all the children so labeled.

### Neurological Handicap (NH)

NH refers to any child who shows signs of a brain or nervous system immaturity or dysfunction that results in disorders of motor, sensory, language, behavior, or learning functions. Most children with so-called minimal brain dysfunction or hyperkinesis actually should fit into this group. The diagnosis of NH is in no way helpful as far as therapeutics or remediation, but is more of a "bookkeeping" term, useful for insurance and hospital forms. *Each child diagnosed as "neurologically handicapped" should have attention given to each problem he has, rather than to the label of "NH."*

### Dyslexia

Dyslexia has been used to describe children who have normal intelligence but cannot learn to read for some unexplained reason. Many other terms such as *word blindness* have been used synonymously with dyslexia. Since we have seen that each child with a reading problem really has his *own* brand of dyslexia, the use of this term can be quite misleading, and it is best forgotten!

### Dysgraphia, Dyscalculia

The terms *dysgraphia* and *dyscalculia* refer to disorders of writing and arithmetic in the same way that dyslexia refers to reading problems. They are not helpful in either diagnosis or remediation and probably should not be used in describing a child's problem.

### Aphasia

*Aphasia* refers to a person who has normal peripheral hearing and speech mechanisms, yet cannot comprehend language or express himself properly (receptive or expressive aphasia). Since the term actually refers to people who have suffered brain damage after having already attained normal language abilities, the term is *incorrect* when applied to children. Children with language disorders should be called "children with language disorders!"

## Maturational or Developmental Lag or Delay (Immaturity)

*Maturational immaturity* refers to a child who has normal intelligence but has a delay in the attainment of one or more skills usually seen at his age. This is frequently seen in the fine motor, perceptual, and social areas, although delays in gross motor and language development are seen also. The term *delay* or *lag* refers to the fact that the child will eventually "catch up" in his area of delay. However, it is often difficult to tell, especially in the child under six, whether we are dealing with a delay or a real disorder. Most children with learning and behavior disorders probably fit into this category. Neurological soft signs, letter reversals, and perceptual problems are part of this problem. If a child shows a delay in *all* areas of development for a long enough period of time, he is actually functioning as a retarded child.

## Specific Learning Disability

*Specific learning disability* refers to an unexpected educational problem that arises in a child who has shown no other areas of physical, emotional, or neurological disturbance. It may be that the child has only a reading disability, or other functions may also be involved. Children with specific learning disabilities may show immaturities in other areas of development, but often have no other problems.

## Autism

*Autism* refers to a child who shows severe signs of emotional disturbance with a total loss of reality. This type of child regards people as objects, displays inappropriate behavioral traits, has absent or delayed language, and is often wild and unmanageable. A young child with autism may be difficult to differentiate from other neurologically handicapped children, especially those with language disorders. The prognosis for the autistic child is poor in most cases.

## Educational Handicap

A child who fails to learn to his full potential because of any problem, be it neurological, medical, psychological, or social, is said to be *educationally handicapped.* This child should be investigated to find out what the specific handicap is and how he can be helped to learn, either by correcting the problem or by working around it if the handicap is not remediable.

## FINAL STATEMENT

A child with educational dysfunction, no matter what the reason, should be thoroughly evaluated educationally, psychologically, and medically. Any and all methods that are necessary for his remediation should be explained to the family, and whatever is necessary should be tried. This means that all of the options including the various educational, psychological, and medical interventions must be thought of in regard to each child. We should not close our minds to one form of remediation or another, so that each child will be able to benefit from all of the knowledge we have accumulated. Remember—each child has his own unique dysfunction! We also have seen that diagnostic labeling in most cases has no real place in the therapy and remediation of any of these children.

It is important that everyone involved with these children be able to contribute whatever they can to the final assessment of the problem. It is equally as important for the various professionals to communicate their findings to each other and to the parents in a concise, meaningful manner (the educational triangle). It then becomes quite important for all concerned to work in close cooperation with each other and not to try to discredit any of the other members of the educational triangle, but to be able to openly discuss differences of approach and opinion.

When each child with a learning handicap is approached in the above manner, the way can be smoothly paved for the ultimate expert— the teacher—to begin the process of reentering the child into a positive educational experience.

# Bibliography and References

Many of the following articles and books have been helpful to the authors in compiling some of the information included in the book. Others are included in order to provide the reader with a source of material for further investigation in this field.

Adams, Jerry, "Clinical Neuropsychology and the Study of Learning Disorders," *Pediatric Clinics of North America,* **20,** No. 3 (August 1973), 587–598.

American Academy of Pediatrics, "The Eye and Learning Disabilities," Joint Organizational Statement, *Pediatrics,* **49,** No. 3 (March 1972), 454–455.

Arena, John I., ed., *Teaching Educationally Handicapped Children.* San Rafael, Calif.: Academic Therapy Publications, 1967.

Barness, Lewis A., et al., "Megavitamin Therapy for Childhood Psychosis and Learning Disabilities," Report of Committee on Nutrition, *Pediatrics,* **58,** No. 6 (December 1976), 910–911.

Bax, Martin C.O., "The Assessment of the Child at School Entry," *Pediatrics,* **58,** No. 3 (September 1976), 403–407.

Becker, Wesley C., *Parents Are Teachers: A Child Management Program.* Champaign, Ill.: Research Press Company, 1971.

Boder, Elena, "School Failure—Evaluation and Treatment," *Pediatrics,* **58,** No. 3 (September 1976), 394–402.

Boyd, Larry, and Kenneth Pandle, "Factor Analysis of the Frostig Developmental Test of Visual Perception," *Journal of Learning Disabilities,* **3,** No. 5 (May 1970), 253–255.

Bradley, Charles, "Benzedrine and Dexedrine in the Treatment of Children's Behavior Disorders," *Pediatrics,* **5,** No. 1 (January 1950), 24–37.

Braud, Lendell W., Mimi N. Lupin, and William G. Braud, "The Use of Electromyographic Biofeedback in the Control of Hyperactivity," *Journal of Learning Disabilities,* **8,** No. 7 (August/September 1975), 420–425.

Bruere, Harriet, "The Dyslexic Child," *Pediatric Annals,* **6,** NO. 2 (February 1977), 129–135.

Brutten, Milton, Sylvia O. Richardson, and Charles Gangel, *Something's Wrong with My Child.* New York: Harcourt, Brace and Jovanovich, Inc., 1973.

*California Master Plan for Special Education.* Sacramento, Calif.: California State Department of Education, 1974.

Chamberlin, Robert W., "The Use of Teacher Checklists to Identify Children at Risk for Later Behavioral and Emotional Problems," *American Journal of Diseases of Children,* **130,** No. 2 (February 1976), 141–145.

Charing, N. G., *Minimal Brain Dysfunction in Children—Educational, Medical and Health-Related Services. Phase Two of a Three-Phase Project,* Public Health Service Publication No. 2015, U.S. Department of Health, Education and Welfare. Washington, D.C.: U.S. Government Printing Office, 1969.

Chess, Stella, Alexander Thomas, and Herbert G. Birch, *Temperament and Behavior Disorders in Children.* New York: New York University Press, 1968.

Clements, Sam D., *Minimal Brain Dysfunction in Children, Terminology and Identification, Phase One of a Three-Phase Project,* National Institute of Neurological Diseases and Blindness Monograph No. 3, Public Health Service Bulletin No. 1415, U.S. Department of Health, Education and Welfare. Washington, D.C.: U.S. Government Printing Office, 1966.

Coleman, Raymond F., and Bernard J. Strenecky, "The Inter-Disciplinary Team: A New Kind of Classroom," *Journal of Learning Disabilities,* **8,** No. 9 (November 1975), 551–554.

Conners, C. Keith, "The Syndrome of Minimal Brain Dysfunction: Psychological Aspects," *Pediatric Clinics of North America,* **14,** No. 4 (November 1967), 749–766.

―――――, "A Teacher Rating Scale for Use in Drug Studies with Children," *American Journal of Psychiatry,* **126,** No. 6 (December 1969), 884–888.

―――――― and Leon Eisenberg, "The Effects of Methylphenidate on Symptomatology and Learning in Disturbed Children," *American Journal of Psychiatry,* **120,** No. 5 (November 1963), 453–459.

Conners, C. Keith, et al., "Food Additives and Hyperkinesis: A Controlled Double-Blind Experiment," *Pediatrics,* **58,** No. 2 (August 1976), 154–166.

Cornblath, Marvin, and Robert Schwartz, *Disorders of Carbohydrate Metabolism in Infancy.* Philadelphia and London: W. B. Saunders Company, 1966.

Critchley, MacDonald, *Developmental Dyslexia.* London: William Heinemann Medical Books, 1964.

Cruickshank, William M., *The Brain-Injured Child in Home, School and Community.* Syracuse, N.Y.: Syracuse University Press, 1967.

_____ and Orville Johnson, eds., *Education of Exceptional Children and Youth.* Englewood Cliffs, N.J.: Prentice-Hall, Inc., 1958.

Dreikurs, Rudolf, and Vicki Stoltz, *Children: The Challenge.* New York: Hawthorne Books, Inc., 1964.

Eisenberg, Leon, "Epidemiology of Reading Retardation," in *The Disabled Reader,* ed. John Money. Baltimore: Johns Hopkins Press, 1966.

_____, "Symposium: Behavior Modification Drugs III. The Clinical Use of Stimulant Drugs in Children," *Pediatrics,* **49,** No. 5 (My 1972), 709–775.

Falik, L. H., "The Effects of Special Perceptual Motor Training in Kindergarten on Reading Readiness and on Second Grade Reading Performance," *Journal of Learning Disabilities,* **2,** No. 8 (August 1969), 395–402.

Feingold, Benjamin F., *Why Your Child Is Hyperactive.* New York: Random House, Inc., 1975.

Frankenburg, William K., and Josiah B. Dodds, "The Denver Developmental Screening Test," *Journal of Pediatrics,* **71,** No. 2 (August 1967), 181–191.

Frostig, Marianne, "Education for Children with Learning Disabilities," in *Progress in Learning Disabilities,* ed. Helmer R. Myklebust. New York: Grune & Stratton, Inc., 1968.

Glenn, Hugh, "The Unimportance of Visual and Auditory Perception in Reading," *Commentary,* School of Education of Pepperdine University, **1,** No. 1 (Fall 1976), 23–27.

Gofman, Helen F., and Bayard W. Allmond, Jr., "Learning and Language Disorders in Children, Part I: The Preschool Child," *Current Problems in Pediatrics,* Vol. 1, No. 10 (August 1971). Chicago: Yearbook Medical Publishers, Inc.

_____, "Learning and Language Disorders, Part II: The School-Age Child," *Current Problems in Pediatrics,* **Vol. 1,** No. 11 (September 1971). Chicago: Yearbook Medical Publishers, Inc.

Gordon, Thomas, *Parent Effectiveness Training.* New York: Peter H. Wyden, Inc., 1970.

Gustafson, Sarah R., and David B. Coursin, eds., "The Minimally Brain Damaged Child," *The Pediatric Patient,* pp. 122–145. Philadelphia: J. B. Lippincott Co., 1968.

Hewett, Frank M., "Strategies of Special Education," *Pediatric Clinics of North America,* **20,** No. 3 (August 1973), 695–704.

Hogan, Gwendolyn R., and Neil J. Ryan, "Evaluation of the Child with a Learning Disorder," *Pediatrics,* **58,** No. 3 (September 1976), 407–409.

Hsai, David Yi-Yung, *Inborn Errors of Metabolism, Part I: Clinical Aspects.* Chicago: Yearbook Medical Publishers, Inc., 1966.

Johnson, Doris J., and H. R. Myklebust, *Learning Disabilities: Educational Principles and Practices.* New York: Grune & Stratton, Inc., 1967.

Kanner, Leon, "Early Infantile Autism," *American Journal of Orthopsychiatry,* **19,** No. 1 (July 1949), 416–426.

Keele, Doman, et al., "Role of Special Pediatric Evaluation in the Evaluation of a Child with Learning Disabilities," *Journal of Learning Disabilities,* **8,** No. 1 (January 1975), 40–45.

Keim, Richard P., "Visual-Motor Training, Readiness and Intelligence of Kindergarten Children," *Journal of Learning Disabilities,* **3,** No. 5 (May 1970), 256–259.

Kinsbourne, Marcel, "Developmental Gertsmann Syndrome," *Pediatric Clinics of North America,* **15,** No. 3 (August 1968), 771–778.

———, "School Problems," *Pediatrics,* **52,** No. 5 (November 1973), 697–710.

Kirk, Samuel A., *Educating Exceptional Children.* Boston: Houghton Mifflin Company, 1962.

Lerner, Robert J., and Pamela M. Lerner, "The Effects of Methylphenidate on the Soft Neurological Signs of Hyperactive Children," *Pediatrics,* **57,** No. 4 (April 1976), 521–525.

Lipton, Morris, *Report on the Meeting of the National Advisory Committee on Hyperkinesis and Food Additives.* New York: The Nutrition Foundation, 1975.

Masland, Richard L., "Foreword" in Lloyd Thompson, *Reading Disability.* Springfield Ill.: Charles C. Thomas, Publisher, 1969.

Mayer, C. Lamar, and Margaret Scheffelin, "State-Wide Planning for Special Education in California," *Journal of Learning Disability,* **8,** No. 4 (April 1975), 238–242.

Menkes, John H., "On Failing in School," *Pediatrics,* **58,** No. 3 (September 1976), 392–394.

Millichap, J. Gordon, et al., "Hyperkinetic Behavior and Learning Disorders," *American Journal of Diseases of Children,* **116,** No. 3 (September 1968), 235–244.

Millichap, F. Gordon, and Glenn W. Fowler, "Treatment of Minimal Brain Dysfunction Syndromes," *Pediatric Clinics of North America,* **14,** No. 4 (November 1967), 767–778.

Myklebust, Helmer R., ed., *Progress in Learning Disabilities,* Vol. 1. New York: Grune & Stratton, Inc., 1969.

Nelson, Waldo E., *Textbook of Pediatrics* (10th ed.), eds. Victor C. Vaughn III and R. James McKay. Philadelphia, London, and Toronto: W. B. Saunders Company, 1975.

Orton, Samuel T., *Reading, Writing and Speech Problems in Children: A Presentation of Certain Types of Disorders in the Development of the Language Faculty.* New York: W. W. Norton and Company, Inc., 1937.

Ott, John N., "Influence of Fluorescent Lights on Hyperactivity and Learning Disabilities," *Journal of Learning Disabilities,* **Vol. 9,** No. 7 (August/September, 1976).

Paine, Richard S., "Syndromes of Minimal Cerebral Damage," *Pediatric Clinics of North America,* **15,** No. 3 (August 1968), 779–799.

Pavy, Robert N., and Jean V. Metcalfe, *The Teacher's and Doctor's Guide to a Practical Approach to Learning Problems.* Springfield, Ill.: Charles C. Thomas, Publisher, 1974.

*Physician's Desk Reference* (31st ed.). Oradell, N.J.: Medical Economics Company, 1977.

Public Law 94-142, "Education for All Handicapped Children Act of 1975." Administered by U.S. Department of Health, Education and Welfare, Washington, D.C., 1975.

Reger, Roger, "What Does 'Mainstreaming' Mean?" *Journal of Learning Disabilities,* **7,** No. 4 (April 1974), 219–231.

*Report of the Conference on the Use of Stimulant Drugs in the Treatment of Behaviorally Disturbed Young School Children,* Sponsored by the Office of Child Development and the Office of the Assistant Secretary for Health and Scientific Affairs. Washington, D.C.: U.S. Government Printing Office, Department of Health, Education and Welfare. January 1971.

Saphier, J. D., "The Relation of Perceptual Motor Skills to Learning and School Success," *Journal of Learning Disabilities,* **6,** No. 9 (November 1973), 583–592.

Sattler, Jerome M., *Assessment of Children's Intelligence* (revised ed.). Philadelphia, London, and Toronto: W. B. Saunders Company, 1974.

Schain, Richard J., "Minimal Brain Dysfunction," *Current Problems in Pediatrics,* **Vol. 5,** No. 10 (August 1975).

———, "Minimal Brain Dysfunction in Children: A Neurological Viewpoint," *Bulletin Los Angeles Neurological Society,* **33,** (1968), 145–155.

———, and Carol L. Reynard, "Observations on Effects of a Central Stimulant Drug (Methylphenidate) in Children with Hyperactive Behavior," *Pediatrics,* **55,** No. 5 (May 1975), 709–715.

Seals, John R., "MBD," in *Advances in Pediatrics,* ed. Lewis A. Barness, **23,** (1976), 113–149.

Senf, Gerald M., "Learning Disabilities," *Pediatric Clinics of North America,* **20,** No. 3 (August 1973), 607–640.

Shiller, Jack G., *Childhood Illness.* New York: Stein and Day, 1972.

Siegel, Ernest, *Special Education in the Regular Classroom.* New York: The John Day Company, Inc., 1969.

Smith, Lendon H., *Improving Your Child's Behavior Chemistry.* Englewood Cliffs, N.J.: Prentice-Hall, Inc., 1976.

Sprague, Robert L., and Esther K. Sleator, "Effects of Psychopharmocologic Agents on Learning Disorders," *Pediatric Clinics of North America,* **20,** No. 3 (August 1973), 719–737.

Spring, Carl, and Jonathan Sandoval, "Food Additives and Hyperkinesis: A Critical Evaluation of the Evidence," *Journal of Learning Disabilities,* **9,** No. 9 (November 1976), 560–569.

Stager, David R., "Amblyopia and the Pediatrician," *Pediatric Annals,* **6,** No. 2 (February 1977), 46–75.

Tarnopol, Lester, ed., *Learning Disabilities: Introduction to Educational and Medical Management.* Springfield, Ill.: Charles C. Thomas, Publisher, 1969.

———, *Learning Disorders in Children—Diagnosis, Medication, Education.* Boston: Little, Brown and Company, 1971.

Thompson, Alice C., *Educationally Handicapped: A Handbook for Teachers.* Los Angeles, Calif.: California State College, 1966.

Thompson, Lloyd J. *Reading Disability.* Springfield, Ill.: Charles C. Thomas, Publisher, 1969.

Trotter, Sharland, "Labeling, It Hurts More than It Helps," *Journal of Learning Disabilities,* **8,** No. 3 (March 1975), 191–193.

Walzer, Stanley, and Julius B. Richmond, "The Epidemiology of Learning Disorders," *Pediatric Clinics of North America,* **20,** No. 3 (August 1973), 549–564.

Weinberg, Warren; Joel Rutman; Leo Sullivan; Elizabeth C. Penick; and Susan Dietz, "Depression in Children Referred to an Educational Diagnostic Center: Diagnosis and Treatment," *Journal of Pediatrics,* **83** No. 6 (Dec. 1973), 1065-72.

Wender, Esther H., "Food Additives and Hyperkinesis," *American Journal of Diseases of Children,* **131,** No. 5 (Nov. 1977), 1204-06.

Wender, Paul H., *The Hyperactive Child—A Handbook for Parents.* New York: Crown Publishers, Inc., 1973.

———, *Minimal Brain Dysfunction in Children.* New York: John Wiley & Sons, Inc., 1971.

Wolraich, Mark L., "Stimulant Drug Therapy in Hyperactive Children: Research and Clinical Implications," *Pediatrics,* **60,** No. 4 (Oct. 1977), 512-518.

Woods, Nancy E., *Delayed Speech and Language Development.* Englewood Cliffs, N.J.: Prentice-Hall, Inc., 1964.

# *Index*